GERMAN OCEAN LINERS OF THE 20TH CENTURY

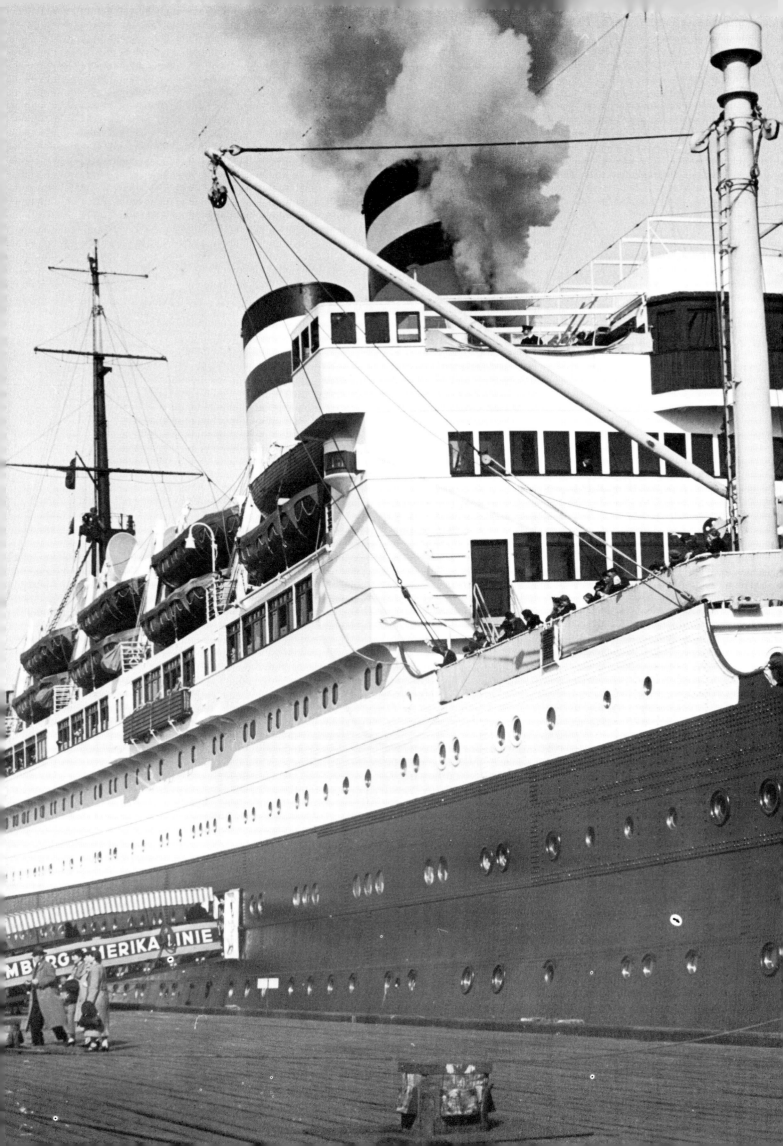

German Ocean Liners
of the 20th Century

William H. Miller

Foreword by Arnold Kludas

Preface by Frank O. Braynard

Patrick Stephens Limited

for
DOREEN HEYWOOD

dear friend, beloved shipmate, always
a source of support and encouragement

First published in 1989

British Library Cataloguing in Publication Data

Miller, William H. (William Henry), 1948–
German ocean liners of the twentieth century.
1. Germany. Passenger transport. Shipping. Liners, 1900–1987
I. Titles
387.2'43

ISBN 0-85059-890-7

Front endpaper *An extremely rare, perhaps the only, occasion when the three
largest and grandest German ocean liners of all, Ballin's immortal 'Big Three', were
berthed together in the same docks. At Southampton's Ocean Dock, they are, however,
under their subsequent names, in their second careers:* Leviathan, *the former* Vaterland,
is to the left; Majestic, *ex-*Bismarck, *is in the centre; and* Berengaria, *once*
Imperator, *is on the right.*

Frontispiece *That special moment: passengers line the outer decks and visitors go
ashore, the whistles are sounded and the ship prepares to make way for her true element
— the sea. In this scene from the 1930s, Hamburg America Line's* Hamburg, *one of
the best known of the German ocean liners of the twentieth century, prepares to depart
on another crossing to New York (Frank O. Braynard Collection).*

Rear endpaper *Long gone are the likes of the Hamburg Sud liners, and* Reliance *and*
Robert Ley *from berths along the Overseas Landing Stage at Hamburg. In this scene,* Europa
makes a special call during a cruise (Hafen Hamburg Authority).

Patrick Stephens Limited is part of the
Thorsons Publishing Group,
Wellingborough, Northamptonshire, NN8 2RQ, England.

Printed in Great Britain by The Bath Press, Bath, Avon

1 3 5 7 9 10 8 6 4 2

Contents

Foreword by Arnold Kludas   6
Preface by Frank O. Braynard   7
Acknowledgements   8
Author's introduction   9
1   The four-stackers   11
2   The *Barbarossa* Class   24
3   The *Pennsylvania* Class   35
4   The North Atlantic 'B' Class   38
5   Other Atlantic ships   42
6   Three four-masted liners   49
7   An intermediate quartet   56
8   Early Hamburg Sud liners   62
9   The 'Big Three'   73
10   Express sisters   88
11   The *Tirpitz* trio   92
12   Intermediate liners of the 'twenties and early 'thirties   97
13   Latin American liners   115
14   Hapag quartet   122
15   The 'Monte' Class and *Cap Arcona*   129
16   North Atlantic superships   143
17   Express liners of the 'thirties   154
18   Two special cruise-ships   165
19   Post-war revival   169
20   Cruising liners   188
Epilogue   197
Bibliography   200
Appendix I: The 25 largest German ocean liners   201
Appendix II: The 25 longest German ocean liners   202
Appendix III: Major German passenger ship losses 1939–45   203
Appendix IV: General reference table for German ocean liners   204
Index   207

Foreword

by Arnold Kludas

When, in 1897, the North German Lloyd liner *Kaiser Wilhelm der Grosse* was commissioned, the Germans for the first time had the biggest ship in the world. And soon, this liner had proved to be the fastest. In 1898, she took the Blue Riband from the Cunarder *Lucania*. But, there was still another superlative for the *Kaiser Wilhelm der Grosse*: for the first time, the biggest, fastest and most luxurious liner in the world had been built in a German shipyard. For the next ten years, the famous 'decade of the Germans on the North Atlantic', the leading position—at least where speed was concerned—remained with those five four-funnel liners of the North German Lloyd and Hamburg America Line until 1907. In that year, *Lusitania* regained the trophy for Britain.

But the loss of the speed record did not affect another outstanding record which both the Lloyd and Hapag liners held: year after year, these two companies carried the largest number of passengers from Europe to the United States. German passenger shipping in those years was second only to Britain. The names of famous German liners were known round the world: *Amerika, Kaiserin Auguste Victoria, George Washington,* the unique cruise-ships of the Hamburg America Line or the giant Far East and Australian liners of the 'Barbarossa' type. Hamburg America and North German Lloyd were by far the biggest shipping lines in the world.

And the Germans did still more to extend their influence. Albert Ballin, perhaps the most outstanding shipping manager of all time, ordered that famous trio of 50,000 tonners, *Imperator, Vaterland* and *Bismarck*, which remained the biggest ships in the world until the advent of *Normandie* in 1935. Most probably these liners would have gained the leading position on the North Atlantic for the Hamburg America Line from 1915 onwards and for many years thereafter.

The First World War intervened, however, and changed almost everything. The German liners thereafter ran under the flags of the former enemies. But, in a remarkably short time, the Germans regained a strong position in passenger shipping. At the end of the 1920s, the superliners *Bremen* and *Europa* not only created new speed records, but also set new scales in building modern passenger liners. They were the forerunners of the giant *Normandie* and the 'Queens'.

Bill Miller, who has written so many interesting books on passenger ships and who is one of the most knowledgeable experts in this field, recalls in this book the fortunes of both the famous as well as the forgotten German passenger ships.

Arnold Kludas
Grünendeich, River Elbe

Preface

by Frank O. Braynard

Human nature in all its good qualities and its worst is well exposed in the beautiful/tragic story of *Vaterland*, the world's undisputed largest ship, in her days at Hoboken from 1914 into 1917. Happily, she receives the special attention she deserves in this, Bill Miller's latest title. Fresh from the Blohm & Voss yards, she arrived to set the Port of New York (and the world) agog in the summer of 1914. Her brilliant owner, Albert Ballin, a man of the world, was leader of the peace party in Germany and did his best to halt the trend toward war. He put his new *Vaterland* into service as 'money on the line' proof that he believed war between England and Germany was not inevitable—and he lost. He lost his company, his great new ship—just about all his ships—and his life! He should be better remembered.

Vaterland docked at Hoboken, which was almost German in its atmosphere and population. She was queen of the world's great liners. Her crew was honoured, fêted and entertained. Her band performed everywhere. She held great events aboard with many distinguished Americans as guests. Famed newspaper publisher William Randolph Hearst was one. Opera stars were among those who gathered for sumptuous dinners, dances and concerts aboard. The vast ship was transformed for these occasions, and electric motor cars sped the guests from the pier's land end down to the gangplank. Officers from *Vaterland* and other German liners were honoured guests in Hoboken homes and the most beautiful young ladies of the area were squired about by them at the best social functions.

Great German war-relief benefits were held in such places as New York City's huge Madison Square Garden. A gigantic model of a Zeppelin was built and hung from the Garden's rafters as a symbol of Germany's conquest of the air at one of these events. The money made was to go to take care of German children who had lost their arms and legs or had been burned or blinded in British air attacks on German cities. Many Americans at that time wished to side with Germany in the war that had come that fateful August of 1914. Anti-British thinking was strong not only in Hoboken, but in many little towns like Sea Cliff, Long Island (my home town) and Milwaukee, Cleveland and Cincinnati— all over America in fact. It went on like this for some time.

Then, almost overnight, like a black cloud dragging its heavy dark shadow over the ocean, the mood changed. It may have been clever British diplomacy like the noted *Dacia* affair (which saw the seizure of an American ship by a French instead of a British warship) that did the trick. Certainly, the sinking of the *Lusitania* played right into the hands of those in America who favoured Britain. Whether this disaster was organized, as some have written, by First Lord of the Admiralty Winston Churchill, is beside the point—but it did happen and the mood switched drastically. Suddenly, the Germans aboard *Vaterland* were spies, conspirators—devils!

We humans have learned little since caveman days. We are blinded by our brainless hates and prejudices, and *Vaterland* was one of the victims. Strange to say, there was one little thing that happened at the end that did not fit into this mindless illustration of human insanity. When the great ship was seized in April 1917, her crew were offered freedom if they would become Americans. Many did, as hundreds of thousands of their immigrant brothers had done in the years before. There was a silver lining.

There have been many reasons that have led to my love and passion for *Vaterland/Leviathan*. She returned to service in 1923 as an American express liner, called by her owners 'the world's greatest ship'. This was when I was attempting for the second time to pass the first grade in school. One of the older school teachers continually gave me clippings about her, which I saved. It was not until fifty years later that I learned that his brother had been navigating officer on her during the First World War, something I found out after I had written Volume I of my six-volume series on the ship. I drew a sketch of her in 1923 and signed it. I was seven at the time and the sketch looks something like her. Then as now, however, I could not spell—even misspelling my own name in the signing!

Ever since, I have carefully saved everything I could about her. In 1929 I bought stock in United States Lines when she became a privately owned vessel and kept it for many, many years. It gave me invitations to parties on United States Lines' ships, to launchings and many other fascinating things such as the annual meetings in Hoboken. When British folders came out saying that *Majestic* was the world's largest ship, contradicting the claim made for *Leviathan*, I childishly corrected each such reference in pencil to 'world's second largest'. I bled for *Leviathan* every time she got bad publicity or was in trouble in any way, and cheered her on for her many brilliant achievements. Whenever anything happened to her, it was front page news worldwide. Similar things would happen to *Majestic*, but the news would end up on page 45!

Many sad things happened to *Leviathan* after the Great Depression: her terrible crack on the Atlantic (*Majestic* had suffered exactly the same, but no one outside the shipping world ever heard about that), her owner's financial difficulties, the fact that she was no longer the world's largest ship (a device in order that her newest owners could save a few pennies on port dues), how she was the world's most unhappy 'white elephant' . . .—all these sad things made me love her even more, defend her more passionately.

And there were many positive things that I discovered when doing my six volumes: her really stupendous First World War record when she carried one out of every ten American soldiers who actually fought on the French front; that she was fitted to transport 14,000 in one crossing; that she was rebuilt as one of the Atlantic's most beautiful and probably best-known liner of the early 'twenties. And I also found out that on many trips she carried many more than *Normandie* or *Queen Mary* ever carried—that she really was remarkably successful despite the handicap of being Government-owned for most of her career. The fact that she was sold for scrap only months before she would have been worth her weight in solid gold as a Second World War troop-ship was the final crime in her heroic, but tragically short, career. She was one of the greatest of all liners – one of the great *German Ocean Liners of the 20th Century*.

Frank O. Braynard
Sea Cliff, Long Island, New York

Acknowledgments

A great many people have been extraordinarily generous in helping me write this book, in sharing prized photos and select brochures and clippings, and in giving me support and encouragement to continue with a project that sometimes seemed lost amidst many other responsibilities.

I especially want to thank two giants of maritime research, Frank O. Braynard and Arnold Kludas, surely without whom this book could not have happened. I want to thank and praise the enormous work of the late Noel Bonsor, and to salute several of the great collectors: Wolfgang Fuchs, Ted Hindmarsh, Charles Sachs, Willie Tinnemeyer and Everett Viez. John Malcolm Brinnin's writings provided, as always, invaluable insights, as did the highly detailed history of Blohm & Voss by Hans Georg Prager. Warmest appreciation also to James Cooper and Michael Dollenbacher, who always add so much to my visits to Germany, particularly to beautiful Hamburg, and to Rolf Finck and Erika Lisson at Hapag-Lloyd, at Hamburg and at Bremen.

I want also to give special thanks to Ernest Arroyo, J. K. Byass, Michael Cassar, Luis Miguel Correia, Frank Duffy of Moran Towing Co, Alex Duncan, John Havers, Michael D. J. Lennon, Jan Loeff, Vincent Messina, Richard K. Morse, Roger Sherlock, Ernst Joseph Weber and Howard Whitford. To these and any others that I might have overlooked, my gratitude.

Author's Introduction

As I write this, on a particularly mild Sunday morning in late winter, I have just returned from a short drive, quite close to my home, to the remnants of the Hoboken steamer piers. I paused for a time and stared at those otherwise empty, desolate, nearly abandoned structures. They were last used by Indian freighters until closed completely in 1978. The redbrick, two-storey façade, which faces River Street, stretching from First to Fourth streets, dates from 1905, when they were built and owned by two of the busiest and mightiest shipping firms on earth, Hamburg America Line (most often referred to more simply as Hapag) and North German Lloyd (often abbreviated to NGL). The gates of this dock area are now locked, doorways and entrances shut, and the shed windows neglected and often broken. The melancholy silence was disrupted only by the cries of the Hudson River gulls. Soon these buildings and the three existing piers are to be removed—crushed by some wrecker's ball. They will be abruptly demolished, then mostly forgotten and replaced instead by a streamlined combination of offices, apartments, a hotel and a marina. The area, once strictly the domain of steamship agents and stevedores, tugboats and freight barges, is now a different kind of prime real estate. After all, sitting just across from the extraordinary Manhattan skyline, the view alone is reason enough.

I thought also of this dock area in earlier times, in fact just 75 years ago, as the biggest ship, liner or otherwise, arrived there for the first time. As horns honked, whistles screeched and flags were waved, the 919-ft (283-m), 52,100-ton *Imperator*—a ship dubbed 'the colossus of the Atlantic'—put into the Third Street pier at the end of her maiden voyage. Her three mustard-coloured funnels and twin masts must have towered over the sheds; one would have thought that she would have been forced to berth in the supposedly larger slips of New York City, at the Chelsea piers at West Twentieth Street.

It was not, however, the first time that these Hoboken piers had received the world's largest ship. Sixteen years before, in 1897, the new speed queen of the North Atlantic, the 14,300-ton *Kaiser Wilhelm der Grosse*, arrived there as well. She was followed by other members, all increasingly larger, of that first generation of aptly named 'superliners' as well as the first 'four-stackers'. They too were Germans, and appropriately named *Deutschland*, *Kronprinz Wilhelm*, *Kaiser Wilhelm II* and finally *Kronprinzessin Cecilie*. Some years later, other big and noteworthy Germans followed, liners such as *Amerika*, *Kaiserin Auguste Victoria* and *George Washington*. These ships were also among the finest and grandest of their day.

That first arrival of the 4,594-passenger *Imperator* was, in fact, a glorious but well intended culmination of this aforementioned group. She was the pride of Imperial Germany, the crowning symbol of German brilliance and technology. It was her creation, her debut 75 years ago, that prompted this book. She was not only the biggest ship afloat, surpassing all of her contemporaries such as the speedy *Mauretania*, the historic *Lusitania*, the innovative *Olympic* and even her immortal sister, the *Titanic*, but this German giant was also the first of a trio of successively larger liners, in fact the very first 'true' superliners. No other ships could statistically compare with them (except, of course, for speed, for which Britain's *Mauretania* remained unchallenged). Within two years, in that fateful, peace-shattering summer of 1914, the second of these Hamburg America behemoths, the 54,300-ton, 950-ft (292-m) long *Vaterland* had her first crossing. She too berthed at the Hoboken piers.

Most unfortunately, however, the cruel untimeliness of war, that so-called 'war to end all wars', changed everything. As an example, the third of the Hapag giants, the largest of all, *Bismarck*, never even made her maiden crossing. Even the Hoboken piers would never again be quite the same. As German and therefore enemy-owned property, they were seized (by the US Government) along with all of the ships at berth (including the flagship *Vaterland*). Later, in a rather strange irony, the same piers were used by the American military forces that were being sent overseas to fight the armies of the same Kaiser who had so inspired and become fascinated by these ships. With German colours lowered and replaced by the Stars and Stripes, and with grey and black 'dazzle' paint masking their earlier Teutonic heritage, they departed the Hoboken shores, mostly under new names: *Vaterland* as USS *Leviathan*, *Kronprinz Wilhelm* as USS *Von Steuben*, *Kaiser Wilhelm II* as USS *Agamemnon* and *Kronprinzessin Cecilie* as USS *Mount Vernon*. There were many other exiled German ships in troop transport service as well.

After the War, the Germans never returned to Hoboken. In fact, by the time the record-breaking new *Bremen* and *Europa* first appeared, in 1929–30, they were relegated to a berth along the distant, far end of the Brooklyn waterfront. (Later, of course, they relocated to New York City's 'Luxury Liner Row' and took their places alongside the likes of *Normandie*, *Queen Mary* and *Rex*.)

Long after that Second World War, when yet another German passenger fleet had all but vanished, either destroyed or under other flags as reparations, I recall the excitement of a July day in 1959. The former *Pasteur* had just arrived in port, but as the vastly refitted *Bremen*. Perhaps more than any other liner, she symbolized the revival, the 'rebirth', of North German Lloyd, even of the West German nation, on the North Atlantic. Coincidentally, she sat at Pier 88 across from the French flagship *Liberté*, herself the former Lloyd *Europa* of prewar service. It was a proud day for the

Germans. However, within a few short years, the emergence of jet aircraft would change the face of passenger shipping forever. Transitionally, the era of ocean liner transportation was over, replaced by the leisure and recreation of vacation cruising.

While it was the 75th anniversary of the completion of *Imperator* that sparked this title, it has also provided an opportunity for yet another nostalgic indulgence: to review a fleet of great ocean liners. Second only to Great Britain, Germany has produced a brilliant list of passenger ships: those first four-stackers; the *Freidrich der Grosse* and her ten near-sisters; the big emigrant ships of the *Pennsylvania* Class; the six-masted *President Lincoln* and *President Grant*; the renowned cruise-ships *Reliance* and *Resolute*; the 'spa ship' *Milwaukee*; the *Albert Ballin* quartet; the brilliant *Cap Arcona*; the speed champions *Bremen* and *Europa*; the intended *Vaterland* of 1940; and more contemporary ships such as the two-funnel *Hanseatic*, *Hamburg*, *Astor* and the current cruise-ship *Europa*. Of course, not all of the listing in these pages, which is restricted to ships mostly over 10,000 gross tons because of the limitations dictated by the size of this book, plied the celebrated North Atlantic run to New York. Many of them worked other trades. *Cordillera* sailed to the West Indies, *Antonio Delfino* to South America, *Windhuk* to West Africa, *Potsdam* to the Far East and the tragic *Wilhelm Gustloff* on so-called 'Strength through Joy' political cruises. In all, well over 100 passenger ships are included and they create a most impressive and very fascinating group.

William H. Miller
Hoboken, New Jersey

1
The four-stackers

They were among the finest ocean liners of all time: large, luxurious, innovative and, perhaps most of all, record-breaking. Apart from their roles in the bid for transatlantic speed supremacy, they were the first so-called 'superliners' and the first of a new and highly popular generation of passenger ships, the 'four-stackers'.

In his splendid book, *The Sway of the Grand Saloon*, author John Malcolm Brinnin wrote, 'By the early years of the 1890s, German firms had become notably prosperous. In one decade, Hamburg America Line alone had carried half a million passengers to New York—half as much again as either Cunard or White Star [the most important British shippers and Hamburg America's rivals]. The German companies basked in Imperial favour, were staffed by brilliant, ambitious executives and, as time would tell, were competitive to the point of madness. The motto on the Hamburg America houseflag was indicative: "Mein Feld Is Die Welt"—"My field is the world".'

Even the Kaiser himself was wildly enthusiastic. He had been to a fleet review at Spithead in 1889, and at the invitation of his grandmother Queen Victoria and under the guidance of his uncle, the Prince of Wales (later Edward VII), he was appropriately impressed with the military craft on display. But he was bewitchingly fascinated by a passenger ship, White Star's *Teutonic*, a 9,000 tonner that was then the biggest ship afloat. That this ship flew the British flag only heightened the Kaiser's sense of challenge. After he returned home, in a story that has often been retold, German shipping was never the same again. Above all, in a grand scale effort to prove herself not only to Britain, but to the world at large, Germany would soon take her rightful international place as an industrial and technological giant. Among the surest avenues of display was passenger ships, then and for some years to come the 'largest moving objects made by man', and specifically those on the most prestigious, most profitable and therefore most competitive trade route on earth: the North Atlantic. Germany was on her expansionist path and shipping was among her priorities.

His Imperial Highness's wishes became well known—in fact, eagerly received—in shipping offices throughout the nation. At Hamburg, the directors of Hamburg America Line were most receptive to such suggestions and began to make plans for bigger and faster passenger ships to augment their already large fleet. However, their enthusiasm was surpassed to some extent by their nearest, and perhaps greatest, rival, North German Lloyd of Bremen. The mood was for record-breaking ships, and Lloyd's first efforts would appear a full three years before a comparable Hamburg America challenger. Consequently, having built not one but several large liners almost immediately following the turn of the century, Lloyd seemed to have the slight competitive edge.

However, Hamburg America was not to be outdone completely. Several larger, very luxurious liners were built between 1905–1907, but were, in fact, a prelude to a trio of giants, scheduled for 1913–15, that would not be simply the world's largest yet, but the most colossal liners ever. Statistically, they would far exceed any other ship then afloat (and, in fact, the third of the trio would remain the world's largest liner until as late as 1935). The German race for shipping supremacy was startling, unstoppable, even mind-boggling to some onlookers. The long-standing British dominance and consequent contentment in deep-sea trade was irrevocably shaken. The likes of the Cunard and White Star lines, from their marble-clad corporate seats in Liverpool and in London, were thrust into a blunt awakening. They had to respond, but any retaliation against these extremely ambitious plans would take time. Steadily, the Kaiser grew more and more pleased as this new breed of 'German monsters', as the British often called them, took one record after another. An envious and undeniably threatened British could only wait and sometimes ask 'Who are these big Germans that sweep past on their way to and from America?'

The world's first so-called superliner, North German Lloyd's Kaiser Wilhelm der Grosse, *is seen at Bremerhaven. Dressed in flags, she is shortly to sail on her maiden run to New York in the late summer of 1897* (Hapag-Lloyd).

This blazing desire by the Germans to develop a mostly unrivalled ocean liner fleet was not simply limited to owning and operating such vessels, however. They wanted to build them as well. Imperial instructions from Berlin were that such record-breaking ships must come from German shipyards. Consequently, agents were sent to the master shipbuilders of the day—at facilities in Glasgow and Newcastle and Belfast—to recruit engineers, designers and craftsmen. The incentives included far better wages, and so this training force was delivered to Hamburg, to Bremen and to Stettin. It was, however, all part of a rather reckless scheme. Once the British methods were adequately learned, copied and then improved and enhanced, all but a small handful of these same technicians and workers were sent packing. By the mid 1890s, some five or so years after the Kaiser's notable visit to the fleet at Spithead, the time had come. The keel plates for the first so-called 'superliner' were laid down. Perhaps even more significantly, she would be a German ship built in a German yard.

Concerning the start of this project, John Malcolm Brinnin wrote 'To put an end to the dominance of rivals like *Campania* and *Lucania* [both Cunarders and both Blue Riband holders] and to halt the leapfrog way in which Cunard alternated with White Star in claiming the fastest speed, the largest menus and the most ornate grand saloons, the North German Lloyd Company adopted Prussian measures. They went to the Vulcan Shipbuilding Company in Stettin with a simple, stark proposal: build us the fastest ship in the world and we'll buy it; give us anything less, and you can keep it.' (As a case in point, one subsequent North German Lloyd liner, the three-funnel, 12,500-ton *Kaiser Friedrich*, completed in 1898, was rejected by the shipowners when she could not muster the contracted speed and then proved mechanically troublesome. Consequently, she was laid up at the shipyards, unwanted and rejected, for twelve years.)

The Vulcan works were only too happy—and honoured—to comply with Lloyd's initial request to build the world's fastest (and the world's largest) ship. John Malcolm Brinnin added 'When the Vulcan yards took the challenge, the immediate result was the tall, fast, always fearsome-looking *Kaiser Wilhelm der Grosse* [named after the Kaiser's grandfather, Wilhelm I, the first emperor of Germany]. This was the ship that would open a new era, a period in steamship history when the landscapes of Valhalla enscrolled on the walls and ceilings of grand saloons would all but collapse under their own weight, as well as a period when Teutonic efficiency united with matchless engine power would give Germany all the honours of the northern seas. And when the wits of the first decade of the century began to say that something or other was "hideously" or "divinely" or "late North German Lloyd", they meant, according to an American contemporary, "two of everything but the kitchen range and then gilded".'

The Kaiser himself attended the launching on 3 May 1897, and his dream ship was soon to become a reality. Four funnels, the first of that number ever to go to sea, and grouped two-and-two, were fitted and painted in Lloyd's mustard yellow colouring. The rigging was set between two tall masts, and altogether the ship had a very deliberate rake and a very sleek, almost serpent-like tone about her. Internally, amidst the gilt and the columned lounges, the over-sized sofas and the marble fireplaces, and public rooms fitted with the highest ceilings yet to go to sea, there were elaborately framed paintings, detailed wood carvings, elaborate bas-reliefs and glittering stained glass. Very special, spectacular even, the object was to awe, even overwhelm, anyone who stepped aboard the brand new Imperial merchant flagship. One reporter, at the end of the maiden voyage, sent the following message: 'Aboard the *Kaiser Wilhelm der Grosse*, a passenger might easily forget that he is at sea and instead imagine himself to be housed in some turreted eyrie on the Upper Rhine'.

After a slight (and somewhat embarrassing) delay when she went aground for a week near Bremen, *Kaiser Wilhelm der Grosse* swept the North Atlantic in the autumn of 1897. She was the new Blue Riband champion, and the first non-British-built speed queen in 40 years. She inaugurated the era of the so-called 'nine-day boat', travelling between Bremerhaven and New York via the Channel ports of Southampton and Cherbourg. The Germans, and particularly the Kaiser and the directors of the North German Lloyd and Vulcan companies, were beaming with pride and satisfaction.

This new 14,300 tonner, the largest ship of all until the appearance of White Star's 17,200-ton *Oceanic* two years later in 1899, was also, for a time, the most popu-

lar passenger ship on the Atlantic Ferry, as it was often called. It hardly seemed to matter that she was a rather notorious roller at sea, having been dubbed the '*Rolling Billy*' soon after her first season. Her four funnels were soon equated by the travelling public and particularly those westbound masses in steerage who were in actuality the most profitable to any passenger shipper, as being symbolic of the largest, fastest and safest ships. Soon after the debut of the subsequent German 'superliners', the 'four-stackers' became the most popular liners to America. So important and influential was the travelling public, that companies often added a fourth 'dummy' funnel just for effect.

But not everyone was pleased with the overwhelming success of the new *Kaiser Wilhelm der Grosse*. No sooner had she left the Bremerhaven docks than the Hamburg offices of Hapag, the abbreviated name for the clearly envious Hamburg America Line, went busily to work planning their own 'wonder ship'. They too would sign up with the Vulcan yards at Stettin. Equally jealous, the Cunard Line could only bide its time, in fact for nearly a decade, until the introduction of the brilliant new team of *Lusitania* and *Mauretania* in 1907. The White Star Line seemed even more overwhelmed, and decided to forget the Blue Riband completely and instead concentrate on future ships of notable size and distinctive luxury. Otherwise, there was no other shipping firm, British, American or wherever, that could seriously and sensibly compete with the victorious, ever-gloating Germans.

The Hapag flagship emphasized and heightened the intense rivalry with Lloyd. Their ship would be 2,000

Kaiser Wilhelm der Grosse *shown as an armed merchant cruiser in the first grey days of the First World War* (Hapag-Lloyd).

Above left *A stern view of* Kaiser Wilhelm der Grosse *while undergoing her annual survey at Bremerhaven* (Hapag-Lloyd).

Above right *Mechanically troublesome and therefore less than satisfactory to her Hamburg America owners, the four-funnel* Deutschland *was the least successful of the first German superliners* (Hapag-Lloyd).

tons larger (at 16,500 tons), more ornate, supposedly more innovative and, perhaps most important of all, faster still. Named *Deutschland* and commissioned in the summer of 1900, she immediately captured the prized Riband. She also became the most publicized and sought-after ship anywhere. Long and low, and a fitting second ship in this new era of the ocean greyhound, she too had four funnels again distinctively grouped in pairs. Unfortunately, however, the early career of this ship was marred by one very serious blemish: she was operationally unsound. Her extremely powerful quadruple-expansion engines caused excessive, passenger-disrupting vibrations, noises and rattling. Her reputation soon lost its glow, and consequently her economic success was far less than Hapag's initial, very promising expectations.

So disappointed were the Company directors that they decided never again to seek the Blue Riband or even very high speed. Like those of White Star Line, the designs for future Hamburg America liners would concentrate on luxury, passenger comfort and, on occasion, statistical one-upmanship. During 1906–7,

albeit for a brief period, Hapag would own the world's largest liner, the 24,300-ton *Kaiserin Auguste Victoria*, and then again, but far more triumphantly, in 1913–14, with the 52,100-ton *Imperator* and then the 54,200-ton *Vaterland*. Under construction before the First World War was an even larger Hapag supership, the 56,200-ton *Bismarck*, but she was never commissioned under the German flag.

Even if she was mechanically and operationally troublesome, *Deutschland* managed to retain the Blue Riband for Germany and for Hapag for six years until 1906. It was then taken for a time by another Lloyd four-stacker, *Kaiser Wilhelm II*, built in 1903. Once surpassed, and with her faults becoming more and more worrisome, *Deutschland* was finally taken in hand in 1910–11 for a full re-engining. She reappeared, however, with far less power than before. Even her role within the fleet was changed: she became a white-hulled, full-time cruise-ship. Her earlier image was discarded and disguised further with a new identity, *Victoria Luise*. Restyled for only 487 all-first-class passengers (downgraded from her earlier transatlantic capacity of 2,050—450 first class, 300 second class, 300 third class and 1,000 in steerage), she remained a very luxurious ship. Hapag literature in 1912 described the liner in detail:

'The *Victoria Luise* compels admiration at first impression by her splendid lines and stately proportions, and also conveys the feeling of stability, security and comfort. Her construction (conforming to and even exceeding the highest legal requirements) and the wonderful arrangements and appointments for the comfort of passengers at once proclaim and endear this vessel to the ocean voyager. Her large capacity and her moderate speed, combined with the Frahm device for stabilizing steamships, ensure an unusual degree of steadiness. The most careful considerations have been given to the passenger accommodations, and the spacious arrangements as to suites, cabins, public rooms and magnificent promenade decks are particularly noticeable. Elegantly decorated and furnished suites have been placed on both the promenade and main decks. The large number of single and two-berth rooms, many with bath and toilet attached, have been furnished and equipped with the idea uppermost of making the traveller feel "at home". Inter-connecting telephones increase the comforts and facilities.

'The dining room, extending the full width of the ship and located amidships, has been exquisitely furnished. A la carte meals are served. Small party tables are fitted to seat two, four, six and eight persons. This is undoubtedly an improvement over the old system of long tables. The promenade deck of the *Victoria Luise* is an important feature of this cruising steamer; it is considered one of the wonders of marine construction, sweeping aft around the stern from near the bow, a total length around the ship of 1,300 feet.

'A social hall or lounge and a music and ladies' saloon on the promenade deck at the head of the grand staircase are masterpieces of the decorator's art. Luxurious divans and chairs invite appealingly, and the whole atmosphere of the rooms breathe of indolent ease. The smoking room is also situated on the promenade deck and practically connected with the music room. A palm garden or tea room is situated on the upper deck aft. The entire treatment is one of artistic harmony, and no incongruous or obtrusive effects appear. As centres of social life on board ship, no finer examples of homelike comfort have ever been devised. In addition to the public rooms mentioned, there are also a gymansium, equipped with Zander electrical apparatus, electric light baths, shower baths, laundry, photographers' dark room, library, book stall and information bureau.'

To not be outdone, and encouraged by ever-increasing numbers of transatlantic passengers particularly in the highly-profitable steerage class, North German Lloyd responded with three more superliners, again all of them four-stackers. The 14,900-ton *Kronprinz Wilhelm* was commissioned in September 1901, just little more than a year after Hapag's *Deutschland*. It was intended that this new liner—one of the 'fleetest of the fleet', as Lloyd advertising literature proclaimed—would take

When she was converted to an all-white, full-time cruise-ship in 1910–11, Deutschland, *renamed* Victoria Luise, *seemed to achieve some operational success after all* (Arnold Kludas Collection).

Above   *After the First World War, the former* Deutschland *was again altered, to the demoded, twin-funnel, all-steerage ship* Hansa (Wolfgang Fuchs Collection).

Below   *A rather imposing view of* Kronprinz Wilhelm *of 1901, Lloyd's response to Hapag's record-breaking* Deutschland (Hapag-Lloyd).

the Blue Riband from the Hapag ship. The plan never came off, however. Her machinery was never quite capable of mustering that slight additional power for a record-breaking passage.

Kronprinz Wilhelm was followed in the spring of 1903 by the largest German liner yet, the 19,300-ton *Kaiser Wilhelm II*. Looking quite similar with her four towering funnels, the only obvious difference was the addition of a third mast. She too was intended to take the Riband, but the attempt was rather long in coming. Not until her fourth Atlantic season, in June 1906, did she finally capture the prized pennant, finally taking it from Hapag, who would never again be able to lay claim to the honour.

The unique celebrity status attached to *Kaiser Wilhelm II* as the world's fastest ocean liner was, however, rather short-lived. It was intended that her near-sister *Kronprinzessin Cecilie* of 1906, the last of the German four-stackers, would be as successful and therefore inherit the coveted title. This never came to pass, again because the ship's machinery was unable to produce the additional power, and consequently the pennant returned to British hands, to Cunard's exceptional *Mauretania*. It remained with her for an unprecedented 22 years, until 1929. Only then did the Germans have another (and final) chance; then the challengers were the giant near sister ships *Bremen* and *Europa* of 1929–30.

Long, slender and very sleek for their time, this view of Lloyd's Kaiser Wilhelm II *clearly shows the fine design of those first German four-stackers* (Everett Viez Collection).

The four-strong team of Lloyd four-stackers—*Kaiser Wilhelm der Grosse, Kronprinz Wilhelm, Kaiser Wilhelm II* and *Kronprinzessin Cecilie*—was extremely successful and superbly popular, perhaps even more so in America than in Europe. At their berths in New York harbour, at the specially owned terminal in Hoboken, they were fondly known as the 'Hohenzollerns of Hoboken'. One of them was in port almost every week of the year and together they provided a prescribed necessity to successful passenger shipping: a predetermined schedule of sailings. Alone, these four liners provided a weekly departure from New York and Bremerhaven as well as calls at Southampton and Cherbourg. Each ship carried passengers in traditionally class-divided accommodation—first class, second class and steerage—offered at fares ranging from over $2,000 for a luxurious first class suite to as little as $10 for a steerage dormitory.

They were a golden foursome, racing back and forth across the North Atlantic, always distinctive with their long and low profiles and the grouping of their funnels in pairs. The Lloyd publicists were understandably proud of them and were often exuberant in the wording of their passenger literature. In 1906, it was written that:

'Of the vessels in the North German Lloyd fleet, this quartet of marvels heads the list. Their completion marked an anachronism which was beyond all power of human imagination a few years ago. While all of these wonders in speed and size were being accomplished, other transformations were in progress. The interior of the ships, instead of stuffy, uncomfortable prisons, were converted into veritable palaces. A decade ago, it would have been considered absurd to spend money for interior decoration of steamships. Today the finest hotels in the world do not boast of more gorgeous splendour.

'It seemed almost impossible to attempt to provide accommodation for 4,000 people of heterogeneous habits and conditions, which would be in accord with their unusual surroundings, for such a short trip. But on the "fleetest of the fleet", no one, be he multi-millionaire or working man, can complain. The splendid suites deluxe and cabins, designed and decorated under the direction of Johann Poppe, the German architect, are as dainty and comfortable as the boudoir of the wealthiest woman in the land. But it is in the grand dining saloons, in the ladies', children's and smoking rooms, the cafes and libraries that the splendour of Poppe shines. German artists vied with each other in originating clever ideas. The most lavish expressions of painting and plastic arts are found, the subjects ranging from the allegorical fancies of the artists, to the portraits of the rulers and greatest public men of the two nations that are so closely linked together by Lloyd—Germany and the United States.

'Poppe's work reached its pinnacle in the decorations of the famous quartette. Above the dining saloon of the *Kaiser Wilhelm II*, the light–well rises three stories and is surrounded by magnificent decorations. The four large paintings on the ceiling represent the seasons. The panels of the walls in this saloon, as well as on the *Kaiser Wilhelm der Grosse*, are

Lloyd's Kronprinzessin Cecilie, *shown departing from her Hoboken berth just opposite the New York City piers, was the last of the German four-funnel liners* (Everett Viez Collection).

decorated with embossed leather designs. The allegorical figures in the great light-well of the *Kronprinz Wilhelm* rank with the works of the most famous artists.

'Of the four flyers, the noblest and most beautiful exemplification of modern naval architecture is found in the *Cecilie*. Here the light-well rises four stories, sixteen isolated columns carrying a new cupola and glass roof. From the balconies a view of unrivalled beauty spreads out when, dazzling in the rays of thousands of electric lights, the magnificently decorated saloon is thronged with 600 or more diners. The walls are ornamented with paintings of ideal landscapes, divided in blue silk material and surmounted by white architecture. In the rear of the room is the grand staircase, with an elaborately ornamented railing of bronze. The children's room, too, is a marvel of dainty beauty. Above the high wainscoting are scenes of child's life, a child's ball, a wedding procession, while between them are bronze reliefs illustrating fairy tales. The pictorial decoration of the smoking room represents exclusively scenes of Mecklenburg-Schwerin, the home of the Crown Princess. The high, vaulted ceiling is finished in the elaborate modern Roman style, bringing into relief a domelike part ornamented with figures of bronze. "The Queen of the Sea" she is called, and no other name would fit the magnificence of this ocean-flyer, which has brought forth admiration and praise from the whole world. And, amid all of this grandeur, what of the fare? With appetites whetted by the sea breezes, it is no small task to feed 3,800 passengers. The culinary department of each of the flyers is provided with every appliance for the preparation of food, which includes every known delicacy. About 20 kinds of warm dishes, besides tea, cocoa, coffee and chocolate, must be provided daily for breakfast. Luncheon comprises, in addition to the introductory courses and salads, three or four different soups, a dozen warm dishes, as many kinds of cold dishes, and four or five vegetables.

'The dinners are too elaborate to describe in detail, consisting as they do of ten to twelve courses and including everything in season and many things that are served only in the most exclusive cafes and hotels. Continuing its policy of progress, the North German Lloyd was first to install the a la carte system. No blare of trumpets now announces dinner, for the meal extends over several hours, passengers come and go at their will. While the table d'hote is still maintained on the "fleetest of the fleet", meals a la carte are served, without additional charge, to those who prefer them. It remained for the Lloyd, to inaugurate the small table system. The dining rooms of the "Four Flyers" are filled with round tables, decorated to harmonize with the surroundings. They are made to accommodate two, five and seven persons, whilst the larger tables are provided along the walls. At bedtime, another innovation. The bane of all travellers, the upper berth, has largely disappeared. Nearly every berth is a lower one, arranged side by side, or at right angles or end to end, so that the space is in nowise encroached upon. With higher ceilings, plenty of ventilation and the splash of waves to soothe you, sleep comes as naturally as to a child. Art and music, comfort and luxury, sumptuous splendour, extravagant living and exquisite surroundings for five days, all too short—that, in brief, is the story of the "fleetest of the fleet".'

Even the envious British were periodically drawn to words of praise. In his *The Sway of the Grand Saloon*, John Malcolm Brinnin noted that journalists at Southampton in 1903 were quite impressed with the then brand new *Kaiser Wilhelm II*. 'It is little less than remarkable that a nation which in the eighties was more or less dependent on this country for the construction of her mail ships should have so rapidly developed her shipbuilding talents that she now produces a vessel which is the largest in the world and which in point of speed promises to equal any steamship yet afloat . . . and there are features about the *Kaiser Wilhelm II* which represent an approach to luxury in voyaging which has as yet been unattained.'

These four-stackers were, in this age of 'bigger and better', surpassed by the likes of the 22,200-ton *Amerika* in 1905, then a year later by the 24,500-ton *Kaiserin Auguste Victoria* and then were completely overshadowed in 1913–14, first by the 52,100-ton *Imperator* and then the 54,200-ton *Vaterland*; but the earlier group remained as very popular ships.

It would be in that peace-breaking summer of 1914 that the careers of these ships—as for those of almost all other German liners—would be changed completely. At the very end, at the time of the Armistice, only *Victoria Luise*, the converted former *Deutschland*, would remain in German hands, and then only as a greatly demoted migrant carrier. Germanic glory seemed to have disappeared.

The eldest of all of the four-stackers, the racy *Kaiser Wilhelm der Grosse*, was the first loss. Interned at Bremerhaven in August 1914, she was requisitioned by the Imperial Navy and converted immediately to a high-speed armed merchant cruiser. Quickly she was ordered into the Atlantic and broke the Allied blockade by steaming northward at first along the Norwegian coast and not turning westward until well into the Northern latitudes. Once at sea, she sank two Allied merchant ships, one of them the British freighter *Hyades*, and later stopped and examined the South African mail boat *Galician*. However, once her coal supplies ran low, she made for the Spanish colony of Rio de Oro on the west coast of Africa. Although she was requested to leave port by the Spanish authorities, she was serviced by three colliers.

The situation grew far more tense by 27 August when the British cadet training ship *Highflyer*, an obsolete cruiser that mounted eleven 6-inch guns, arrived and ordered the former German flagship to leave immediately. The Germans refused and *Highflyer* opened fire. Sadly, after a short but very fierce action, the former transatlantic speed champion, whose armament of ten 4-inch guns was no match for the British vessel, was sunk. One of her shots killed one sailor and wounded five others on *Highflyer*, but suddenly the first superliner was gone forever.

At about the same time, *Kronprinzessin Cecilie* was in rather serious trouble as well. Eastbound out of New York, on 29 July, she was still off the North American coast when word was received that war was imminent. Most worrisome, she was not only carrying many German passengers but also $10 million in gold bars and $1 million in silver which were bound for the treasury in Berlin. A safe passage to Bremerhaven, avoiding capture by the British, seemed impossible. Consequently, the captain reversed course and announced that he would take his ship to a still neutral American port. Taking all precautions, however, she sailed in blackout and with radio silence. While not all of her passengers were pleased with this new plan,

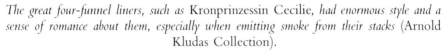

The great four-funnel liners, such as Kronprinzessin Cecilie, *had enormous style and a sense of romance about them, especially when emitting smoke from their stacks* (Arnold Kludas Collection).

Seized by the Americans during the First World War, Kronprinzessin Cecilie *was among a sizeable number of exiled German liners that were outfitted to serve the Allies against their creators. She is seen in this view as the troop transport USS* Mount Vernon *(Hapag-Lloyd).*

others became excited with the drama of it all and several of them, all businessmen and politicians travelling in first class, offered to buy the ship on the spot for $5 million. An extra sum was even offered to the captain if he agreed. They felt, in rather misguided determination, that *Kronprinzessin Cecilie* could then raise the US flag and sail onward to Germany untouched.

Instead, the Captain sensibly declined the offer and had his deck crews paint black bands around the tops of the four enormous funnels. His purpose was rather startling: at a distance, the ship was to resemble the British *Olympic*. Several days later, the disguised German liner appeared in the tiny harbour of Bar Harbour, Maine, an otherwise tranquil summer resort. At first, the scheme seemed to work—word spread that *Olympic* was, much to everyone's surprise, in port. The excitement was calmed rather quickly, however, when a message from New York reported that *Olympic* was, in fact, berthed at her Hudson River pier. The German's actual identity was soon discovered.

The exiled superliner was soon moved to Boston, laid up and later, following America's official entry into the War in 1917, was seized officially, never again to sail as a German ship. Following a full refit, she reappeared but as the Allied trooper USS *Mount Vernon*. She now served against the very country that had created her. To many of the servicemen, the affectionately dubbed 'doughboys', who sailed eastbound in her to the trenches of Western Europe, her earlier heritage hardly seemed to matter.

Kaiser Wilhelm II was caught, along with several other German liners including the giant flagship *Vaterland*, at her Hoboken berth. At first these ships were left in something of a political limbo, especially in respect to America's long existing neutrality, but then they too were seized by US authorities. *Kaiser Wilhelm II* was refitted as a troop transport as well and, in 1917, began sailing as USS *Agamemnon*.

The fourth of this group, *Kronprinz Wilhelm*, saw the most service under the German flag during the War. She was converted to an armed merchant cruiser, but one that established a particularly tragic record: she sank 15 Allied ships in all, totalling over 60,000 tons. John Malcolm Brinnin rightly labelled her 'the terror of the Southern Seas'.

As *Kronprinz Wilhelm* moved to more distant Southern waters, cloaked in various shades of grey, she became less and less the peaceful express liner of earlier days. Perhaps most sinister, she was fitted with guns, including an especially powerful machine-gun that was placed in the centre of her bridge, but which could also be moved to either side as needed. Internally, her once magnificent grand saloon was dismantled by her own carpenters while at sea, and converted to a huge coal storage hold. The smoking room underwent similar gutting and transformation, but into a large hospital ward, with endless rows of beds and bunks and white-painted cabinets. Mattresses were secured to the walls in this area so as to prevent further injury to the sick and wounded should the ship be damaged or tossed in heavy weather.

This role for *Kronprinz Wilhelm* was exhausting. Continuously at sea for just over eight months, she was in a badly deteriorating condition. Coaled at sea in special rendezvous with German and other sympathetic ships, her hull was frequently dented, serious leaks developed and her bow section had to be filled repeatedly with cement to plug holes and avoid flooding. Complicating all of this, her boiler tubes began to blow up, the ammunition supplies dwindled and all the while disease began to spread amongst her badly strained crew.

In due course, she fled northward to the safety of a neutral American port. Her captain selected Norfolk, Virginia, and once there, while her commander had hoped to return to sea after suitable repairs and provisioning, she was interned for the remainder of the War. In the spring of 1917 she was officially seized by the US Government, just after America's formal entry into the hostilities. Soon afterwards, she was reconditioned as the troopship *USS Von Steuben*.

By 1920, with the War over and their trooping duties past, the three remaining four-stackers became redundant within the US fleet. It was decided, however, that the well-worn *Von Steuben* was beyond any further use. Accordingly, in 1923 she was sold to Baltimore shipbreakers. Of the two survivors, *Mount Vernon* (ex-*Kronprinzessin Cecilie*) and *Agamemnon* (ex-*Kaiser Wilhelm II* and later renamed *Monticello*) spent the remainder of their days riding at anchor in a tributary of Chesapeake Bay in Maryland. There were over a dozen proposals set forth to reactivate them, including use as industrial trade fair ships and another that would have had them restored on the North Atlantic but as diesel-driven liners and in company with another former German, *Leviathan*. Even early attempts to sell them for scrap seemed to fail. It was not until the dramatic summer of 1940, when Germany was again at war and when they might have been refitted as troopers once again, that the scrappers were seriously interested. Both ships finished their days at Baltimore. Rusted, long ignored and mostly forgotten, this was a sad ending for those five once glorious superliners, the first four-stackers.

Kaiser Wilhelm der Grosse
(North German Lloyd)

Service Bremerhaven to New York via Southampton and Cherbourg.
Specifications 14,349 gross tons, 655 × 66 ft (201 × 20 m).
Builder Vulcan Works, Stettin, Germany, 1897.
Machinery Steam, triple expansion, twin screw. Service speed 22 knots.
Capacity 558 first class, 338 second class, 1,074 steerage.

1897 4 May: Launched in the presence of the Kaiser. Completed in Sept and established as world's largest ship, a record held until 1899. Captured Blue Riband in Nov with eastbound run of 22.35 knots.
1900 30 June: Slightly damaged in the great Hoboken pier fire at New York; later repaired. Also used during the year for some of the earliest Marconi wireless experiments.
1906 21 Nov: Collision at Cherbourg with Royal Mail Lines' *Orinoco*; 8 killed. German liner later found to be at fault.
1907 Oct: Rudder ripped off in North Atlantic storm; continued voyage using twin screws only.
1913 Tonnage revised to 13,952 and accommodation restyled for third and steerage class passengers only.
1914 2 Aug: Requisitioned by Imperial German Navy for wartime use as armed merchant cruiser. Travelled into Atlantic and sank three Allied ships. Put into Rio de Oro in Spanish West Africa on 26 Aug for bunkering. Converted British cruiser HMS *Highflyer* requested she depart immediately; German commander refused. Confrontation developed and German liner sunk.

Deutschland
(Hamburg America Line)

Service Bremerhaven to New York via Southampton and Cherbourg.
Specifications 16,502 gross tons, 684 × 67 ft (210 × 21 m).
Builder Vulcan Works, Stettin, Germany, 1900.
Machinery Steam, quadruple expansion, twin screw. Service speed 22½ knots.
Capacity 450 first class, 300 second class, 300 third class and 1,000 steerage.

1900 10 Jan: Launched. Completed in June and captured Blue Riband in following month during westbound maiden passage, with record of 22.42 knots.
1902 Apr: Lost rudder and stern post during storm in North Atlantic. During repairs, attempts made to recondition otherwise noisy and troublesome engines; ship also plagued with great vibrations. Returned to service in Oct, but little improvement. Thereafter considered less than successful by owners, thoroughly dissuading them from ever again seeking Blue Riband.
1910 Oct–**1911** Sept: Kept at Vulcan yards at Stettin and rebuilt as all-white cruising ship *Victoria Luise*. New engines fitted with service speed of 17½ knots. Tonnage revised to 16,703 and accommodation restyled for 487 all-first class passengers. Also used periodically as royal review ship.
1914 Aug: Fitted out for intended service with Imperial German Navy as armed merchant cruiser, but once again proved inefficient. No longer capable of any high speed. Laid up for duration of War.
1919 Allied Reparations Committee decide against taking vessel because of poor mechanical state. Retained as largest liner left under German flag.
1920–21 Rebuilt at Vulcan yards at Hamburg, but progress delayed by no less than three separate fires.
1921 Oct: Resumed Hamburg America service but as two-funnel migrant carrier *Hansa*, with restyled accommodation for 36 first class and 1,350 third class passengers. Tonnage revised to 16,333 and later to 16,376. Hamburg-New York service and later some migrant voyages to Canada.
1922 Accommodation restyled to 200 cabin class and 664 third class.
1925 Outmoded and exhausted; sold and handed over in May to Hamburg breakers.

Kronprinz Wilhelm
(North German Lloyd)

Service Bremerhaven to New York via Southampton and Cherbourg.
Specifications 14,908 gross tons, 664 × 66 ft (204 × 20 m).
Builder Vulcan Works, Stettin, Germany, 1901.
Machinery Steam, quadruple expansion, twin screw. Service speed 22½ knots.
Capacity 367 first class, 340 second class, 1,054 steerage.

1901 30 Mar: Launched. Completed in Aug. Crossed to New York on maiden voyage in September.
1902 8 Oct: Rammed small collier *Robert Ingham* in North Sea; 2 killed.
1907 8 July: Rammed small iceberg off Newfoundland.
1914 Aug: Departed from New York and converted at sea to armed merchant cruiser. Served mostly in South Atlantic and consequently sank 15 Allied ships, total 60,000 tons. At sea for 251 days.
1915 Apr: Sought safety of neutral American port, Norfolk, Virginia, for repairs and provisioning. Quickly interned by US authorities and laid up.
1917 Apr: Officially seized by US Government and refitted as troop-ship *USS Von Steuben*.
1917 9 Nov: During eastbound convoy, collided with transport *Agamemnon* (ex-*Kaiser Wilhelm II*). Later repaired.
1919 Decommissioned from war duties; laid up amidst various schemes to reactivate for commercial purposes, but with greatly deteriorated condition.
1923 Sold to scrappers at Baltimore.

Kaiser Wilhelm II
(North German Lloyd)

Service Bremerhaven to New York via Southampton and Cherbourg.
Specifications 19,361 gross tons, 707 × 72 ft (217 × 22 m).
Builder Vulcan Works, Stettin, Germany, 1903.
Machinery Steam, quadruple expansion engines, twin screw. Service speed 23 knots.
Capacity 775 first class, 343 second class, 770 steerage.

1902 12 Aug: Launched.
1903 Apr: Completed maiden voyage to New York.
1906 June: Took Blue Riband from Hapag's *Deutschland* with eastbound record of 23.58 knots.
1914 17 June: Collided with British freighter *Incemore* off Needles; damage repaired. Two months later (Aug) interned at berth at Hoboken in New York harbour. Idle for nearly three years.
1917 Apr: Officially seized by US authorities and afterwards converted to troop transport USS *Agamemnon*.
1919 Decommissioned and later thought to be used by United States Lines for transatlantic passenger service. Other schemes for revival included trade fair ship and diesel-powered passenger ship; none materialized and ship remained in lay-up.
1929 Renamed *Monticello*, but remained in idle state. Later plans to sell ship for scrap failed to materialize.
1940 Offered to British Government for use as troop-ship but rejected due to age and general condition. Sold in June to scrappers at Baltimore and delivered a month later.

Kronprinzessin Cecilie
(North German Lloyd)

Service Bremerhaven to New York via Southampton and Cherbourg.
Specifications 19,360 gross tons, 707 × 72 ft (217 × 22 m).
Builder Vulcan Works, Stettin, Germany, 1907.
Machinery Steam, quadruple expansion engines, twin screw. Service speed 23 knots.
Capacity 742 first class, 326 second class, 740 steerage.

1906 1 Dec: Launched.
1907 20 July: Sank alongside Bremerhaven dock just prior to maiden voyage; later pumped out and repaired. Crossed to New York on maiden voyage in Aug.
1914 July: Received word that war was imminent during early stages of eastbound run. Carrying large gold and silver shipments, and a number of German passengers, her captain especially wanted to avoid capture by British. Consequently, reversed course and repainted funnels in disguise as White Star *Olympic*. Sought refuge at Bar Harbour, Maine. Soon afterwards, ship moved to Boston and interned. Idle for nearly three years.
1917 Apr: Seized by US authorities and refitted as troop transport USS *Mount Vernon*.
1918 5 Sept: During westbound troop voyage with 2,500 onboard, torpedoed by German U-82; 37 killed. Returned to Brest for temporary repairs and later sailed to Boston for complete overhaul. Returned to service and later made special voyage from New York to Vladivostock via Panama to evacuate troops and refugees. Only German four-stacker to sail in Pacific.
1919 Decommissioned and laid up; many subsequent proposals submitted for revival, including conversion to diesel for transatlantic passenger service with United States Lines. Subsequently laid up in Chesapeake Bay with near sister *Agamemnon* (ex-*Kaiser Wilhelm II*).
1940 Offered to British for use as troop transport, but offer declined in view of age. Sold in June to scrappers at Baltimore for $178,300.

2

The *Barbarossa* Class

At the turn of the century, German passenger ship building efforts were not only encouraged by the Government, in the form of the Kaiser himself, but by the ever-improving trading conditions. For example, in the years between 1898 and 1899, first class traffic in German passenger ships increased from 15,700 to 17,700, and, in a far greater jump, steerage went from 32,200 to 53,600. Further expansion was also under way on some of the other German liner services, namely the migrant runs from Italy to New York (which was supported heavily not only by Germans and Italians, but by Austrians and Eastern Europeans), out to Australia from Germany via Suez and another long-distance run to the Far East via Suez. Consequently, and among many other projects, eleven sister ships and near sister ships, commonly known as the *Barbarossa* Class, were created. Seven went to North German Lloyd—*Freidrich der Grosse* (1896), *Barbarossa* (1897), *Konigin Luise* (1897), *Bremen* (1897), *Konig Albert* (1899), *Grosser Kurfurst* (1900) and *Prinzess Irene* (1900). Hamburg America Line had the other four—*Hamburg* (1900), *Kiautschou* (1900), *Moltke* (1902) and *Blucher* (1902).

They were built by three German yards: Vulcan at Stettin, Blohm & Voss at Hamburg and Schichau, also at Hamburg. Their measurements varied, ranging from approximately 10,000 gross tons to the 13,100 tons of the largest member of the group, *Grosser Kurfurst*. In length, they ranged from 521 to 581 ft (160 to 179 m). Their profiles consisted of two rather thin funnels, two tall masts, three-deck high superstructures, a straight bow and a counter stern. Variously they had, in addition to their passenger spaces, as many as six cargo holds each. Freight was very much a part of their projected revenues, so much so that parts of their austere, lower-deck steerage quarters could be easily dismantled and used for the stowage of smaller crates and other items.

Despite their comparatively moderate sizes, their passenger accommodation was substantial. For example,

Konigin Luise could take 225 in first class, 235 in second class and 1,940 in third class or steerage. The migrant passengers, no matter how low the respective fares, were another strong consideration for their profitability.

Hamburg America Line seemed to be particularly proud of their four ships in this class and, while they were often used on the Genoa-Naples-New York migrant run, their first class virtues were emphasized as 'ships with remarkable steadiness under all conditions of sea weather, and with such added comforts as a grill room, gymnasium and superior deck accommodation'. Hapag literature also duly noted that 'The *Hamburg* is distinguished for having more than once been singled out for royal patronage of an exceptional nature. She has been chartered by the German Emperor at different times, and used by him as his private yacht during his cruises to the Mediterranean as well as to Norway. Also, Colonel Theodore Roosevelt [by then, the former President of the United States], on the trip to Italy, en route to Africa on his hunting expedition, used the *Hamburg*.' Hapag also used *Hamburg* and her sister ships for periodic cruising.

All of these ships served until the start of the First World War in the summer of 1914. Several were interned in US ports, others at such diverse places as Manila and Naples, Genoa and Pernambuco (Brazil). Still others were kept in German ports.

Almost amazingly, the eleven sisters and near sisters of the *Barbarossa* Class survived the Great War and then afterwards, like almost all other German ships, were given over to the Allied victors. Most of this particular class went to the Americans, first serving as troop-ships and then on commercial services in more distant waters. For example, the former *Freidrich der Grosse* went into Hawaiian islands service as the white-hulled *City of Honolulu*. Of the few exceptions, *Koningin Luise* and *Bremen* went to the British, *Konig Albert* and *Moltke* to the Italians, and *Blucher* first to the Brazilians and then to the French.

Above   *North German Lloyd's* Konigin Luise, *completed in 1897, is shown after receiving some structural alterations in 1912* (Hapag-Lloyd).

Below   *After the First War, the former* Konigin Luise *was sold to National Steam Navigation of Greece and sailed in the Mediterranean–New York service as* Edison (Eric Johnson).

Above   Bremen *of 1897, repainted in white during the period she served as a cruise-ship* (Arnold Kludas Collection).

Below   Konig Albert *finished her long career with the Italians, as* Italia *and serving as a peacetime troop transport* (Willie Tinnemeyer Collection).

The former Grosser Kurfurst *of North German Lloyd is shown resting in drydock in her post-war career in the 1920s as the white-hulled cruise-ship* City of Los Angeles (Willie Tinnemeyer Collection).

It is important to note at this point the Great Hoboken Pier Fire of 1900, as *Bremen* was among the German liners involved. It was the worst tragedy of its kind yet to occur within the confines of New York Harbour and surely one of the most destructive. Author Irving Wagen wrote in considerable detail of this immortal day:

'A brisk wind sweeping the crowded Hoboken waterfront on a Saturday afternoon in 1900 was to be the death agent for more than 400 persons.

'Longshoremen were wrestling with cargo. Men in top hats and bowlers, and women in puff sleeves gaped at the towering steel hulls tied to the wooden docks. Sailors performed routine chores as passengers lolled aboard the ships. A watchman patrolling Pier 3 of the North German Lloyd was making his rounds on that mild day, checking over the bales of cotton and stacks of turpentine and oil-filled barrels stored on the pier. It was 4 pm on June 30th when a thin streak of orange flame issued from one of the cotton bales. The watchman saw it. He ran and sounded the alarm, but it was too late. Within seconds the blaze enveloped the cotton bales. The watchman's shouts were drowned out in the roar. For many, in the dock buildings, and below decks on the ships, the first warning came when the fire struck the barrels of oil. They exploded with a staccato sound of a rapid fire weapon.

'The wind carried the fire southward for a moment, then shifted to the opposite direction. Panic-stricken men, women and children trampled each other in their effort to escape. For most, escape to the landward side was impossible. The fire had travelled with incredible speed. In 15 minutes, it engulfed a quarter-of-a-mile of dock area. Hundreds aboard the piers and ships hurled themselves into the Hudson River. Many who could not swim died in minutes. Others clung to the piling of the piers until the fire forced them to let go and drown.

'The fire swept northward toward the big passenger ships, the cream of the North German Lloyd fleet. The nearest and the first to be hit was the *Saale*. She had 150 men aboard. Next in line was the *Bremen* with 200 persons aboard. In the next berth, tugs and crewmen worked frantically to move the mighty *Kaiser Wilhelm der Grosse* into the middle of the Hudson and out of danger. She was the queen of the German passenger fleet and the fastest ship afloat. Fifteen minutes after the fire broke out, she was in midstream, clear of danger, scorched, but not seriously damaged.

'Not so lucky was the *Main* with 150 men aboard. It had taken 25 minutes to push the blazing, ruined hulks of the *Bremen* and *Saale* into the River channel. The *Main* stayed at her berth for 11 hours. Miraculously, 16 men survived in her lowest compartment. All other hands perished. Firemen could not get close to fight the inferno, so intense was the

Above *Hapag's* Hamburg, *completed in 1900, was typical of her class of passenger ship: she served on the North Atlantic run to New York, out of the Mediterranean and on the long-distance Far East service via Suez* (Arnold Kludas Collection).

Right *A rather poetic view of the outbound* Karlsruhe, *the former* Prinzess Irene *of 1900, as seen in 1930* (Everett Viez Collection).

heat. The sun was a red ball shining through the smoke. Crowds gathered blocks away to gape at the spectacle.

'The *Bremen* drifted, toward the New York side of the River, scorching several piers there before she and the *Saale* were taken in tow, and beached at Liberty Island in New York Bay. Time and again, the New York shore was menaced by the drifting hulks of the 15 canal boats and 12 lighters [barges] caught in the Hoboken pier fire. Captain Mirow of the *Saale* made his way to the bridge of his ship where he was burned to death. The captains of the other ships escaped.

'The fire burned for three days, laying waste to the dockside area. The four piers were burned to the waterline. Warehouses along River Street were partially crumbled. Everything was covered with grey ash. Damage was estimated at $10 million, an extremely high amount for that day.

'On Thursday, July 5th, following the fire, seven flat bed horse-drawn carts, piled high with coffins, covered with black tarpaulins with a single wreath of flowers on each, left Hoffman's Funeral Home in lower Hoboken, proceeding up Washington Street. People fell in line behind the carts as the procession containing the bodies of 102 persons, known and unknown, victims of the fire, were carried to a common grave in Flower Hill Cemetery in nearby North Bergen.'

Decades later, on a mild afternoon in the autumn of 1982, I gave a filmed interview for German television on those same, but then rebuilt, docks where that devastating fire had occurred. It was a rather brief session that was to be inserted into a documentary about the great liners and was done with a style and panache that included a monocled director, smoking endless cigarettes in an enamel holder and wearing his long leather coat draped over his shoulders. He barked orders to his cameramen and other assistants, and insisted on a retake despite the presence of a patiently waiting New York City taxi-cab. The cab fare was already well over $200.

I spoke of the big liners, of the excitement that once prevailed on those now lonely docks and of my grandmother's distinct recollection of the fire itself. She was eleven, out for a Saturday afternoon on her roller skates, when the fire began. 'The smoke was so thick and so black,' she told me, 'that all of us thought that it was the end of the world!'

Friedrich der Grosse

(North German Lloyd)

Service Bremerhaven or Mediterranean ports to New York alternating with sailings from Bremerhaven to Australia via Suez.
Specifications 10,531 gross tons, 546 × 60 ft (168 × 19 m).
Builder Vulcan Works, Stettin, Germany, 1896.
Machinery Steam, quadruple expansion, twin screw. Service speed 14.5 knots.
Capacity 216 first class, 243 second class, 1,964 steerage.

1896 1 Aug: Launched. Completed in Nov.
1902 Tonnage relisted as 10,696.
1914 Aug: Interned at Hoboken owing to outbreak of First World War.
1917 Apr: Seized by US Navy and outfitted as troop transport USS *Huron*.
1919 Transferred to US Shipping Board and converted at Brooklyn to oil-burning ship.
1922 Chartered to Los Angeles Steamship Co and renamed *City of Honolulu* for California-Hawaii service. Caught fire on 12 Oct on return passage to Los Angeles and had to be abandoned. Deliberately sunk on 17 Oct by US warship.

Barbarossa

(North German Lloyd)

Service Bremerhaven to New York and Bremerhaven to Australia via Suez.
Specifications 10,769 gross tons, 548 × 60 ft (169 × 19 m).
Builder Blohm & Voss, Hamburg, Germany, 1897.
Machinery Steam, quadruple expansion, twin screw. Service speed 14.5 knots.
Capacity 230 first class, 227 second class, 1,935 steerage.

1896 5 Sept: Launched.
1897 Jan: Entered service, first to Australia and later to New York.
1902 Refitted and tonnage relisted as 10,915.
1914 Aug: Interned at Hoboken when war broke out.
1917 Apr: Formally seized by US Navy and outfitted as troop transport USS *Mercury*.
1919 Transferred to US Shipping Board and chartered to short-lived Baltic Steamship Corporation of America; never completed a voyage as company soon bankrupt. Laid up.
1924 Scrapped in USA.

Konigin Luise

(North German Lloyd)

Service Bremerhaven-Channel ports-New York, Bremerhaven to Australia via Suez, Mediterranean ports to New York.
Specifications 10,566 gross tons, 552 × 60 ft (170 × 19 m).
Builder Vulcan Works, Stettin, Germany, 1897.
Machinery Steam, quadruple expansion, twin screw. Service speed 14.5 knots.
Capacity 225 first class, 235 second class, 1,940 steerage.

1896 17 Oct: Launched.
1897 Mar: Entered service, first to New York and later on Australian trade.
1902 Extensively refitted and tonnage relisted as 10,711.
1912 Again refitted and tonnage relisted as 10,785.
1914 Laid up throughout First World War.
1919 Apr: Given to Great Britain as reparations and assigned to Orient Line. Refitted.
1920 Sept: Began commercial service from London to Australian ports via Suez. Tonnage relisted as 11,103. During first sailing collided at Lisbon with British freighter *Loughborough*, which sank.
1921 Jan: Purchased from the British Government by Orient Line and renamed *Omar*.
1924 Sold to Byron Steamship Company of London and renamed *Edison* for Piraeus-Mediterranean ports-New York service.
1929 Transferred to Greek registry.
1935 Scrapped in Italy.

Bremen

(North German Lloyd)

Service Bremerhaven to New York, Bremerhaven to Australia via Suez, Mediterranean ports to New York.
Specifications 10,552 gross tons, 550 × 60 ft (169 × 19 m).
Builder Schichau Works, Danzig, Germany, 1897.
Machinery Steam, quadruple expansion, twin screw. Service speed 14.5 knots.
Capacity 230 first class, 250 second class, 1,850 steerage.

1896 14 Nov: Launched.
1897 May: Completed.
1900 30 June: Caught in Great Hoboken Pier Fire; later run aground deliberately and with loss of 12 crew. Temporarily repaired. Sailed for Germany in Oct. Repaired at Vulcan yards, Stettin.
1901 Oct: Returned to service following extensive refit. Tonnage relisted as 11,540 and length increased to 575 ft (177 m).
1905 Sept: Lost propeller during transatlantic crossing and later had to be towed to Halifax.
1908 Dec: Used to evacuate refugees from Messina, Sicily, following eruption of Mount Etna.
1914: Laid up throughout First World War.
1919 Apr: Given to Great Britain as reparations and managed by P&O Lines. Used briefly in their Australian passenger service.
1921 Sold to Byron Steam Navigation Co of London; renamed *Constantinople* for Piraeus-Mediterranean ports-New York service.
1924 Renamed *King Alexander*.
1929 Broken up in Italy.

Konig Albert

(North German Lloyd)

Service Bremerhaven to New York, Bremerhaven to Far East via Suez. Later, mostly Mediterranean ports-New York.

Specifications 10,643 gross tons, 521 × 60 ft (160 × 19 m).

Builder Vulcan Works, Stettin, Germany, 1899.

Machinery Steam, quadruple expansion, twin screw. Service speed 15½ knots.

Capacity 257 first class, 119 second class, 1,799 steerage.

1899 24 June: Launched. Completed in Sept and maiden voyage from Bremerhaven to Yokohama via Suez in Oct.

1914 Aug: Laid up at Genoa due to outbreak of First World War.

1915 May: Seized by Italian Government and refitted as hospital ship *Ferdinando Palasciano*.

1920 Sold to Navigazione Generale Italiana and used on Naples-Genoa-New York run.

1923 Became transport in Italian Navy, renamed *Italia*.

1925 Laid up.

1926 Broken up in Italy.

Hamburg

(Hamburg America Line)

Service Hamburg to Far East via Suez, Hamburg-New York, Genoa-New York.

Specifications 10,532 gross tons, 521 × 60 ft (160 × 19 m).

Builder Vulcan Works, Stettin, Germany, 1900.

Machinery Steam, quadruple expansion, twin screw. Service speed 15.5 knots.

Capacity 290 first class, 100 second class, 80 third class, 1,700 steerage.

1899 25 Nov: Launched. Original intended name had been *Bavaria*.

1900 Mar: Completed. Maiden voyage from Hamburg to Far Eastern ports.

1910 27 Feb: Collided with tugboat *Eolo* in Naples harbour.

1914 Aug: Interned at New York due to outbreak of First World War. Chartered to American Red Cross (renamed *Red Cross*) for one round voyage to Rotterdam then returned to New York and reverted to *Hamburg*. Laid up.

1917 Apr: Seized by US Navy and renamed *Powhatan*. Refitted as hospital ship.

1919 Transferred to US Shipping Board.

1920 Aug: Chartered to short-lived Baltic Steamship Corporation of America, renamed *New Rochelle*. New York-Danzig service.

1921 Feb: Chartered to United States Mail Steamship Co and used again on New York-Danzig service. Renamed *Hudson*. Charter changed in Aug to United States Lines and transferred to New York-Bremerhaven service.

1922 July: Renamed *President Fillmore*.

1924 Transferred to Dollar Line, also US flag, and used on round-the-world passenger service from San Francisco.

1928 Scrapped.

Grosser Kurfurst
(North German Lloyd)

Service Bremerhaven to New York, Bremerhaven to Australia via Suez.
Specifications 13,182 gross tons, 581 × 62 ft (179 × 19 m).
Builder Schichau Works, Danzig, Germany, 1900.
Machinery Steam, triple expansion, twin screw. Service speed 15 knots.
Capacity 299 first class, 317 second class, 172 third class, 2,201 steerage.

1899 2 Dec: Launched.
1900 Apr: Completed.
1913 9 Oct: Involved in rescue operation of burning British passenger ship *Volturno* in mid-Atlantic.
1914 Aug: Interned in New York.
1917 Apr: Formally acquired by US Navy and refitted as transport *Aeolus*.
1919 Transferred to US Shipping Board.
1920 Chartered to US-flag Munson Line. Refitted at Baltimore including conversion to oil burning. Explosion on 10 Sept; four killed. Entered service in Dec from New York to Rio de Janeiro, Santos, Montevideo and Buenos Aires.
1922 Mar: Rammed and sank British freighter *Zero* in South Atlantic. Sold in June to Los Angeles Steamship Co and underwent extensive refit at Bethlehem Steel shipyards at Quincy, Massachusetts. Renamed *City of Los Angeles* and restyled as luxury cruise-ship with 446 first class berths only. Tonnage relisted as 12,642. Used in Hawaiian islands cruise service.
1932 Laid up owing to Depression.
1933 Transferred to Matson Line, but laid up after only a few voyages.
1937 Crossed Pacific to Japan for scrapping.

Prinzess Irene
(North German Lloyd)

Service Bremerhaven-New York, Bremerhaven to Australia via Suez.
Specifications 10,881 gross tons, 540 × 60 ft (166 × 19 m).
Builder Vulcan Works, Stettin, Germany, 1900.
Machinery Steam, quadruple expansion, twin screw. Service speed 15.5 knots.
Capacity 268 first class, 132 second class, 1,954 steerage.

1900 19 June: Launched. Completed in Sept. Maiden voyage to Far Eastern ports.
1909 10 June: Rescued 110 survivors from Cunard liner *Slavonia*, stranded off Azores.
1910 6 Apr: Stranded off Long Island, New York; later refloated and repaired at Newport News, Virginia.
1914 Aug: Interned at New York.
1917 Apr: Transferred to US Navy and outfitted as transport *Pocahontas*.
1919 Handed over to US Shipping Board and chartered to United States Mail Steamship Co. Used on New York-Genoa-Naples service with restyled accommodation for 350 cabin class and 900 third class passengers.
1921 May: Laid up at Gibraltar with machinery defects; soon afterwards bought by North German Lloyd and towed to Bremerhaven for full repairs. Renamed *Bremen* and tonnage relisted as 10,826.
1923 Apr: Resumed Bremerhaven-New York sailings with cabin, tourist third and third class accommodation.
1928 Jan: Renamed *Karlsruhe* to allow *Bremen* to be used as name of new express liner. Thereafter mostly used on Gulf of Mexico service to Galveston, Havana, Veracruz and Tampico.
1932 Scrapped at Bremerhaven.

Kiautschou

(Hamburg America Line)

Service Hamburg-Far East, Hamburg-Channel ports-New York.
Specifications 10,911 gross tons, 540 × 60 ft (166 × 19 m).
Builder Vulcan Works, Stettin, Germany, 1900.
Machinery Steam, quadruple expansion, twin screw. Service speed 15.5 knots.
Capacity 327 first class, 103 second class, 80 third class, 1,700 steerage.

1900 14 Sept: Launched. Original name to be *Borussia*, then *Teutonia*. Completed in Dec.
1904 Feb: Sold to North German Lloyd and renamed *Prinzess Alice* for Bremerhaven-Suez-Far East service. Also transatlantic service to New York.
1914 Aug: Interned at Manila; laid up.
1917 Apr: Seized by US Government and renamed *Princess Matoika*; refitted as troop transport.
1919 Assigned to US Shipping Board and allocated to United States Mail Steamship Co; used on New York-Genoa-Naples service. Accommodation restyled for 350 cabin and 500 third class passengers. Subsequent voyages to Bremen and Danzig.
1922 Renamed *President Arthur*.
1925 Sold to newly formed American Palestine Line for New York-Haifa service; shortlived. Ship again offered for sale. Was to have been renamed *White Palace*, but sold to New York buyers then resold to Los Angeles Steamship Co and rebuilt at San Pedro, California, for Hawaiian islands cruise service. Renamed *City of Honolulu* and fitted with restyled accommodation for 445 first class and 50 third class passengers. Tonnage relisted as 10,860.
1927 June: Entered Hawaiian service.
1930 25 May: Burnt out at Honolulu and later brought to Los Angeles and laid up.
1933 Aug: Sold to Japanese shipbreakers and broken up at Osaka.

Moltke

(Hamburg America Line)

Service Hamburg-Channel ports-New York, Genoa-Naples-New York.
Specifications 12,335 gross tons, 550 × 60 ft (169 × 19 m).
Builder Blohm & Voss, Hamburg, Germany, 1902.
Machinery Steam, quadruple expansion, twin screw. Service speed 16 knots.
Capacity 333 first class, 169 second class, 1,600 steerage.

1901 27 Aug: Launched.
1902 Mar: Maiden voyage to New York.
1915 May: Interned at Genoa owing to outbreak of First World War; transferred to Italian Government and then to Italian State Railways, renamed *Pesaro*.
1919 Apr: Transferred to Lloyd Sabaudo and used on Genoa-Naples-New York service. Later used on South American run to Rio de Janeiro and Beunos Aires.
1925 Scrapped in Italy.

Blucher

(Hamburg America Line)

Service Hamburg and Channel ports to New York, Hamburg to South America.
Specifications 12,334 gross tons, 550 × 62 ft (169 × 19 m).
Builder Blohm & Voss, Hamburg, Germany, 1902.
Machinery Steam, quadruple expansion, twin screw. Service speed 16.5 knots.
Capacity 333 first class, 169 second class, 1,600 steerage.

1901 23 Nov: Launched.
1902 June: Maiden crossing to New York.
1914 Aug: Interned at Perambuco, Brazil.
1917 June: Formally seized by Brazilian Government and renamed *Leopoldina*.
1919 Transferred to French Government.
1920 Mar: Chartered to Compagnie Générale Trans-atlantique (French Line) for Le Havre-New York service.
1921 Dec: Laid up.
1923 Mar: Sold outright to CGT and renamed *Suffren*. Accommodation restyled as 500 second class and 250 third class. Le Havre-New York service.
1928 Sept: Laid up.
1929 May: Scrapped at Genoa, Italy.

3
The *Pennsylvania* Class

Again, this was a group, although only a quartet, of sisters and near sisters. Each was owned by Hamburg America Line and they were named *Pennsylvania*, *Pretoria*, *Graf Waldersee* (she was to have used the 'P' nomenclature as well and been called *Pavia*) and finally *Patricia*. Rather large four-masters, they were built to earn their keep both with passengers, particularly for the ever-increasing numbers travelling westbound to America in steerage, and as large cargo carriers (each ship had seven holds). In fact, on their return eastward crossings to Germany the austere steerage quarters could be partially dismantled and used as additional cargo space.

Completed just before the turn of the century, this foursome served until the outbreak of war in 1914.

Popular ships, Hapag literature described them aptly as

'. . . among the largest and best known vessels in the world. These ships embody and exemplify a distinct modern type, responding to the demand for steamers of unusual size and exceptional carrying capacity. In their construction and equipment, the passenger accommodations have received the most careful attention and are of superior order, and their huge cargo capacity imparts unusual stability and steadiness under all conditions of wind and water. While not so swift as some of the ocean greyhounds of the fleet, many travellers select these vessels on account of their steadiness and their manifold comforts.

'When the colossal *Pennsylvania* was constructed, she was justly considered the leviathan of her day. So successful was

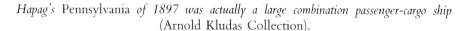

Hapag's Pennsylvania *of 1897 was actually a large combination passenger-cargo ship* (Arnold Kludas Collection).

Pretoria of 1898 finished her career in the years following the First World War as a freighter for the British-flag Ellerman Lines (Willie Tinnemeyer Collection).

this advance in the building of giant ships that the *Pretoria*, *Patricia* and *Graf Waldersee*, built on similar lines, naturally followed as a legitimate development. The *Pennsylvania* has carried in one trip more freight than the entire sailing force of the Line in its early days took across in a year. Some idea of the size of these steamships may be gained from the fact that in the holds of such vessels, there is room for so great a cargo that it would take 616 large American freight cars to transport it or, in other words, a train of cars reaching from Trinity Church, at the head of Wall Street, to Central Park in New York City.

'The second class accommodations on these ships would have made luxurious first class quarters a decade earlier. As to the first-cabin accommodations, it is enough to say that they conform to the highest standards of comfort and convenience consistently maintained by the Line. Their roomy and home-like staterooms, broad stretches of deck, invariable steadiness, excellent cuisine and superior service, combine to render them justly popular with discriminating travellers.'

They had passed into American hands by the end of the First World War, but saw comparatively little service thereafter. All of them were scrapped by the mid-'twenties.

Pennsylvania
(Hamburg America Line)

Service Hamburg-Channel ports-New York.
Specifications 12,891 gross tons, 579 × 62 ft (178 × 19 m).
Builder Harland & Wolff Ltd, Belfast, Northern Ireland, 1897.
Machinery Steam, quadruple expansion, twin screw. Service speed 13 knots.
Capacity 162 first class, 180 second class, 2,382 steerage; later 404 second class, 2,200 steerage.

1896 10 Sept: Launched.
1897 Jan: Maiden voyage to New York.
1900 Tonnage relisted as 13,333.
1914 Aug: Interned at New York.
1917 Apr: Officially seized by US Government and refitted as Navy transport *Nansemond*.
1919 Handed over to US Shipping Board and laid up in upper Hudson River, New York.
1924 Scrapped.

Pretoria
(Hamburg America Line)

Service Hamburg-Channel ports-New York.
Specifications 12,800 gross tons, 586 × 62 ft (180 × 19 m).
Builder Blohm & Voss, Hamburg, Germany, 1898.
Machinery Steam, quadruple expansion, twin screw. Service speed 13 knots.
Capacity 197 second class, 2,382 steerage class; later 400 second class, 2,200 steerage.

1897 9 Oct: Launched.
1898 Feb: Maiden voyage to New York.
1900 Tonnage relisted as 13,324.
1908 9 Oct: Collided with steamer *Nipponia* near Texel, which was lost with all hands.
1914 12 June: Damaged in collision near Nantucket Lightship with American liner *New York*. Sailed to Hamburg for repairs, then laid up due to outbreak of war.
1919 Mar: Surrendered to US Government for use as Army transport.
1920 Sept: Transferred to British Government and managed by Ellerman Lines.
1921 Nov: Scrapped.

Graf Waldersee
(Hamburg America Line)

Service Hamburg-Channel ports-New York.
Specifications 12,830 gross tons, 586 × 62 ft (180 × 19 m).
Builder Blohm & Voss, Hamburg, Germany, 1899.
Machinery Steam, quadruple expansion, twin screw. Service speed 13 knots.
Capacity 162 first class, 184 second class, 2,200 steerage; later 408 second class, 2,300 steerage.

1898 10 Dec: Launched. Intended name was *Pavia*, but changed prior to launching.
1899 Apr: Maiden voyage to New York.
1900 Tonnage relisted as 13,193.
1914–19 Laid up during war.
1919 Mar: Handed over to US Navy for use as transport.
1920 Transferred to British Government and managed by P&O Lines.
1921 Aug: Sold to British shipbreakers, then resold to Hamburg breakers.
1922 Scrapped.

Patricia
(Hamburg America Line)

Service Hamburg-Channel ports-New York.
Specificiations 13,023 gross tons, 585 × 62 ft (180 × 19 m).
Builder Vulcan Works, Stettin, Germany, 1899.
Machinery Steam, quadruple expansion, twin screw. Service speed 13 knots.
Capacity 162 first class, 184 second class, 2,143 steerage.

1899 20 Feb: Launched. June: Maiden voyage to New York.
1900 Tonnage relisted as 13,424.
1910 2 Jan: Collided and sank lightship *Elbe V*.
1914–19 Laid up during war.
1919 Mar: Handed over to US Government for use as Navy transport.
1920 Transferred to British Government and managed by Ellerman Lines.
1921 Scrapped.

4
The North Atlantic 'B' Class

These were refined, slightly smaller and slower (a mere 12½ knots at maximum speed) versions of *Pennsylvania* and her sisters. Given 'B' names— *Brasilia, Bulgaria, Batavia, Belgravia* and *Belgia*—they were again designed as combination passenger and cargo vessels. Also, and as an alternative to the ever-growing New York service, this group was intended especially for service between Hamburg, the Channel ports and Baltimore. In their passenger quarters, while lacking provision for first class, they each had a capacity for approximately 2,700—300 in second class and, most lucrative of all, some 2,400 in steerage. Often filled to capacity with westbound settlers, that same steerage space could also be used for cargo on eastbound voyages. Otherwise, the large pieces of freight were handled in the seven holds.

From the start, however, the ships did not come up to expectations and consequently there was some rethinking on the part of their owners. In fact, *Belgia* was sold off just before completion, in the autumn of 1899, to Britain's Atlantic Transport Line and was finished as the freighter *Michigan*. Slightly later, in 1900, after just a little more than a year in Hamburg America service, *Brasilia* was sold to her builders, Harland & Wolff shipyards of Belfast in Northern Ireland, who then rebuilt her for North Atlantic service as Dominion Line's *Norseman*. A few years afterwards, in 1905, *Belgravia* went to the Russians, becoming the Naval ship *Riga*. While the others would be broken up by the early 'twenties, it was this Soviet vessel that survived the longest of the group, 46 years, until torpedoed in 1945.

Also, and particularly notable in the annals of maritime history, *Bulgaria* survived an especially perilous eastward crossing in February 1899. Carrying some passengers and a cargo of grain, she was caught in a particularly nasty hurricane. Her hatch covers began to break and the ship quickly started to flood. The rudder was ripped off, a sailor was swept overboard and the 517-ft ship was listing so badly that she could not be steered even by the propellers. After a day, over 100 injured horses housed in the forward hold had to be killed. Distress rockets were fired and, in due course, three nearby British ships responded. A child was killed in the difficult transfer of passengers from *Bulgaria*, and soon afterwards the rescue ships lost sight of the German vessel and later reported that she had most likely sunk. In fact, she was still afloat, carrying most of her crew. After wallowing for five days, the storm briefly subsided and the rotting horse carcasses were thrown over the side. Later, however, the storm resumed and *Bulgaria* was 'lost' for another four days, before being sighted by a British freighter. Five attempts to tow the battered German were made, but each failed. After another week, the crew constructed an emergency rudder and, within several days, *Bulgaria*, which by then had made international headlines, was safely at anchor at Ponta Delgada in the Azores. Once back in Germany, this 'heroic ship', as she was called, was given a joyous welcome. Kaiser Wilhelm presented her captain with a medal of the House of Hohenzollern and the crew were treated to an enormous town hall reception given by the Hamburg senate.

Top right *Hapag's* Bulgaria *of 1898 and her near sisters were very basic ships; they were large cargo carriers as well as being fitted with extensive steerage capacities* (Willie Tinnemeyer Collection).

Middle right Batavia *sailed for her Hamburg America owners on the Hamburg-Baltimore service* (Arnold Kludas Collection).

Right Belgravia *of 1899 was the longest lasting of Hapag's 'B' Class. She survived until torpedoed in the Pacific in June 1945* (Arnold Kludas Collection).

Brasilia

(Hamburg America Line)

Service Hamburg-Baltimore.
Specifications 10,336 gross tons, 516 × 62 ft (159 × 19 m).
Builder Harland & Wolff, Belfast, Northern Ireland, 1898.
Machinery Steam, quadruple expansion, twin screw. Service speed 12 knots.
Capacity 300 second class, 2,400 steerage.

1897 27 Nov: Launched.
1898 Mar: Maiden voyage.
1900 Feb: Sold to Harland & Wolff, then resold to Dominion Line of Liverpool and renamed *Norseman*. Refitted as freighter with four masts and steerage accommodation. Tonnage relisted as 9,546. Used on Liverpool-South African service as transport for Boer War.
1910 Transferred to Aberdeen Line and used on London-Cape Town-Sydney service.
1914 Wartime transport.
1916 22 Jan: Torpedoed by German submarine in Gulf of Salonika. Later towed to Mudros, again torpedoed and later sank. Sold to Italian salvage company for scrapping.
1920 Broken up.

Bulgaria

(Hamburg America Line)

Service Hamburg-New York, Hamburg-Boston or Baltimore.
Specifications 10,237 gross tons, 517 × 62 ft (159 × 19 m).
Builder Blohm & Voss, Hamburg, Germany, 1898.
Machinery Steam, quadruple expansion, twin screw. Service speed 12.5 knots.
Capacity 300 second class, 2,400 steerage.

1898 5 Feb: Launched. April: Maiden voyage.
1899 Feb: Survived extraordinary hurricane during homeward voyage in eastern Atlantic. Rudder lost and numerous rescue attempts; ship given up as lost. Received international attention. After three weeks, emergency rudder created and ship later put into Ponta Delgada, Azores. Subsequently returned to Hamburg for heroic welcome and full repairs.
1906 Refitted and tonnage relisted as 11,494.
1913 Apr: Sold to Unione Austriaca of Trieste and renamed *Canada* for short-lived Trieste-Quebec City-Montreal service. Aug: Resold to Hamburg America and reverted to original name.
1914 Aug: Interned at Baltimore on outbreak of war.
1917 Apr: Formally seized by US Government and outfitted as Army transport *Hercules*.
1919 Transferred to US Shipping Board and renamed *Philippines*.
1920 Laid up.
1924 Scrapped at New York.

Batavia
(Hamburg America Line)

Service Hamburg-Baltimore, Hamburg-Boston, Mediterranean ports-New York.
Specifications 10,178 gross tons, 517 × 62 ft (159 × 19 m).
Builder Blohm & Voss, Hamburg, Germany, 1899.
Machinery Steam, quadruple expansion, twin screw. Service speed 12½ knots.
Capacity 300 second class, 2,400 steerage.

1899 11 Mar: Launched. May: Maiden voyage.
1906 Refitted and tonnage relisted as 11,464.
1909 11 June: Rescued 300 passengers from stranded Cunarder *Slavonia*, aground off the Azores.
1913 Temporary transfer to Unione Austriaca of Trieste and renamed *Polonia* for short-lived Trieste-Quebec City-Montreal service. Returned to Hamburg America and reverted to original name.
1914 Aug: Laid up at Hamburg owing to outbreak of war.
1917 Briefly used as German transport *Batavia 7* in Baltic waters.
1919 Dec: Transferred to French Government and operated by Messageries Maritimes as *Batavia*.
1924 Scrapped.

Belgravia
(Hamburg America Line)

Service Hamburg-New York, Hamburg-Baltimore, Genoa-Naples-New York.
Specifications 10,155 gross tons, 516 × 62 ft (159 × 19 m).
Builder Blohm & Voss, Hamburg, Germany, 1899.
Machinery Steam, quadruple expansion, twin screw. Service speed 12½ knots.
Capacity 300 second class, 2,400 steerage.

1899 11 May: Launched. Aug: Maiden voyage.
1900 Tonnage relisted as 10,982.
1905 May: Sold to Russian Navy and refitted for use as transport *Riga*.
1906 Transferred to Black Sea Steamship Co of Odessa.
1920 Transferred to Sovtorgflot and renamed *Transbalt*. Used as hospital ship until 1923.
1945 13 June: Accidentally torpedoed by US submarine *Spadefish* after having been misidentified as Japanese freighter.

Belgia
(Hamburg America Line)

Service Intended for Hamburg-New York run.
Specifications 11,585 gross tons, 516 × 62 ft (159 × 19 m).
Builder Harland & Wolff, Belfast, Northern Ireland, 1899.
Machinery Steam, quadruple expansion, twin screw. Service speed 12½ knots.
Capacity 300 second class, 2,400 steerage.

1899 5 Oct: Launched. Prior to completion, sold to Atlantic Transport Line of London and renamed *Michigan*. Completed as cargo ship with steerage accommodation. Tonnage listed as 9,501. Shortly thereafter sold to Dominion Line of Liverpool and renamed *Irishman*.
1914–18 War service.
1921 Sold to F. Leyland & Co, Liverpool.
1924 Sold to Dutch shipbreakers.
1925 Scrapped.

5
Other Atlantic ships

So far groups of ships have been considered which were sister ships or near sisters, or obviously linked, comparable fleetmates such as the four-stackers. This section, however, deals with more specific ships—the unsuccessful *Kaiser Friedrich*, the twin sisters *Rhein* and *Main*, and two other sister ships, and the only six-masted liners ever to sail the North Atlantic, *President Lincoln* and *President Grant*.

Lloyd's three-funnel *Kaiser Friedrich* was intended to sail with the larger and faster *Kaiser Wilhelm der Grosse*, which was completed about six months earlier and which was the first of the four-stackers. Built at Schichau yards at Danzig, *Kaiser Friedrich* was just short of a complete failure, at least for the Germans. Required to achieve a 22-knot top speed, the ship could barely manage 20 knots during her trials and maiden voyage in the spring of 1898. Consequently, North German Lloyd refused to accept her. Returned to her builders, the ship was overhauled and returned to Lloyd, but only with the slightest improvement in her speed. Lloyd was deeply dissatisfied, the ship was again declined and returned to her builders, and all the while a highly publicized scandal developed. A court battle followed and, in due course, the shipyard was found to be at fault.

After considerable lay-ups, *Kaiser Friedrich* was chartered in October 1899 for about a year by the rival Hamburg America Line. It too was less than pleased with the ship and so she went back to the Schichau Company once again and was subsequently laid up at Hamburg for 12 years, until the spring of 1912. She was then purchased by the newly created French firm, Compagnie Navigation de Sud Atlantique. Given an extensive refit as well as new, more efficient boilers, she was renamed *Burdigala* and used on the Bordeaux-South America run. Regrettably, her new commercial life was all too brief. Converted to a trooper for the First World War, she was subsequently mined in the Aegean in November 1916.

Soon after the completion of *Kaiser Friedrich* in 1899–1900, Lloyd built two supplemental, medium-sized liners, the 10,000-ton sisters *Rhein* and *Main*. With four tall masts in a design based on the earlier sailing ships, they had three-class passenger quarters, but with especially extensive berthing for steerage travellers. They were used on the busy New York service as well as on the run to Baltimore and even further afield to Australia via Suez. While *Main* was burnt and sank during the Great Hoboken Pier Fire in June 1900, she was later salvaged and repaired and returned to passenger service. Both ships continued until the outbreak of war in August 1914; *Rhein* was caught at Baltimore, laid up and later, in April 1917, formally seized by the US Navy and outfitted as the troop transport *Susquehanna*. Laid up again after the hostilities, she was reactivated in 1920 for the resumption of German passenger service, but under American colours, first for United States Mail Lines and then United States Lines. Within two years, however, she was again idle and then finally broken up in 1928. *Main* was kept at Antwerp throughout the war years and was then surrendered to the British, who used her for a very short time before handing her over to the French. She was scrapped in 1925.

The other two ships in this section, *President Lincoln* and *President Grant*, were built for Hamburg America Line, which, by 1905, was both the biggest and busiest passenger ship firm in the world. Their staple seems to have been to provide, and often aboard the very same ships, some of the most luxuriously decorated, well-served first class accommodation as well as extensive third class and steerage quarters for the huge ever-increasing westbound migrant trade to North America.

After the turn of the century, the Hapag Company was under the guidance of a shipping genius, Albert Ballin. He followed and studied every aspect of shipping, and noted every detail both ashore and afloat. He often travelled on Hapag ships with pad and pencil in hand, carefully noting details from the emission of smoke from the funnels, the adequacy of the safety equipment and the efficiency of the kitchens to the

Above *The most troublesome of all the big German liners,* Kaiser Friedrich, *spent twelve years in lay-up, from 1900 until 1912* (Arnold Kludas Collection).

Below *Completed in 1899, North German Lloyd's* Rhein *finished her career in the hands of Japanese shipbreakers in 1928* (Arnold Kludas Collection).

fullness of the pillows in the passenger cabins. Furthermore, as a proud nationalist, Ballin wanted to increase the size, and with competitive superiority as well, of the Hapag fleet and, in fact, bring it to the 'crowning glory' of building the biggest ships ever, a trio of superliners that would begin to appear in 1913.

In his *The Sway of the Grand Saloon*, John Malcolm Brinnin wrote:

'Albert Ballin was one of the most imaginative and humane figures in the whole cold, Roman-eyed pantheon of shipping executives. Ballin had come up the hard way and in the course of ascent had brought Germany to first place on the waterways of the world. Starting with a job in a small Hamburg agency that, for a fee, packed off emigrants to New York and Baltimore, Ballin soon became an operator of ships himself. Still in his early twenties when he joined the Carr Line, he parlayed that company's six rusty little ships into a combine with two other emigrant services—Sloman's American Line and the Union Line—and gave Hamburg America so much competition that they decided to get rid of him. To do this, they simply incorporated him and his hard-working fleet into their own operations. Their drastic step proved to be a brilliant one. In no time at all, Ballin rose from manager of Hamburg America's passenger department to become director of the whole company. Since it had by then become the biggest shipping firm on earth, Ballin's position, at the age of thirty-one, made him the wunderkind.'

While Ballin, other Hapag directors and sponsors and supporters in Berlin preferred to build brand new passenger ships, and in home yards, they were not above buying ships to expand their fleet even further. The sister ships *Scotian* and *Servian* were launched at Belfast in 1903 for the Furness-Leyland Line, but then, prior to completion, the order was suddenly cancelled. They sat incomplete at the shipbuilder's yard for three years until late in 1906, when Ballin himself thought them to be the ideal ships for transatlantic service, especially for the booming migrant business. In fact, this steerage traffic had become the most profitable and consequently the most sought-after part of the Atlantic trade. (Of course, although somewhat less profit-making on paper, the first class trade was still immensely important, and every luxury and novelty was put aboard Hapag ships to recruit and then cater for these mostly demanding voyagers.)

By 1907, immigrants were arriving in New York Harbour at the astonishing rate of 12,000 a day. All of them came by ship. Consequently, ocean shippers—including the Germans—wanted their share. Hamburg America felt, in an early form of market research and among serveral other calculations, that passenger ships with American or at least American-sounding names lured even more immigrant passengers. It seems that these steerage passengers felt that if they travelled and

One of the North Atlantic's only six-masted passenger ships, Hapag's President Lincoln, *was originally designed for British owners as* Scotian *(Arnold Kludas Collection).*

Given an American name so as to attract more European migrants, President Grant *later went into US-flag service as* Republic *and then was not scrapped until as late as 1952* (Arnold Kludas Collection).

then arrived at American shores in a ship with such a name, their formal entry into the United States would be eased. Many had already heard of the often complicated, sometimes sinister, receptions and processing at Ellis Island, the immigrant receiving station in New York Harbour, which had also come to be known as the 'Island of Tears'.

Consequently, soon after Hapag bought *Scotian* and *Servian*, they were renamed, not after German cities or Hohenzollern princesses, but as *President Lincoln* and *President Grant*. Both ships were completed by 1907 to Hapag specifications and with appropriate accommodation, in fact the largest then on the Atlantic—a capacity of 3,828 in all. This was divided between 324 first class, 152 second class, 1,004 third class and 2,348 in steerage. The ships were placed on the express run between Hamburg and New York, with calls at Plymouth and Cherbourg. Large ships, they became quickly known for their novelty within the Atlantic passenger fleet: the only liners with six masts.

Hapag, in their advertising literature for the two ships, stated that:

'Accommodations are provided for first class passengers on the promenade, bridge, awning and upper decks, with a large number of these staterooms being arranged for one passenger only. The various staterooms are fitted up with all the latest improvements for the comfort of passengers. The first class dining saloon is situated on the upper deck amidships and extends the full breadth of the vessel. Seating accommodations are provided for 228 persons at one sitting. On the *President Lincoln*, small party tables, seating two, four, six and eight persons, have been installed in place of long tables.

'The apartment is tastefully decorated and furnished in polished hardwood, with satinwood and Lincrusta panels, and parquet floor, the whole forming a very fine and spacious saloon. A large smoking room is arranged aft on the boat deck, the panelling and framing being of carved oak, and the seat and chairs upholstered in leather. The library or ladies room at the forward end of the boat deck is panelled in carved satinwood, inlaid, and upholstered in moquette, these forming a very pleasing effect. The main staircase leading from the saloon to the boat deck is finished in polished oak, and the spacious entrances on the various decks are decorated in oak. There is also arranged on the boat deck, convenient to the main entrance, a gymnasium with the complete outfit of Zander vibratory appliances, electrically operated, and on the bridge deck a special room is fitted for electric light baths and massage.

'The second class accommodations are provided aft of the first class accommodations, and are fitted with two-, three- and four-berth rooms. The dining saloon is arranged to seat all the second cabin passengers at one sitting, and is finished and decorated in white, with medallion in panels, forming a fine and spacious apartment. A smoking room and ladies room or library are also provided, the decorations and furnishings of which are tastefully carried out.

'Third class passengers are accommodated on the middle and lower decks aft, all of them being in enclosed rooms. The dining saloon, which is situated on the upper deck aft, is arranged to seat 400, and is panelled and decorated in white. A neatly decorated smoking room for this class is also provided on the aft promenade deck. Accommodations for fourth class passengers are provided on the middle and lower 'tween decks, in open steerage berths.'

The North Atlantic's only six-masted passenger steamers saw just about seven years of service. They were caught, like several other German liners, at their Hoboken berths and interned there for several years, then both were later seized by the American Navy in April 1917. Refitted as troop transports, they kept, quite sensibly, their original names and began sailing on the Atlantic troop shuttle as USS *President Lincoln* and USS *President Grant*. Unfortunately, *Lincoln* survived for only another year. On 31 May 1918, on a westbound passage to New York, she was torpedoed by a German submarine and then quickly sank. There were 26 casualties.

The Germans could not have imagined that their original *President Grant* would survive for 49 years from her keel laying in 1903 to her demise at the scrapyard in 1952. After yeoman service as a Navy trooper, she was laid up for several years before being passed to United States Lines for commercial service on the same New York-Channel ports-Hamburg run that she ran in the prewar years. She was extensively rebuilt in 1923–24 at the big Newport News Shipyard in Virginia and had two of her six masts removed, her superstructure enlarged and her accommodation reduced. With the far more stringent US immigration quotas then in effect, greatly curtailing those seemingly endless and exceptionally profitable flows of westbound steerage passengers, the enormous capacity from her Hapag days was no longer necessary. The revised berthing was for 619 in cabin class and 1,332 in third class. While it had been intended to rename her *President Buchanan*, which would have been in keeping with the naming theme for United States Lines' ships at the time, she was named *Republic* instead. She resumed sailing in the spring of 1924.

In 1931, having been adversely affected by the Depression on her transatlantic sailings, but then avoiding the prospect of lay-up, *Republic* was transferred to the US Army and used as a peacetime troop transport. A decade later, she was painted grey and began service, for the second time, in a World War. Towards the end of the hostilities, she assumed yet another role as a hospital ship. She then reverted to trooping before finishing her long career at the scrappers.

Kaiser Friedrich
(North German Lloyd)

Service Bremerhaven-Channel ports-New York.
Specifications 12,481 gross tons, 600 × 63 ft (185 × 19 m).
Builder Schichau Works, Danzig, Germany, 1898
Machinery Steam, quadruple expansion, twin screw. Service speed 19 knots.
Capacity 400 first class, 250 second class, 700 steerage.

1897 5 Oct: Launched.
1898 May: Completed. Unsuccessful trials—contracted for 22-knot top speed, but barely managed 20 knots. Attempted repairs. June: Maiden voyage to New York, then again returned to shipbuilders. Sept: Returned to service. After only three voyages, again returned to builders as mechanically unsatisfactory.
1899 Used briefly by North German Lloyd, then returned once again to builders. Scandalous court battle followed, later settled in favour of the shipowner. Oct: Began unsuccessful one-year charter for Hamburg America Line on Hamburg-New York run.
1900 Oct: Laid up at Hamburg for 12 years.
1912 May: Sold to Compagnie Navigation de Sud Atlantique, French flag. Refitted extensively, given new boilers and renamed *Burdigala* for Bordeaux-Rio de Janeiro-Santos-Montevideo-Buenos Aires service.
1915–16 French troop transport.
1916 14 Nov: Sunk in Aegean off Mykonos by underwater mines.

Rhein
(North German Lloyd)

Service Bremerhaven-Channel ports-New York, and Bremerhaven-Channel ports-Baltimore to Philadelphia, Australia via Suez.
Specifications 10,058 gross tons, 520 × 58 ft (160 × 18 m).
Builder Blohm & Voss, Hamburg, Germany, 1899.
Machinery Steam, quadruple expansion, twin screw. Service speed 14½ knots.
Capacity 369 second class, 217 third class, 2,865 steerage; third class later renamed second class.

1899 20 Sept: Launched. Dec: Maiden voyage to New York.
1914 Aug: Interned at Baltimore and laid up.
1917 Apr: Formally transferred to US Government and refitted as troop transport *Susquehanna*. Tonnage relisted as 9,959.
1920 Aug: Commercial service for United States Mail Lines from New York to Bremerhaven and Danzig. Accommodation restyled for 500 cabin class and 2,500 third class passengers. Later transferred to United States Lines and reassigned to New York-Plymouth-Cherbourg-Bremerhaven service.
1922 Laid up.
1928 Nov: Sold to Japanese shipbreakers.

Main
(North German Lloyd)

Service Bremerhaven-Channel ports, Bremerhaven-Baltimore.
Specifications 10,067 gross tons, 520 × 58 ft (160 × 18 m).
Builder Blohm & Voss, Hamburg, Germany, 1900.
Machinery Steam, quadruple expansion, twin screw. Service speed 14½ knots.
Capacity 369 second class, 217 third class, 2,865 steerage; later revised as 369 first class, 217 second class, 2,865 steerage.

1900 10 Feb: Launched. Apr: Maiden voyage to New York. 30 June: Burnt out and sunk in Great Hoboken Pier Fire, New York. Later salvaged and fully repaired at Newport News, Virginia.
1901 Oct: Resumed commercial service.
1914–18 Laid up at Antwerp.
1919 May: To British Government; managed by Turner, Brightman & Co, then Alfred Holt & Co.
1921 June: Transferred to French Government.
1925 Broken up.

President Lincoln

(Hamburg America Line)

Service Hamburg-Channel ports-New York.
Specifications 18,168 gross tons, 616 × 68 ft (189 × 21 m).
Builder Harland & Wolff Ltd, Belfast, Northern Ireland, 1903–07.
Machinery Steam, quadruple expansion, twin screw. Service speed 14½ knots.
Capacity 324 first class, 152 second class, 1,004 third class, 2,348 steerage.

1903 Oct: To be launched as *Scotian* for Furness-Leyland Line, British flag, but cancelled just prior to launching. With sister ship, the intended *Servian*, launched by Harland & Wolff, then laid up.
1906 Dec: Bought by Hamburg America Line and completed. Intended name (*Berlin*) later changed to *President Lincoln*.
1907 May: Maiden voyage for Hamburg America Line.
1914 Aug: Interned at New York.
1917 Apr: Officially seized by US Government and refitted as troop transport.
1918 31 May: Torpedoed during westbound transatlantic crossing to New York; 26 lost.

President Grant

(Hamburg America Line)

Service Hamburg-Channel ports-New York.
Specifications 18,072 gross tons, 616 × 68 ft (189 × 21 m).
Builder Harland & Wolff Ltd, Belfast, Northern Ireland, 1903–07.
Machinery Steam, quadruple expansion, twin screw. Service speed 14½ knots.
Capacity 326 first class, 152 second class, 1,004 third class, 2,348 steerage.

1903 Dec: To be launched as *Servian* for Furness-Leyland Line, British flag, but order cancelled and ship completed instead by Harland & Wolff, then laid up.
1906 Dec: Bought by Hamburg America Line. Intended name *Boston*, but completed as *President Grant*.
1907 Aug: Maiden voyage to New York.
1914 Aug: Interned at New York.
1917 Apr: Formally seized by US Government and refitted as troop transport.
1921 Transferred to US Shipping Board but laid up at Norfolk.
1923–24 Rebuilt at Newport News Shipyard, Virginia, for further commerical service. Six masts reduced to four, accommodation restyled for 619 cabin class, 1,332 third class. Tonnage relisted as 17,910. Intended new name *President Buchanan*, but instead became *Republic*. New York-Plymouth-Cherbourg-Bremerhaven service for United States Lines.
1931 Aug: Withdrawn from commercial service owing to Depression. Transferred to US Army and used as peacetime trooper.
1941 June: Transferred to US Navy for wartime service.
1945 Jan: Refitted as hospital ship.
1946 Further troop-ship service, then laid up.
1951 Broken up at Baltimore.

6
Three four-masted liners

They were three superb ships, the first two for Hamburg America and the third for North German Lloyd, each progressively larger and more luxurious. They used the twin-funnel, four-masted design that was both conservative looking as well as reminiscent of the greatly respected sailing ships of the previous century, and therein lay part of their appeal with the travelling public. They were also styled after (and in direct competition with) a quartet of highly successful ships, White Star Line's 'Big Four'—*Cedric*, *Celtic*, *Adriatic* and *Baltic*—which ran on the Liverpool-New York service.

While these newest German liners were especially noted for their first class quarters and the special amenities therein, their biggest profits, just as with most of the earlier ships discussed in these pages, would come from their third and fourth class

passengers. Consequently, they too were to be given specially selected names that would appeal directly to the steerage class passengers. Both Hamburg America and North German Lloyd were in fierce competition for the largest share of this migrant trade, attempting to lure these passengers not only from Germany but also from Poland, Scandinavia, Eastern Europe, Russia and wherever else possible on continental Europe. Subsequently, the first of these new four-masted liners was, quite cleverly, named *Amerika*.

The second ship, in consideration of the origins of many of her passengers, was to have the complimentary name of *Europa*. However, there was some rethinking on this choice and, in view of the strong interest, even keen watchfulness, of the Kaiser himself on the growth and development of German merchant shipping, the ship was named instead after his wife and

The 25,500-ton George Washington *of 1909 was the largest North German Lloyd liner to date and was quite similar in design to Hapag's* Amerika *and* Kaiserin Auguste Victoria *(Arnold Kludas Collection).*

Above *The world's largest ocean liner for one year (1905–06), the 22,200-ton* Amerika *used the conservative profile of two thin funnels and four tall masts* (Everett Viez Collection).

Below *Originally to have been named* Europa, *the name was changed to* Kaiserin Auguste Victoria *when the Empress of Germany consented to launch her in the summer of 1906* (Arnold Kludas Collection).

After the First World War, Amerika *returned to commercial service, but for United States
Lines and with the spelling of her name changed to* America *(United States Lines).*

christened *Kaiserin Auguste Victoria*.

The third of the group, built for Lloyd, had perhaps the boldest name of all, *George Washington*, honouring America's first president. At this distance in time, some eighty years later, this selection of names for large ocean liners might seem somewhat strange. I dare say that it would seem quite odd to have a contemporary German cruise-ship, sailing in the Caribbean and marketed mostly to Americans, named *George Washington* or *Abraham Lincoln*. It was, of course, for a far different trade and different clientele that the earlier ships were created.

Amerika, completed in the autumn of 1905, was alone in having been built abroad, at the renowned Harland & Wolff yards at Belfast. In fact, her creation was fitted in between two of those big White Star liners, *Baltic*, which was finished in the summer of 1904, and *Adriatic*, which appeared in the spring of 1907. These ships, together with the new German, were the biggest ships of their day, passenger or otherwise. In fact, the 22,225-ton *Amerika* was listed for at least a year as the 'world's largest ship'. She was displaced by the 24,541-ton *Adriatic*, which was then very quickly eclipsed by the 31,550-ton Cunarder *Lusitania*, which swept across the North Atlantic for the first time in September 1907. The Atlantic race for maritime honours—for biggest and longest and fastest—grew more and more intense. The Germans would not,

much to their regret, have the world's largest liner until the exceptional 52,100-ton *Imperator*, which was delivered in the spring of 1913.

In Hapag's advertising literature of 1908, it was said that *Amerika* and the subsequent *Kaiserin Auguste Victoria*

'. . . were planned to be the highest type of passenger and freight vessels ever built—having great promenade decks, large cabins with lower berths only, grand combinations of suites and, in addition to the grand dining saloon, a perfectly equipped restaurant a la carte, the latter under the supervision of the famed Ritz-Carlton Hotel of London [*Kaiserin Auguste Victoria* was also fitted with a palm court]. In the dining saloon, small party tables have been provided in place of long tables and an a la carte service has been added. They also have a gymnasium, Turkish and electric baths, and, last but not least, passenger elevators running through the five decks'.

Used on the express route between Hamburg and New York, and via Cherbourg and Plymouth, it is especially interesting to note that in the advertising literature, strong attention was paid to the safety features of the ships. This was an area of particular concern to the steerage passengers, especially as they were often deeply intimidated by the prospect of making a passage across the notorious North Atlantic. Of course, after April 1912, this became a paramount concern. The so-called 'unsinkable' *Titanic* had been lost, on her maiden voyage no less, and claimed over 1,500 lives. Every liner company on the Atlantic improved and increased its safety provisions quickly thereafter.

In describing *Amerika* and *Kaiserin Auguste Victoria*, Hapag publicists wrote:

'For the safety of the ships, the hulls are provided with a double bottom as a safeguard in case of grounding. Above this double bottom, there are watertight steel bulkheads, extending to the upper deck, and the engine compartment is divided by a longitudinal bulkhead. These watertight compartments make the ship practically unsinkable [a term that would have been clearly avoided following the tragedy of the *Titanic*]. All the bulkhead doors can be closed in a few seconds, either individually or collectively, from the captain's bridge, and the mere entrance of water into any one or several of the compartments would automatically close the bulkhead doors in the compartments affected in the event of any defect in the connection with the bridge. The power needed to operate the system is quite independent of the ship's engines, being derived from hydraulic pressure from accumulators. It is easy to understand the absolute safety thus provided'.

While these two ships were later surpassed by the giant *Imperator* and then *Vaterland* within the Hapag fleet, the 25,500-ton *George Washington* remained the largest and finest liner in the North German Lloyd fleet until the outbreak of war in the summer of 1914. Just before, however, Lloyd had ordered two 32,300-ton tonners, *Columbus* and *Hindenburg*. However, the plans for all ships would be greatly changed by the advent of war.

When that 'war to end all wars' began, *Amerika* and *George Washington* were caught in US ports, the former at Boston, the latter at Hoboken. *Kaiserin Auguste Victoria* was laid up at Hamburg. In the spring of 1917, with the USA now involved in the war, the two interned liners were converted into valuable, high-capacity troopers and began sailing as USS *America* (the slightly revised spelling had been adopted) and USS *George Washington*. *America* was nearly lost in October 1918 when, while docked at her Hoboken berth, she partially sank due to tidal changes and open portholes. Fortunately, she could be salvaged and was later repaired, resuming military service in early 1919. *George Washington*—which became known to most of her soldier-passengers as the 'Big George'—achieved special notoriety when she carried President Woodrow Wilson and his staff to and from the historic Peace Conference at Versailles during 1919.

Later, with the return of international peace and the

After the First World War, George Washington retained her original name but sailed under the Stars and Stripes for United States Lines. She was affectionately known as 'Big George' and survived until 1951 (Everett Viez Collection).

In the 'twenties, the former Kaiserin Auguste Victoria *sailed for the British as the well-known Canadian Pacific transatlantic and cruising liner* Empress of Scotland (Everett Viez Collection).

revival of commercial transatlantic passenger service, both *America* and *George Washington* were transferred to United States Lines and placed on the same Northern service to the Channel ports and Germany. With altered and reduced capacities, they joined several other ex-German liners now also sailing under the Stars and Stripes. This group included the giant ex-*Vaterland*, renamed *Leviathan*, and the former *President Grant*, which became *Republic*. Also, for a time, there was a plan to revive four other large ex-Germans, the four-stackers *Kaiser Wilhelm II* (renamed *Agamemnon*) and *Kronprinzessin Cecilie* (renamed *Mount Vernon*). However, this project—including proposed conversion of these ships to diesel drive—never materialized. Unfortunately, each of the other German liners would see comparatively little service. Within less than a decade, by the early 'thirties, they would become victims of the sinister, trade-disrupting Depression. Both *America* and *George Washington* were laid up in 1931.

While both ships might well have been scrapped if it had not been for the Second World War, further military service was accomplished only by great effort and expense. Aged, somewhat deteriorated and with greatly exhausted machinery, they were revived only after extensive and expensive refits. The former *America* sailed as the trooper *Edmund B Alexander*; *George Washington*, briefly renamed *Catlin*, reverted to her original name. Both were laid up in the late 'forties and then later scrapped—*America* in 1957, at the age of 52, and *George Washington* in 1951, aged 42.

At the end of the First World War, *Kaiserin Auguste Victoria* also went on to a new life. In 1919 she was awarded to the British as reparations and, while used briefly as an American troop-ship and then for a short charter to Cunard Line, she was fully restored and reactivated by 1921–22 for Canadian Pacific Steamships as their *Empress of Scotland*. Quite sensibly, she had been refitted by her original builders, Vulcan Works, but at their Hamburg yard instead of at Stettin. Later used as both a transatlantic and cruising liner, she too was an early victim of the Depression and was retired in 1930 and almost immediately sold to shipbreakers.

Ironically, fire played a decisive part in the later careers of each of this trio of former Germans. The former *Amerika*, then sailing as the US-flag *Republic*, was nearly destroyed completely in a shipyard fire in March 1926. So extensive was the damage that she might have been scrapped, but instead was repaird and later reactivated. *Empress of Scotland*, ex-*Kaiserin Auguste Victoria*, burnt out completely at the scrappers' yard in Scotland in 1931, and then sank. Her charred wreckage was later salvaged, but then only to break in half before being scrapped completely. *George Washington* was damaged in a fire in 1947 and then, far more seriously, in a pier fire in 1951. By then, she was beyond economic repair and was subsequently sold for scrap.

In 1957, when the former *Amerika* was sold for scrap, she was the last of the large ex-German liners to be built before the First World War, and the final member of a glorious group of great passenger ships.

Amerika
(Hamburg America Line)

Service Hamburg-Southampton-Cherbourg-New York.
Specifications 22,225 gross tons, 700 × 74 ft (215 × 23 m).
Builder Harland & Wolff Ltd, Belfast, Northern Ireland, 1905.
Machinery Steam, quadruple expansion, twin screw. Service speed 17½ knots.
Capacity 420 first class, 254 second class, 223 third class, 1,765 steerage.

1905 20 Apr: Launched. Sept: Completed. 11 Oct: Maiden voyage from Hamburg. World's largest liner for one year, until 1906. Remeasured later as 22,622 gross tons.
1912 4 Oct: Collided with and sank British submarine B2 off Dover; 15 lost.
1914 June: Reassigned to Hamburg-Boulogne-Southampton-Boston service. Aug: Interned at Boston at outbreak of war.
1917 Apr: Formally seized by US Government and name altered to *America*. Outfitted as troop-ship for US Navy.
1918 14 July: Collided with and sank British freighter *Instructor*; 16 lost.
1918 15 Oct: Sank at Hoboken pier while being coaled; 6 killed. Later raised and repaired at Brooklyn Navy Yard.
1919 Feb: Resumed troop-ship service. Sept: laid up.
1920 Jan: Sailed on special voyage, New York-Panama Canal-Vladivostock-Suez-Trieste-New York; brought troops from Vladivostock to Trieste and then migrants from Trieste to New York.
1920–21 Thorough overhaul and refitting at Brooklyn; converted to oil fuel. Accommodation restyled for 225 first class, 425 second class, 1,500 third class. Assigned to United States Lines and used on New York-Channel ports-Bremerhaven service.
1923 Accommodation again restyled for 692 cabin class, 1,056 third class. Tonnage relisted as 21,114.
1926 10 Mar: Badly damaged in shipyard fire at Newport News, Virginia. Thought to be worthy only of scrapping, but later repaired and rebuilt. Tonnage relisted as 21,329. Further transatlantic service.
1931 Sept: Laid up in Chesapeake Bay.
1940 Oct: Converted to accommodation ship at Baltimore and renamed *Edmund B Alexander*. Sent to Newfoundland.
1941 June: Further conversion work at Brooklyn to troop-ship. Mechanically troublesome. Further alter-

ations carried out at Baltimore; rebuilt with one funnel.

1949 Laid up at Baltimore.

1951 Moved to US Government Reserve fleet at Jones Point, upper Hudson River, New York.

1957 Sold to shipbreakers at Baltimore.

1958 Broken up.

Kaiserin Auguste Victoria
(Hamburg America Line)

Service   Hamburg-Southampton-Cherbourg-New York.

Specifications 24,581 gross tons, 705 × 77 ft (217 × 24 m).

Builder Vulcan Works, Stettin, Germany, 1906.

Machinery Steam, quadruple expansion, twin screw. Service speed 17½ knots.

Capacity 652 first class, 286 second class, 1,842 steerage.

1905 29 Aug: Launched. Proposed name *Europa* changed prior to launching ceremonies.

1906 May: Maiden voyage to New York. Ranked as world's largest liner until 1907.

1914 Aug: Laid up at Hamburg.

1919 Mar: Surrendered to British Government and chartered to US Government for troop-ship service.

1920 Chartered to Cunard Line for Liverpool-New York service.

1921 May: Sold outright to Canadian Pacific Steamships, British flag. Renamed *Empress of Scotland* and refitted with accommodation for 459 first class, 478 second class and 960 third class passengers. Converted to oil fuel and tonnage relisted as 25,037. Mostly Southampton-Cherbourg-Quebec City service and winter cruising.

1930 Dec: Sold to shipbreakers at Blyth, Scotland. Burnt out at breakers' yard and sank.

1931 May: Wreck salvaged, but broke apart.

1931 Oct: Demolition completed.

George Washington
(North German Lloyd)

Service   Bremerhaven-Southampton-Cherbourg-New York.

Specifications 25,570 gross tons, 723 × 72 ft (222 × 22 m).

Builder Vulcan Works, Strettin, Germany, 1909.

Machinery Steam, quadruple expansion, twin screw. Service speed 18½ knots.

Capacity 568 first class, 433 second class, 452 third class, 1,226 steerage.

1908 10 Nov: Launched.

1909 June: Maiden voyage to New York.

1914 Aug: Interned at New York.

1917 Apr: Seized by US Government and refitted as troop-ship USS *George Washington*.

1919 Mar: Carried President Woodrow Wilson and party to Peace Conference at Versailles.

1920 Transferred to US Shipping Board and laid up at Boston. Later chartered to United States Mail Lines, then United States Lines. Thoroughly overhauled at Hoboken; tonnage relisted as 23,788 and accommodation restyled for 573 first class, 442 second class, 1,485 third class.

1921 Aug: Resumed commercial service, New York-Channel ports-Bremerhaven.

1931 Nov: Laid up.

1932 Aug: Moved to Patuxent River, Maryland, and laid up alongside *America*, *Monticello* (ex-*Kaiser Wilhelm II*) and *Mount Vernon* (ex-*Kronprinzessin Cecilie*).

1940 Reactivated for troop-ship service. Renamed *Catlin* by US Navy.

1941 Briefly loaned to British Government, but quickly returned to US Government and reverted to *George Washington*.

1942 Mechanically exhausted and initial wartime service complicated; refitted thoroughly at Brooklyn and rebuilt with oil-fired engines and single funnel. Further troop service.

1947 Mar: Seriously damaged by fire at New York; laid up at Baltimore.

1951 17 Jan: Destroyed in Baltimore pier fire; remains then scrapped.

7
An intermediate quartet

To support their increasingly larger and more lucrative passenger services, particularly the steerage trade, a quartet of 17,000-ton ships was added to the North German Lloyd and Hamburg America North Atlantic fleets in 1908–9. There were two sets of sister ships, Lloyd's *Prinz Freidrich Wilhelm* and *Berlin*; and Hapag's *Cincinnati* and *Cleveland* (which once again used American names so to especially appeal to the immigrant passengers).

The two Lloyd liners copied a basic design: twin funnels and twin masts. By contrast, the Hapag ships copied the design of the earlier *Amerika* and *Kaiserin Auguste Victoria* by using twin funnels and four masts. Rather interestingly, each of these ships came from a different German shipbuilder—the Tecklenborg works at Geestemunde, the Weser yards at Bremen, Schichau at Danzig and, surely most famous of all, Blohm & Voss at Hamburg.

The first and second class accommodation, particularly aboard *Cincinnati* and *Cleveland*, were most comfortable and very much in keeping with Hapag's high standards of the day. Publicity material for *Cincinnati* stated that

'. . . the first class passengers' accommodations are situated amidships and extend over four decks, namely the saloon, upper, bridge and promenade. They are connected by a grand and smaller companionway, and also by an electric passenger elevator. The grand entrance hall and companionway have received special attention, and by somewhat unusual treatment of the staircase itself, a result has been achieved which is not only novel but very pleasing.

'The dining room, extending the full width of the ship, has been exquisitely furnished. Small tables, seating two, four or six persons, have been provided and each table has an electric lamp with decorative lampshade, making the room one of the most pleasing ever seen on a vessel. The recent introduction of an a la carte service on various Hamburg America Line steamers also includes the *Cincinnati* [and the *Cleveland*].

'A social hall or lounge on the promenade deck, at the head of the grand staircase, is a masterpiece of the decorator's art. Luxurious divans and chairs invite appealingly, and the whole atmosphere of the room, with its library of carefully selected volumes, breathes of luxury ease. The writing room is conveniently near. The music and ladies' saloon also provides delightful opportunity for entertainment and recreation. The smoking room is situated on the aft end of the bridge deck, and connected with the music room and lounge by a beautifully decorated vestibule and covered passage. Entrance by staircase from the lower decks and to the open-air promenade and sheltered corners are conveniently situated. High panelled wainscoting of dark woods, the artistically carved capitals, charming electroliers, the harmonious lines of the furniture covered with red leather, and the magnificent mantelpiece, combine to make this room a credit to the designer. A dome of delightfully tinted glass softens the abundance of light.

'In addition to the public rooms mentioned, there are also a gymnasium equipped with Zander electrical apparatus, light baths, photographers' dark room, library, book stall and information bureau.'

While both North German Lloyd and Hamburg America Line were engaged in considerable cruising by this time (1908–09)—winters in the Caribbean and Mediterranean, with summer trips to the Norwegian fjords and even remote Iceland and Spitzbergen—it was Hapag that seemed to have the keener interest in this alternate luxury trade. In 1911 they introduced the

Two intermediate North Atlantic liners, Lloyd's Prinz Friedrich Wilhelm (**top right**) *and* Berlin (**middle right**) *(Arnold Kludas Collection).*

Right *Cincinnati and her sister ship* Cleveland *used a general exterior design that followed the earlier* Amerika *and* Kaiserin Auguste Victoria *(Arnold Kludas Collection).*

Above *After having been in British and then American hands, the former* Cleveland *was repurchased by her original Hapag owners in 1926, and again sailed in German-flag transatlantic service* (Arnold Kludas Collection).

Below *USS* Covington, *ex-*Cincinnati, *sinking in the North Atlantic on 1 July 1918* (Hapag-Lloyd).

all-white, four-funnel, 16,500-ton *Victoria Luise*, which had been specially refitted for 487 first class passengers for cruise service. Having been the transatlantic Blue Riband holder *Deutschland* (see Chapter 1), she was by far the largest liner thus far engaged in such vacation voyaging. Hapag, and in particular Albert Ballin, saw great potential in the future of cruising. Consequently, from the very beginning of their sea-going careers, the sisters *Cincinnati* and *Cleveland* were used for luxury and mostly longer cruise voyages. Their around-the-world voyages, usually run from New York twice a year, one in autumn and the other in the early winter, completely circled the globe in approximately 125 days. Passage fares, which seem quite inexpensive from this distance in time, ranged from $650 (in third class cabins 'for gentlemen only') to $6,600 in top-deck suites. (Comparatively, Cunard's *Queen Elizabeth 2*'s circumnavigation of 1986 had passage fares ranging from a minimum of $16,000 to a penthouse suite fare of $325,000.)

Such was the success of German-flag cruising that, by 1914, two simultaneous world cruises were planned for the following winter. A short advertisement read 'Around the world through the new Panama Canal. Two grand cruises by the sister ships *Cincinnati*, on January 16th 1915, and the *Cleveland* on January 31st. From New York, the principal cities of the world—including visits to the San Diego (*Cincinnati*) and Panama Pacific (*Cleveland*) Expositions. 135 days, $900 up and which includes all necessary expenses afloat and ashore [including shore excursions]'. In addition, in a smaller space in the right-hand corner of the same advertisement, Hapag's transatlantic service was also mentioned. 'Send 25 cents [to the Hapag offices at 41–45 Broadway in lower New York City] for a double-disc travel record and picture booklet, "A Day in Berlin", by well-known lecturer E. M. Newman. It may be played on any other talking machine. Other records are in preparation.'

While both *Cleveland* and *Cincinnati* were later used on North Atlantic services to Boston, they too had rather short-lived, albeit successful, careers by the time the First World War erupted in August 1914. Among others, those projected twin-world cruises were cancelled. *Cleveland* was laid up at Hamburg; *Cincinnati*—

along with a considerable number of other Germans—was kept at Hoboken.

Although her owners had attempted, even as the hostilities were already under way, to sell her to neutral Swedish interests, *Cleveland* was finally surrendered to the invading Americans and refitted as the Navy trooper USS *Mobile*. Once this task ended, she was briefly chartered to Britain's White Star Line, who were short of adequate ships in those initial postwar years. The former *Cleveland* was then ideally suited for several 'austerity' sailings between Liverpool and New York. Soon after, her career began even further change. Found to be surplus by the American authorities, she was sold to the Byron Steamship Co, a London-based firm with Greek financial backing (the Embiricos Brothers), and was renamed *King Alexander* for further transatlantic service but out of Mediterranean waters. Unfortunately, this proved to be rather unsuccessful, lasting little more than two years.

In 1923, she was sold to United American Lines, an American-owned company, but one which was forced to use Panamanian registry to avoid the stringencies of newly enacted American Prohibition. Similar to the subsequent *Reliance* and *Resolute*, it was surely one of the earliest occasions involving a so-called 'flag of convenience' (and one which is so common to present-day cruise liners which often fly the Panamanian flag as well as the colours of the Bahamas, Liberia and even in one instance of far-off Mauritius). After a full refit and modernization (conducted at Hamburg), she reverted to her original Hapag name and was soon back on the Northern run to New York. Her operations were, at first, jointly coordinated with Hamburg America and then by 1926 her original owners were sufficiently recovered from the deprivations of war and also free of further Allied restrictions to repurchase their former ship. So she was again under German colours for the last seven years until she was scrapped—by her original builders, no less—in 1933.

Cincinnati was taken from her Hoboken berth in April 1917, just as the US entered the war, and was renovated as the troop-ship USS *Covington*. Unfortunately, she survived for little more than a year, being torpedoed, ironically by a German sub, in July 1918.

Prinz Friedrich Wilhelm
(North German Lloyd)

Service Bremerhaven-Southampton-Cherbourg-New York.
Specifications 17,082 gross tons, 613 × 68 ft (189 × 21 m).
Builder Tecklenborg Shipyard, Geestemunde, Germany, 1908.
Machinery Steam, quadruple expansion, twin screw. Service speed 17 knots.
Capacity 425 first class, 338 second class, 1,756 steerage.

1907 21 Oct: Launched.
1908 June: Maiden crossing to New York.
1914 Aug: During pleasure cruise to Fjords, took refuge on outbreak of war at Norwegian port of Odda.
1916 Attempted to return to Germany, but ran aground in Danish waters; later salvaged and eventually arrived at Kiel.
1919 Mar: Surrendered to British Government and chartered to US Navy for trooping duties.
1920 Feb: Chartered to Canadian Pacific Steamships for Liverpool-Quebec City service.
1921 May: Bought outright by Canadian Pacific and extensively refitted; tonnage relisted as 17,282. Renamed *Empress of China* and then *Empress of India* before entering service.
1922 June: Entered Canadian Pacific Liverpool–Quebec City service.
1922 Dec: Renamed *Montlaurier*.
1925 Feb: Grounded off Queenstown, Ireland, following rudder damage; later towed to Liverpool for repairs. Apr: Badly damaged by fire while undergoing repairs at Cammell Laird shipyards, Birkenhead.
1925 June: Renamed *Monteith* and placed on Glasgow–Montreal service; within one month, renamed *Montnairn*.
1927 Reassigned to Antwerp-Quebec City service.
1930 Scrapped at Genoa.

Berlin
(North German Lloyd)

Service Bremerhaven-Southampton-Cherbourg-New York.
Specifications 17,323 gross tons, 613 × 69 ft (189 × 21 m).
Builder AG Weser, Bremen, Germany, 1909.
Machinery Steam, quadruple expansion, twin screw. Service speed 19 knots.
Capacity 266 first class, 246 second class, 2,700 steerage.

1908 7 Nov: Launched.
1909 May: Maiden voyage to New York; also used in Naples-Genoa-New York service.
1914 Aug: Fitted out as mine-layer in Germany Navy. Oct: One of her mines sank British battleship HMS *Audacious*. Nov: Interned at Trondheim, Norway.
1919 Dec: Surrendered to British Government and used for troop-ship services under P&O Lines management.
1920 Nov: Sold to White Star Line, British flag; refitted at Portsmouth. Renamed *Arabic*.
1921 Sept: Entered White Star service, Southampton-New York and Genoa-Naples-New York.
1924 Hamburg-Channel ports-New York service. Accommodation restyled for 500 cabin class and 1,200 third class passengers.
1926 Oct: Chartered to Red Star Line and reassigned to the Antwerp-Southampton-Cherbourg-New York service.
1930 Returned to White Star Line service and used on Liverpool-Cobh-New York service. Accommodation again restyled as 177 cabin class, 319 tourist class and 823 third class.
1930 Laid up.
1931 Dec: Delivered to shipbreakers at Genoa.

Cincinnati

(Hamburg America Line)

Service Hamburg-Southampton-Cherbourg-New York; later used on Hamburg-Channel ports-Boston service. Also considerable cruising, especially longer voyages.
Specifications 16,339 gross tons, 603 × 63 ft (185 × 19 m).
Builder Schichau Works, Danzig, Germany, 1909.
Machinery Steam, quadruple expansion, twin screw. Service speed 15½ knots.
Capacity 246 first class, 332 second class, 448 third class, 1,801 steerage.

1908 24 July: Launched.
1909 May: Maiden voyage to New York.
1914 Aug: Interned at Boston.
1917 Apr: Formally seized by US Government and refitted as Navy transport *Covington*.
1918 1 July: Torpedoed by German submarine in North Atlantic and sank on following day.

Cleveland

(Hamburg America Line)

Service Hamburg-Southampton-Cherbourg-New York; later Hamburg-Channel ports-Boston as well as considerable winter cruising, especially longer cruises.
Specifications 16,960 gross tons, 607 × 63 ft (187 × 19 m).
Builder Blohm & Voss, Hamburg, Germany, 1909.
Machinery Steam, quadruple expansion, twin screw. Service speed 15½ knots.
Capacity 239 first class, 224 second class, 496 third class, 1,882 steerage.

1908 26 Sept: Launched.
1909 Mar: Entered service to New York.
1914 Aug: Laid up at Hamburg for remainder of war.
1917 Attempted sale to Swedish interests not recognized by Allies following German defeat in late 1918.
1919 Mar: Surrendered to US Government and refitted as Navy troop transport *Mobile*.
1920 Chartered to White Star Line for several Liverpool-New York sailings.
1920 Oct: Sold to Byron Steamship Co, British flag; renamed *King Alexander* and used in Piraeus-Mediterranean ports-New York service.
1923 Sold to United American Lines, US flag; renamed *Cleveland*. Sent to builders' yard at Hamburg, refitted as oil-fired vessel. Tonnage relisted as 15,746, accommodation restyled for 600 cabin class and 1,000 third class. Placed under Panamanian flag and entered Hamburg-Channel ports-New York service.
1926 July: Sold to Hamburg America Line (original owners) and refitted for further service to New York.
1931 Laid up at Hamburg.
1933 Sold to her builders' for scrapping.

8
Early Hamburg Sud liners

The Hamburg-South America Line—commonly referred to as Hamburg Sud—was perhaps largely overshadowed at this point in passenger ship history by both the Hamburg America Line and North German Lloyd. It was Germany's 'third' passenger ship firm and had had considerable interests in South Atlantic passenger services for many years. Regrettably, they barely resumed their passenger services after the Second World War (and then only with smaller combination passenger-cargo ships), and today concentrate all of their deep-sea operations in freight, mostly with sizeable container-ships.

The Company was formed from a combination of British and German shipping interests in 1871. Its primary trading interests were to the East Coast of South America, principally to the main-line ports of Rio de Janeiro, Santos, Montevideo and Buenos Aires. While the cargo business was important as well as profitable, such as taking German manufactured goods outbound and then returning with the likes of Brazilian coffee and Argentine beef, the passenger business developed as well. Of particular importance was the provision of adequately comfortable—and, in later years, very luxurious—first class quarters for business-men, traders and merchants and their respective families who began to travel regularly to and from Latin America. Also, a sizeable, ever-expanding and therefore encouraging migrant trade emerged, both of Germans as well as other Europeans seeking 'new life and economic opportunity' in the New World lands of Brazil, Uruguay and Argentina.

Like the North Atlantic passenger business during the same turn-of-the-century period, this steerage business caused Hamburg Sud to build increasingly larger ships. By 1906–07, its biggest passenger ships were the 9,400-ton *Cap Vilano* and the 9,800-ton *Cap Arcona*. But, the management of Hamburg Sud saw even better times ahead—and were surely influenced by the expansion of Hamburg America and North German Lloyd as well. Consequently, the company went to the renowned Blohm & Voss shipyards and there, in August 1911, launched their largest liner yet, the 14,500-ton *Cap Finisterre*. A twin-stacker that resembled some of Lloyd's North Atlantic passenger ships, her accommodation was similarly fashioned: 297 in first class, 222 in second class and 870 in third class.

In Prager's history of the Blohm & Voss Co, special attention was given to the new Hamburg Sud flagship.

'The *Cap Finisterre* was so long [591 ft overall] that the stem jetted out beyond the framework of Slipway No 6. The keel blocks had to be laid in such a way that the railway trains passed beneath the stem. The ship caused a sensation with its numerous innovations. For the first time, a large dining hall going through two decks was created. This was a major problem for an all-steel built vessel, since despite this, the ship still had to have the necessary strength in the longitudinal and transverse structures. Altogether, this ship represented an entirely new type. The dining hall referred to, two decks high and occupying the full width of the ship, was by no means the only innovation as regards comfort. Others included a large, hall-like winter garden complete with fountains, a flower shop, a conservatory, a dark room for amateur photographers, a hairdresser's salon, a complete large scale laundry, insulating holds with the Linde refrigerating machines which had reached their final, functional maturity at that time, special dining rooms for children and individual cuisine for Jewish, Spanish and Portugese passengers [Hamburg Sud liners also called en route at such ports as Vigo and Lisbon to collect further passengers].

'Nor does this exhaust the list of novelties on this vessel, which naturally is equipped with the Frahm anti-roll tanks. All the rooms had artificial, that is to say, electrical ventilation. To top it all, on the boat deck, there was a real, firmly built-in swimming pool. In view of the impending maiden voyage [December 1911], a trial trip was carried out with the vessel fully loaded, which meant that the swimming pool was filled for the first time. From then onwards, the somewhat "crank" *Cap Finisterre*, having relatively low

Above *The largest German liner yet built for the Latin American service,* Cap Finisterre *of 1911, is shown in the River Elbe* (Arnold Kludas Collection).

Below *Immortalized because of her sea battle in September 1914 with the Cunarder* Carmania, *Hamburg Sud's* Cap Trafalgar *was later sunk* (Arnold Kludas Collection).

Above *Hamburg Sud's* Cap Polonio *was the finest German luxury liner in service to South America until the advent of another three-stacker,* Cap Arcona, *completed in 1927 (Willie Tinnemeyer Collection).*

Below *In a scene dating from the late 'twenties,* Cap Polonio *is berthed at the Hamburg Landing Stage while, on the right,* Monte Sarmiento *is outbound (Hamburg-South American Line).*

Above *The 707-ft long* Kronprinzessin Cecilie *superimposed amidst the vast grandeur of St Peters in Rome* (Charles Sachs Collection).

Below Kaiser Welhelm der Grosse *taking on passengers at her home port of Bremerhaven* (Charles Sachs Collection).

Hamburg-
Amerika
Linie.

Am Bord
des Doppelschrauben - Postdampfers
„PATRICIA"

den

Left　*A maiden voyage rendering of Hapag's* Patricia *(Charles Sachs Collection).*

Above　*Sweeping the North Atlantic,* Deutschland *of 1900 was the only Blue Riband champion in the Hamburg America fleet (Charles Sachs Collection).*

Below　*A first class sitting room aboard* Kronprinzessin Cecilie, *with a portrait of Her Imperial Highness to the left (Charles Sachs Collection).*

Grandeur and glitter on the high seas: the first class dining saloon aboard Deutschland *of 1900 (Charles Sachs Collection).*

stability, began to heel over precariously every time the wheel was rolled. The swimming pool was obviously making the ship somewhat top-heavy. Finally, there was no alternative but to retrospectively add "pockets" on each side of the ship so that she was sufficiently stable on the high seas.'

Encouraged by increasing and improving trading prospects in the passenger division, Hamburg Sud soon decided on two larger liners—the 18,800-ton *Cap Trafalgar* and then the 20,500-ton *Cap Polonio*. Both were three-stackers, fashioned deliberately after the large, well-known North Atlantic liners; the former came from the Vulcan yards at Stettin and the latter from Blohm & Voss again. Most unfortunately, the outbreak of war was to interrupt their early careers.

Cap Trafalgar, commissioned in March 1914, barely saw five months of active service before being interned at Beunos Aires when war was officially declared. But her days were numbered. Later ordered to Montevideo and then fitted with guns and ammunition, and with her third stack removed for disguise, she was sent—as a German armed raider—out into the South Atlantic. Once there, she was to encounter a more powerful rival and this was to bring about her end. It was the tragic demise of a fine liner that was just a few months old.

John Malcolm Brinnin, in his *The Sway of the Grand Saloon*, detailed *Cap Trafalgar*'s end.

'Correctly, as it would appear, the British Admiralty suspected that the German Navy had established a number of secret depots in the South Atlantic where colliers from Europe could rendezvous with German sea raiders. When the *Carmania* [a 19,500-ton Cunard liner, which had been converted to an armed merchant cruiser] arrived off Trinidad Island [a remote South Atlantic isle and not to be confused with the more popular Caribbean island of the same name] one bright morning, her officers—lifting their binoculars—saw just what they were looking for: a ship as big as their own, quietly riding at anchor, while two small ships—with all derricks up—busily filled her bunkers with coal.

'This was the *Cap Trafalgar*, the finest liner on the German South American run. Far grander in the matter of palm gardens and suites de luxe than the *Carmania*, and considerably newer [the Cunarder dated from 1905], she had been a cruiser for hardly two weeks. Docked in the River Plate when War was declared, she had made a successful run for it and rendezvoused with a German gunboat from South Africa that supplied her with officers and armament. Then, quite like the *Carmania*, she had immediately started looking for enemy ships to sink—in the natural expectation that those she might find would be far smaller and more vulnerable than herself.

'Almost as soon as she was spotted, on the morning of September 14th, the *Cap Trafalgar* put up steam, indicating to the *Carmania*'s officers that she was aware of being observed and that she was getting ready for whatever the encounter might lead to. The *Carmania*'s commander thought that the ship in view was North German Lloyd's *Berlin*. His mistake was explicable: while the *Cap Trafalgar* was known to have three funnels, one of these—a dummy ventilator—had been jettisoned when the ship cleared Montevideo. The *Cap Trafalgar*'s captain, on the other hand, knew exactly who the British ship was and that she was far bigger game than anything he had ever expected to meet in these remote waters. As the two erstwhile floating palaces looked each other over through telescopes and glasses, they could see that they were more or less the same size, more the same hastily assumed disguises and guessed that they were about evenly matched in the matter of speed and perhaps of armament. "It promised," said a British chronicler, "to be an equal fight and, in preparation for it, dinner was ordered for all hands that could be excused duty, for the hour of 11.30, in accordance with the old naval principle—food before fighting."

'In a brief ballet of chivalric thrusts and manoeuvres that seem hardly credible in the century of total war, the two ships moved almost merrily toward the fray, guns up and banners flying. The *Carmania*'s ensign flew from both the flagstaff aft and the masthead. The *Cap Trafalgar* ran up the white flag with the blue cross of the German Navy. As if to throw down the gauntlet, the *Carmania* fired a shot across the *Cap Trafalgar*'s bow. The German ship replied in kind and the battle was joined. Within minutes, both were on fire, paint began to flake from blistered gun emplacements and both began to list. As the two ships closed in, the German brought out machine guns and raked the *Carmania*'s open decks. The British plugged away at the *Cap Trafalgar*'s waterline as if it were a jugular vein. German shells demolished the *Carmania*'s bridge, rendered almost all of her controls inactive and penetrated her side seventy-nine times. As bucket brigades were attempting to dampen down the worst fires on the decks of the British ship, the *Cap Trafalgar* suddenly veered to port and started for shore. Her list had increased steeply, her boats were being swung out yet she kept going on, perhaps with the idea of beaching herself. "More and more," said an eyewitness, "the big liner fell over until at last her funnels lay upon the water, and then, after a moment's apparent hesitation, with her bow submerged, she heaved herself upright and sank bodily." It had been a good fight and she had fought honorably to the end and gone down with her ensign flying, and when, as she vanished, the men of the *Carmania* raised a cheer, it was hardly less for their own victory as a tribute to their enemy.'

The third of these larger Hamburg Sud liners, *Cap Polonio*, was to have come into service in late 1914, but this too was disrupted by the war. While her completion had been halted that August, it was later resumed, but under German Navy plans for her to be finished as an armed merchant cruiser. Temporarily renamed *Vineta*, her trials as a warship could not have been less success-

Above *Crowds gather to watch the arrival of* Cap Polonio *at the Overseas Landing Stage at Hamburg* (Hamburg-South America Line).

Below *River traffic at Hamburg: the tugboat* Emil *assists the freighter* Lahn *as Cap Polonio rests majestically at her berth on the left* (Hamburg-South America Line).

ful. She was returned to her builders, decisions were reversed and she was outfitted to her original design as a passenger ship. She also reverted to her original name. She sat unused, however, for the duration of the war and was then surrendered to the British. Briefly used by Union Castle and P&O, her engines proved faulty and consequently, with supposed little commercial value, she was sold to her original German owners. With far more faith in the vessel, she was returned to Blohm & Voss and thoroughly rebuilt. Thereafter followed nearly a decade of good service on the South American run as well as considerable cruising. A victim of the Depression, she was laid up in 1931 and then scrapped four years later.

The aforementioned *Cap Finisterre* actually survived the longest of this pre-First World War group. She was also surrendered at the end of the hostilities, going first to the Americans, then to the British and finally to the Japanese. She saw Pacific passenger service with them as *Taiyo Maru*, until torpedoed in May 1942 during the next world conflict.

Cap Finisterre
(Hamburg-South America Line)

Service Hamburg-Rio de Janeiro, Santos, Montevideo and Buenos Aires.
Specifications 14,503 gross tons, 591 × 65 ft (182 × 20 m).
Builder Blohm & Voss, Hamburg, Germany, 1911.
Machinery Steam, quadruple expansion, twin screw. Service speed 16½ knots.
Capacity 297 first class, 222 second class, 870 third class.

1911 8 Aug: Launched. Dec: Maiden voyage.
1914 Aug: Laid up at Hamburg owing to outbreak of war.
1919 Apr: Surrendered to US Government and later transferred to British Government; managed by Orient Line.
1920 July: Transferred to Japanese Government as wartime reparations.
1921 Assigned to Toyo Kisen KK of Tokyo and renamed *Taiyo Maru*. Tonnage relisted as 14,457. Yokohama-San Francisco service.
1926 Toyo Kisen integrated into Nippon Yusen Kaisha (NYK Line).
1934 Refitted and machinery overhauled; service speed relisted as 19 knots.
1941 Dec: Used for Pacific patrol duties by Japanese Navy.
1942 8 May: Sunk by US submarine *Grenadier* southwest of Kyushu island.

Cap Trafalgar

(Hamburg-South America Line)

Service Hamburg-Rio de Janeiro, Santos, Montevideo and Buenos Aires.
Specifications 18,805 gross tons, 613 × 72 ft (189 × 22 m).
Builder Vulcan Works, Hamburg, Germany, 1914.
Machinery Steam, triple expansion, triple screw. Service speed 17 knots.
Capacity 400 first class, 274 second class, 913 third class.

1913 31 July: Launched.
1914 Mar: Completed. Maiden voyage to South America.
1914 Aug: Caught at Buenos Aires on outbreak of war; later ordered to Montevideo for coal. Rendezvous on 23 Aug with German gunboat *Eber*; given ammunition and guns. Third funnel removed for disguise. Proceeded to Trinidad Island. 14 Sept: Gun duel with auxiliary cruiser *Carmania*, former Cunard liner. *Cap Trafalgar* sunk; 16 casualties.

Cap Polonio

(Hamburg-South America Line)

Service Hamburg-Rio de Janeiro, Santos, Montevideo and Buenos Aires.
Specifications 20,576 gross tons, 662 × 72 ft (204 × 22 m).
Builder Blohm & Voss, Hamburg, Germany, 1914–15.
Machinery Steam, triple expansion, triple screw. Service speed 17 knots.
Capacity 356 first class, 250 second class, 949 third class.

1914 25 Mar: Launched. Aug: Construction halted due outbreak of war. Fitted out as armed merchant cruiser; third funnel removed.
1915 Feb: Completed as auxiliary cruiser; briefly renamed *Vineta*. Trials unsatisfactory and returned to Blohm & Voss for refitting as passenger ship; renamed *Cap Polonio*.
1916 Construction completed but laid up for duration of war.
1919 Apr: Transferred to British Government. Briefly used by Union-Castle Line for one voyage to South Africa and then by P&O Lines for one sailing to Bombay.
1920 Laid up at Liverpool; troublesome engines only capable of 12 knots or less.
1921 July: Sold to Hamburg–South America Line; given extended refit at Blohm & Voss, and converted to oil-firing.
1922 Feb: Entered commercial service to South America.
1931 Laid up owing to Depression.
1935 Scrapped at North German Lloyd shipyard at Bremerhaven.

9
The 'Big Three'

It was perhaps the greatest and most ambitious plan ever for a German shipping company, and it was undoubtedly intended to achieve that persistent goal: German supremacy on the high seas. Represented by the Hamburg America Line, Imperial Germany wanted to outdo Imperial Britain. Cunard Line already had the speed queens *Lusitania* and *Mauretania*, both of nearly 32,000 tons, and were planning for a third major ship, the 45,600-ton *Aquitania*. Their British-flag, but American-owned, rival, White Star Line, had a three-liner plan of its own—the 46,000-ton sisters *Olympic* and *Titanic*, and the 48,000-ton *Britannic* (originally to be named *Gigantic*). Hapag's designers and engineers responded with a trio of successively larger liners that would be the largest and most extravagant ocean super-ships ever seen.

The keel plates for the first of these German giants, already known as 'the colossus of the Atlantic', were put into place in June 1910. Meanwhile, the sisters *Olympic* and *Titanic* were already under construction and the order had been placed for *Aquitania*. Cunard claimed that this ship, to exceed 45,000 tons, would be the largest liner on the Atlantic run. Shortly thereafter, the Germans announced that their new ship would surpass 52,000 tons. The race had begun. (It should be noted, however, that none of these giant liners was ever intended to be in the Blue Riband class. Expensive, record-breaking speed was left to Cunard's *Mauretania*, which remained the unrivalled transatlantic champion from 1907 until 1929. Instead, these new liners vied with one another in size and grandeur.)

Hapag selected a three-funnel design (not the mighty four-stack style which was then so popular) for their new flagship. In fact, standing nearly 70 ft above the upper deck, these funnels were among the largest ever fitted to a liner. (Later, they would add considerably to the ship's balance problems and would be cut down by 9 ft.) Along her decks were no fewer than 83 lifeboats and two motor launches (impressive, but overly cautious numbers that were no doubt prompted by the *Titanic* disaster). Her four four-bladed propellers could make 185 revolutions per minute and her twin engine rooms were 69 and 95 ft long. The massive bunkers had space for 8,500 tons of coal.

In a bid to attract more Continental passengers, the new vessel was to be named *Europa*. However, the Kaiser himself became so intrigued and even fascinated by the new ship, that it seemed an even more fitting choice to name her *Imperator*. His Imperial Majesty launched her on 23 May 1912, a triumphant, high-spirited occasion, but one which was still partly overshadowed by the tragic loss of *Titanic* five weeks before. The Kaiser shared the elaborate launching platform with Albert Ballin, the genius director of Hamburg America and master architect of this three-superliner plan. So delighted with this glittering symbol of Imperial Germany's technological might were the shipyard directors that they presented the Kaiser with a 3-ft long model of the liner, executed completely in silver. Equally impressed, the Kaiser in turn presented the model to Ballin himself.

The construction of this new 'sea monster' was not without its problems, however. In *Blohm & Voss: Ships and Machinery for the World*, it was noted that:

'To the annoyance of Blohm & Voss, the Hapag director general placed the order for the first giant ship, the *Imperator*, with the rival Vulcan shipyards, which had only opened its Hamburg works in 1910. After a very short time, however, Blohm & Voss realized that it could not have wished for anything better; the Vulcan work had to put up with all the difficulties which inevitably resulted from a newbuilding of proportions never tackled before. The worries and problems were considerable, and financially the *Imperator* was a failure to the shipyard. What's more, the ship could only be drydocked at Blohm & Voss in any case. Incidentally, there was another reason why they were happy that this building order had been placed with Vulcan. In 1910, the new [Blohm & Voss] slipway was still not completely ready, and the shipyard would inevitably have been unable to observe the deadlines.'

Above left *The biggest ship of any kind built at that time, the mighty bow of the 52,200-ton* Imperator *towers above the dockyard at Hamburg* (Hapag-Lloyd).

Above right *Kaiser Wilhelm II and Albert Ballin are among the dignitaries assembled on the podium just after the naming of* Imperator *in May 1912* (Hapag-Lloyd).

Below *Just a month after the tragic demise of* Titanic, *great excitement and pride prevail at the Vulcan shipyards as* Imperator *is launched* (Hapag-Lloyd).

Imperator was also, as intended, a ship of enormous statistics and wonders. John Malcolm Brinnin wrote that,

'Nothing but a troop transport had accommodations for so great a number of passengers and crew. As originally equipped, the *Imperator* could carry 908 passengers in first class, 972 in second class, 942 in third class and 1,772 steerage. Her crew numbered about 1,200. Fully booked, she would sail with nearly 5,000 souls on board—a figure ships of later decades would not even remotely approach. Another notable feature of the *Imperator* was a pillar-free vista the whole, end-to-end length of her enormous first class lounge. This was made possible when architects divided the uptakes of her two functional smoke-stacks (the third was a dummy) so that they ran up the side of the superstructure rather than through the middle of the ship. Another feature was the swimming pool that gave the appearance of being set in a mosaic temple supported by Doric columns. Another was a large searchlight, set up on its own platform on the foremast, presumably meant to comfort passengers by giving them visible evidence of an eye out for icebergs.

'But, without question, the most striking thing about the new *Imperator* was a crudely grotesque and scarifying

Above   *After launching,* Imperator *was moved to a floating drydock for fitting-out and completion. Only two of her three enormous funnels have been installed in this view* (Hapag-Lloyd).

Below   *A* Zeppelin *hovers above the* Imperator, *almost complete and ready for her maiden crossing to New York* (Hapag-Lloyd).

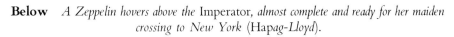

Above left   *Top-heavy and largely unstable,* Imperator *is even listing slightly to star-board in this dramatic view. Her funnels were later cut down in size and the large eagle and globe, which was ripped from her bow in a ferocious storm, was never replaced* (Hapag-Lloyd).

Above right   *The enormous tower crane at the Blohm & Voss yards lifts the forward mast in place aboard* Vaterland (Hapag-Lloyd).

Below   *With her funnels trimmed by nearly 10 ft,* Imperator *had a somewhat better look. She is shown outbound in the Elbe in 1914* (Hapag-Lloyd).

Right   *Another triumphant occasion, 3 April 1913: Prince Rupert of Bavaria and Albert Ballin are at the Blohm & Voss shipyards in Hamburg for the launching of* Vaterland, *the next German supership* (Frank O. Braynard Collection).

Above left *A historic meeting in Cowes Roads of the two largest liners afloat — the bow of the 52,100-ton* Imperator *and the brand new 54,200-ton* Vaterland *(Hapag-Lloyd).*

Above right *The maiden arrival at New York:* Vaterland *is anchored in the Lower Bay prior to making her run to Hoboken docks (Frank O. Braynard Collection).*

Below *Proud and majestic, the 950-ft long* Vaterland *leaves her birthplace at the port of Hamburg for her sea trials and then formal delivery to her Hapag owners (Hapag-Lloyd).*

One of Hapag's own tugs at New York assists as Vaterland *is berthed for the first time at the foot of Third Street in Hoboken* (Frank O. Braynard Collection).

figurehead. Ugly as sin, this device was a huge bland-eyed eagle with a dainty little crown on its snakelike head. Its cast-iron claws gripped a cast-iron globe that was bolted to a cast-iron sunburst of flashing golden spikes. Around the globe ran a gilded ribbon of iron embossed boldly with the familiar Hamburg America motto: "Mein Feld Ist die Welt". Straining for length [to outpace all other liners], the *Imperator*'s architects had also given her a deep overhang out of all proportions. These fore and aft features made her the longest thing afloat [the German measured 919 ft overall compared to the next largest, Cunard's *Aquitania*, at 901 ft], but were scant help in modifying her bulkiness or her worrisome heaviness. Enthroned in its flashy gear, the imperial eagle ruffled the Atlantic waves until the ship's third voyage. Then, an angry wave reached up, ripped the whole business from the prow and drowned it.'

Imperator was completed in the late spring of 1913, and departed from Cuxhaven (Hamburg) on 13 June on her maiden trip to New York. This otherwise gloriously exuberant occasion was marked, however, by one very serious flaw: she was exceedingly top-heavy. She rolled terribly even in the calmest seas—a fault, so her Hapag owners accurately felt, which could ruin her financially. Therefore, in her first annual overhaul and drydocking, her three funnels were cut down, all upper deck panels and fittings were replaced by ones in

lighter materials and a substantial amount of cement was poured along her bottom. To this, John Malcolm Brinnin added:

'First, Hapag ordered the removal of truckloads of ponderous ornamental furniture, then the marble baths in the luxury suites. The mahogany and marble fixtures in the Continental Grill on the promenade deck were taken away and the space transformed into a garden with lightweight cane furniture. Denuded inside and slightly disfigured outside [primarily by the cutting down of her three monstrous funnels], the *Imperator* had still to endure further ignominy: 2,000 tons of concrete were poured into the bottom.'

To some extent, *Imperator*'s rolling was curtailed, and so attention was focused on the second of the Hapag trio. If *Imperator* was the largest ocean liner yet, at 52,100 tons, the second of these German giants was bigger still. This ship was, at best estimations, expected to exceed 54,000 tons. Once again, and to the Kaiser's delight, the Germans would surely have the world's largest ship of any kind and, perhaps even more importantly, would greatly surpass the British. Also, according to Prager's *Blohm & Voss*,

'The new *Vaterland* [as the new ship was named even though

Above left *The third and last of Ballin's 'Big Three', Bismarck, is launched to great cheers and excitement in the summer sunshine of June 1914 (Hapag-Lloyd).*

Left *Completed in March 1922, and still bearing the name Bismarck, the liner is to sail shortly for British waters to become Majestic of White Star Line (Hapag-Lloyd).*

Above *Throughout the 'twenties and 'thirties, there was a near-continual battle for the distinction of 'world's largest liner' between the British Majestic, and former Bismarck, and the American Leviathan, ex-Vaterland. The two ships are shown together at Southampton in July 1925 (Frank O. Braynard Collection).*

Europa was once again the intended choice] became the top-class ship of the world merchant fleet at that time. She possessed a wonderfully large dining hall running through several decks. Above it were festive rooms, a Ritz Carlton restaurant, the Winter Garden, the hall and an elegant smoking room. Everywhere the ship provided a host of uninterrupted, pleasant internal vistas, thanks to the divided boiler shafts which Nordhausen had thought out and which were a complete innovation in shipbuilding.

'The ship had an entire row of shops, with a bank and a travel bureau, its own telephone exchange and a large [indoor] swimming pool. The spacious cabins in the first class sector, equipped like real miniature apartments, had 752 beds. In addition, there were two particularly luxurious emperor suites and ten staterooms, consisting of saloon, bedroom and bathroom. Counting all the classes, the *Vaterland* transported over 4,000 people across the Atlantic. The 46 watertube boilers for the 60,000 hp liner were all installed, with the aid of six cranes each, at the slipway.

Thus, a 950 ft long superlative vessel was created, run by a commodore and four assistant captains, seven nautical officers, 29 engineers and was to feature a 1,180-man crew. The ship's bunkers held about 9,000 tons of coal, the holds 12,000 tons of cargo. Some 15,000 electric light bulbs illuminated the floating town, which in addition had an emergency lighting system with a dynamo in a special space above the waterline. A station for wireless telegraphy, staffed by three telegraphists, was located on the Boat Deck and had 3 transmitters. Among these was a large scale telegraph sender ensuring almost constant touch with the mainland, even at that time.'

Vaterland was launched on 3 April 1913 and was named by Prince Rupert of Bavaria. One of the oddities about these three great German liners was that their christenings, in contrast to prevailing tradition, were done by men. The Kaiser himself had done the honours for

Above   *Transatlantic service in the early 'thirties: the former* Imperator, *as Cunard's* Berengaria, *departs from New York's Pier 54 while* Leviathan, *ex-*Vaterland, *is on the left at berth at her pier in Hoboken* (Frank O. Braynard Collection).

Below   *Postwar, in 1919, USS* Imperator, *now in American hands, 'swaps' berths at Hoboken with the grey-painted USS* Leviathan, *ex-*Vaterland (Frank O. Braynard Collection).

Above   *No longer looking like the pride of the Imperial German fleet,* Vaterland, *as the rust-streaked trooper* USS Leviathan, *returns to New York with yet another load of 10,000 soldiers* (Frank O. Braynard Collection).

Below   *Two generations of German flagships meet at Southampton in September 1935:* Berengaria, *the former* Imperator, *is about to sail, as* Bremen *is at berth across the slip* (Frank O. Braynard Collection).

Above *Dressed overall, and still the world's largest liner in the twilight years of her career,* Majestic *became, in January 1934, the first liner to use the then newly finished King George V graving dock at Southampton* (Frank O. Braynard Collection).

Above right *In peacetime service in the 'twenties,* Leviathan — *with a special aircraft catapult temporarily erected just aft of her wheelhouse* — *is at berth between transatlantic crossings. At New York's Pier 86, the Hapag* New York *is to the right* (Frank O. Braynard Collection).

Imperator, Prince Rupert for *Vaterland* and, on the occasion of the launching of *Bismarck,* the Kaiser unexpectedly took the role after the intended sponsor, Countess Hanna von Bismarck, had failed it. *Vaterland*'s launching was a specially planned and carefully orchestrated affair. According to *Blohm & Voss,*

'The launching of the *Vaterland* was kept to schedule, even if after several days of persistent east winds, the Elbe had dangerously little water. Hermann Blohm nevertheless decided to take the risk and send the newbuilding into its element. He felt confident that the ensuing higher stern wave, resulting from higher launching speed of the large vessel, would guard the giant's hull against "dumping".

'Launching of the *Vaterland* was a glorious event, which was reported in the international press. 15,000 tickets had been issued for the spectators' stands erected on the shipyard terrain especially for the purpose. These guests

came across the Elbe in ferryboats. Another large contingent of onlookers came through the newly built Elbe tunnel. Furthermore, all the married shipyard workers were allowed to give their wives a complimentary ticket, so that according to an estimate by Edward Blohm, about 40,000 people attended this launching.'

However, commercial life for the world's largest ship was all too short. She left Hamburg on her maiden passage to New York on 14 May 1914, and by August she was interned at New York (Hoboken) when war erupted.

Sadly, the Germans were never able to enjoy the third and largest of their intended super-threesome—the 'Big Three' as they became known. She was launched as *Bismarck,* on 20 June 1914. Eight days later, the gunshots at Sarajevo shattered and then fully

Right *Albert Ballin's projected trio of superliners all finished their days at the hands of shipbreakers in Scotland. The once pristine Boat Deck of* Leviathan, *ex-*Vaterland, *is soon to be invaded by armies of men with acetylene torches and hammers. The location is Rosyth and the date 1938 (Frank O. Braynard Collection).*

destroyed world peace. Archduke Ferdinand was killed, the scenario for war was set and *Bismarck* would never sail for the Germans.

Throughout the war years, *Bismarck* sat at her berth at her builder's yard, rusting, forlorn and mostly neglected. It was rumoured, however, that once the war was over she would be outfitted as a giant royal yacht for a celebratory around-the-world victory cruise by the Imperial family. Instead, by 1919, Germany was in pitiful defeat, the Kaiser was sent into exile and even Albert Ballin, Hapag's guiding force, was so shattered and demoralized that he took his own life. However, with rather blind, misguided enthusiasm, the Germans had actually hoped that the victorious Allies would permit *Bismarck* to be completed for a luxury revival of German-flag North Atlantic service. The Allied commanders had other plans, however.

Hapag's 'Big Three' went to the Allies and then into commercial service as competitors to their original owners. It was a strange irony. *Imperator*, left at Hamburg throughout the war years and then surrendered and briefly used as an American troop transport, sailing as USS *Imperator*, was soon thereafter ceded to the British and then more specifically to Cunard Line as reparations for the sinking of their *Lusitania*. *Vaterland*, left in American waters throughout the early war years, became the trooper USS *Leviathan* and delivered tens of thousands of soldiers to accomplish the defeat of her creators. After military service and then after suitable refitting and alterations, she reappeared on the transatlantic passenger run, sailing under the banner of United States Lines and as the largest liner (even at this distance in time) ever to fly the Stars and Stripes. The incomplete *Bismarck* also went to the British. When finally completed in 1922, she was transferred to White Star Line and became their *Majestic*, a replacement for their sunken *Britannic*. The three were, as planned, the largest ships afloat, but flying the British and American colours.

In many ways they were the finest ocean liners of their time. They briefly elevated Germany to the very highest maritime and therefore technological pinnacle. But the glory was all too brief—the brilliant plans were shattered. It was surely one of the more tragic aspects of war.

Imperator
(Hamburg America Line)

Service Hamburg-Southampton-Cherbourg-New York.
Specifications 52,117 gross tons, 909 × 98 ft (280 × 30 m).
Builder Vulcan Works, Hamburg, Germany, 1913.
Machinery Steam turbines, quadruple screw. Service speed 23 knots.
Capacity 908 first class, 972 second class, 949 third class, 1,772 steerage.

1912 23 May: Launched.
1913 June: Maiden voyage to New York; world's largest ship for one year until advent of *Vaterland*. Stability and other problems. Nov: Altered and funnels shortened by 9 ft.
1914 Aug: Laid up at Hamburg throughout the war years.
1919 Apr: Surrendered to US Government and reactivated as troop transport; sailed as USS *Imperator*.
1920 Feb: Handed over to British Government as reparations; chartered to Cunard Line for Liverpool-New York service.
1921 Feb: Sold outright to Cunard and renamed *Berengaria*.
1921 Sept–**1922** May: Extensive refit at Newcastle; tonnage relisted as 52,226. Berthing rearranged for 972 first class, 630 second class, 606 third class, 515 tourist class. Converted to oil fuel.
1938 3 Mar: Damaged by fire at New York; later sailed empty to Southampton and then laid up. Nov: Sold to be scrapped at Jarrow.
1939 Sept: Ship scrapped to double bottom, then work ceased on outbreak of Second World War.
1946 Last remains towed to Rosyth and broken up.

Vaterland

(Hamburg America Line)

Service Hamburg-Southampton-Cherbourg-New York.
Specifications 54,282 gross tons, 950 × 100 ft (292 × 31 m).
Builder Blohm & Voss, Hamburg, Germany, 1914.
Machinery Steam turbines, quadruple screw. Service speed 23 knots.
Capacity 752 first class, 535 second class, 850 third class, 1,772 steerage.

1913 3 Apr: Launched.
1914 May: Maiden voyage to New York as world's largest ship. Aug: Laid up at New York owing to outbreak of war.
1917 Apr: Formal seizure by US Government met with some opposition from loyalist crew members. Jul: Entered service as US Navy troop transport. Sept: Renamed *Leviathan*.
1919 Sept: Laid up at New York; disposition uncertain.
1922 Feb–**1923** May: Extensive refit at Newport News, Virginia, for further commerical passenger service for United States Lines. Tonnage relisted as 59,956; berthing rearranged for 970 first class, 542 second class, 944 third class and 935 fourth class. Berthing later rearranged for 750 first class, 535 second class and 2,000 third class. New York-Cherbourg-Southampton service.
1931 Official tonnage relisted as 48,932 in effort to save harbour fees.
1932 Laid up although briefly reactivated for some sailings during 1933 and 1934.
1934 Sept: Laid up at New York.
1938 Jan: Departed from New York bound for shipbreakers at Rosyth, Scotland.

Bismarck

(Hamburg America Line)

Service Intended for Hamburg-Southampton-Cherbourg-New York service but prevented by First World War.
Specifications 56,551 gross tons, 956 × 100 ft (294 × 31 m).
Builder Blohm & Voss, Hamburg, Germany, 1914–22.
Machinery Steam turbines, quadruple screw. Service speed 23½ knots.
Capacity Total 3,500 passengers in first, second and third class and steerage; exact numbers never determined.

1914 20 June: Launched. Aug: All construction ceased on outbreak of war.
1919 June: Transferred to British Government as reparations; construction resumed under British supervision.
1920 5 Oct: Construction delayed owing to fire at shipyard berth.
1921 Feb: Still incomplete but formally sold by British Government to White Star Line.
1922 Mar: Completed and sailed to Liverpool; world's largest ship until advent of French *Normandie* in 1935. Apr: Ran trials then renamed *Majestic*. May: Entered Southampton-New York service.
1934 Feb: Transferred to newly created Cunard-White Star Ltd.
1936 Feb: Laid up. May: Sold to British shipbreakers then promptly resold to British Admiralty for use as cadet training ship for 2,000 young men and boys. Renamed *Caledonia* and permanently positioned at Rosyth for training purposes.
1939 29 Sept: Was to have been converted to wartime troop transport for further service but caught fire and burnt out. Sank in shallow water.
1940 Mar: Wreckage scrapped on the spot.
1943 July: Last pieces raised and towed to Inverkeithing for final demolition.

10
Express sisters

While an always serious and ever-competing rival, North German Lloyd had no intention of challenging the 'Big Three' of Hamburg America. (More importantly, it is doubtful whether North Atlantic trade could have withstood, at least at that time, further tonnage of such great proportion and capacity.) Following the completion of Lloyd's largest liner to date, the 25,500-ton *George Washington* of 1909 (see page 51), the next ships in the Company's plans were a pair of 32,000-ton sisters, to be named *Columbus* and *Hindenburg*. They were to have been completed in 1914–15 and run on the transatlantic express service to New York via Southampton and Cherbourg. If completed as planned, they would have competed directly with the likes of Hapag's 52,100-ton *Imperator* and 54,200-ton *Vaterland*, but, once more, plans were disrupted by war.

Columbus was nearly complete by August 1914, but then sat idle for well over four years. Then, like so many other German liners, and including the afore-mentioned Hapag superliners, her fate was in the hands of the Allied reparations committees. *Columbus* went to the British Government and was completed under their supervision. Later she was sold outright to White Star Line and then commissioned as their *Homeric*. Used in the Atlantic express run to New York, she was teamed with the giant *Majestic* (the former *Bismarck*) and *Olympic*, near sister to the tragic *Titanic*. While smaller than the other two, *Homeric* was one of the best known and most popular transatlantic liners of the 'twenties. However, in the following decade, in the harsh economic climate of the early 'thirties, her fate was reversed. With too few passengers and therefore unable to earn her keep on the New York run, she was, as an alternative, sent on inexpensive cruises. But before long, she was completely out of work and was laid up in 1935, after having seen only a scant 13 years of active service. A year later, she went to the breakers.

The proposed *Hindenburg* fared differently, however.

Also incomplete during the war years, she was not included in the Allied reparations group for reasons unknown at this distance in time, but possibly as a generous gesture towards German passenger ship renewal. She was left in German hands and was to be finished for her original owners, North German Lloyd. Construction was resumed by 1920, although at a rather sluggish pace (caused mostly by material short-ages and strikes in a postwar, defeated Germany), and later there was a change in plans. She took the name of her intended first sister ship. Among other consider-ations, the name *Columbus* sounded less Germanic, especially at a time when deep bitterness lingered among sea travellers from other nations, particularly in the highly sought-after American market. Finally launched after still further delays in the summer of 1922, her debut was also delayed from the autumn of 1923 until the following spring. Technically her construction—from keel laying to completion—took a full decade. However, once in service, the new *Columbus* was heralded as 'the largest German liner of her time'.

Later refitted with new, squat funnels, she took on the low, flat, rather racy appearance of the later 'twenties and was, more specifically, something of a prelude to the streamlined Art Deco age of the 'thirties. This also made her seem a more appropriate companion to the then brand new *Bremen* and *Europa*, which also had squat funnels as built.

Columbus was an especially beautifully decorated liner. In A. G. Horton White's *Ships of the North Atlantic*, it was stated that,

'Most of the first class cabins have a private bathroom, and most are furnished as bed-sitting rooms. There are also several suites comprising bedroom, sitting room and bathroom. There are also large and comfortable public rooms in first class. On the Boat Deck is the Verandah and the Gymnasium, and on the Promenade Deck further aft is the Smoking Room. In one corner is a smaller Smoking

Room, and in another, a Bar. A passage leads forward to the library, which has a skylight.

'On each side of the engine room, two wide furnished corridors lead to the immense Social Hall, which is also fitted with a big skylight. The Dining Saloon is two decks in height in the centre, having a square gallery enclosed by windows. It has over 50 tables. Annexing are four smaller Dining Saloons, each with five or six tables. There is also a Children's Dining Saloon. The first class is also fitted with elevators.'

While used throughout the 'thirties as a transatlantic peak season companion to the far larger and faster *Bremen* and *Europa*, *Columbus* also developed considerable acclaim as a cruise-ship, particularly on longer, more expensive trips in the winter months. She was in fact on a cruise, although a shorter trip to the Caribbean, in the late summer of 1939 when the Second World War was just about to explode. In a flash command from Berlin, she abruptly off-loaded her American passengers at Havana and then fled to the safety of neutral Vera Cruz in Mexico. Three months later, she was ordered to return to home waters. However, in the course of this daring passage, she became the first large German liner to be a casualty of the war. Intercepted by a British warship off the Virginia coast, she was deliberately scuttled by her crew to avoid capture. One of Germany's finest liners, she finished her days, her Nazi banners flying, as a blazing inferno before slipping beneath the waves.

Below *As built, with two tall funnels, Lloyd's* Columbus *was the largest and grandest post-war German luxury liner until the advent of* Bremen *in 1929 (Hapag-Lloyd).*

Bottom *Re-engined and fitted with new squat funnels,* Columbus *is nearing the end of her extensive refit at the Blohm & Voss yards in 1929 (Hapag-Lloyd).*

Above   *Given shorter funnels so as to resemble the larger* Bremen *and* Europa, *the two bigger ships were rather quickly fitted with taller stacks instead and so the intended similarity was spoiled* (Everett Viez Collection).

Below   *A blazing inferno off the Virginia coast in December 1939, HMS* Hyperion *stands by the ill-fated* Columbus (Arnold Kludas Collection).

Columbus

(North German Lloyd)

Service Intended for Bremerhaven-Southampton-Cherbourg-New York, but not completed owing to outbreak of war.
Specifications Projected at approx 32,000 gross tons; 774 × 82 ft (238 × 25 m).
Builder Schichau Works, Danzig, Germany, 1913–22.
Machinery Steam, triple expansion, twin screw. Service speed 18 knots.
Capacity Approx 2,750 passengers. Berthing for German passenger service never determined.

1913 17 Dec: Launched.
1914 Aug: Although nearly complete, construction halted during war; ship remained idle.
1919 June: Transferred to British Government as reparations; construction resumed under British supervision.
1920 June: Sold to White Star Line and completed as *Homeric*.
1922 Jan: Maiden arrival at Southampton. Feb: Maiden voyage to New York. Tonnage listed as 34,351 and berthing arranged as 529 first class, 487 second class, 1,750 third class.
1923 Oct–**1924** Mar: Converted to oil firing and service speed relisted as 19 knots.
1932 June: Owing to Depression, removed from regular transatlantic service and used solely for cruising.
1934 Feb: Transferred to newly formed Cunard-White Star Ltd.
1935 Sept: Laid up as uneconomic.
1936 Feb: Sold to shipbreakers and broken up at Inverkeithing.

Hindenburg/Columbus

(North German Lloyd)

Service Bremerhaven-Southampton-Cherbourg-New York, and considerable cruising.
Specifications 32,354 gross tons, 775 × 83 ft (238 × 26 m).
Builder Schichau Works, Danzig, Germany, 1914–23.
Machinery Steam, triple expansion, twin screw. Service speed 19 knots.
Capacity 513 first class, 574 second class, 705 third class.

1914 Laid down. Intended name *Hindenburg*, sister to *Columbus* (see above). Aug: Construction halted owing to outbreak of war; left untouched.
1919 Not included in Allied reparations agreements and consequently remained with North German Lloyd.
1920 Construction resumed.
1922 June: Named *Columbus*. 12 Aug: Launched after several unsuccessful attempts.
1923 Nov: Completed, but entry into service delayed.
1924 Apr: Maiden crossing to New York; largest German passenger liner until advent of *Bremen* in 1929.
1927 Aug: Damaged during Atlantic crossing; machinery and engines ruined; returned to Germany and underwent extensive repairs. Temporarily fitted with triple expansion engines from freighter *Schwaben*.
1929 Extensive refit at Blohm & Voss yards at Hamburg; fitted with new, shorter funnels and new steam turbine machinery. Service speed increased to 22 knots and tonnage relisted as 32,565.
1939 Aug: During Caribbean cruise from New York, ordered to Havana to off-load passengers, then to safety of Vera Cruz, Mexico, owing to threat of war. 19 Dec: Attempting to return to Bremerhaven, ordered to stop by British destroyer *Hyperion*. To avoid capture, crew set fire to and scuttled liner 320 miles east of Cape Hatteras, Virginia. Crew rescued by a nearby US warship.

11
The *Tirpitz* trio

They were smaller, modified versions of the giant *Imperator* and her two near sisters, and were intended not for the North Atlantic, but to challenge the new luxury ships of Hamburg South America Line to Latin America. Similar to Hamburg Sud's *Cap Trafalgar* and *Cap Polonio*, this new Hapag trio used the same three-funnel design (a reminder of the more celebrated transatlantic ships) and had superb first class quarters as well as accommodation in second class, third class and steerage. The first of them, *Admiral von Tirpitz*, was launched in December 1913, just six months after *Imperator* had been commissioned and just a few months before Hamburg Sud's new flagship *Cap Polonio*. She was followed in February 1914 by *Johann Heinrich Burchard* and, a month later, by *William O'Swald*.

Once again, the war interrupted the plans for these ships. All completion and subsequent maiden voyage plans were cancelled, and the three ships were left virtually untouched during the war years. There were rumours, however, that *Admiral von Tirpitz*, which had been renamed more simply as *Tirpitz*, would be specially completed so as to serve as a Kaiser's 'victory yacht' when he reviewed the defeated British fleet. Instead, she was finished for the Allies and was then handed over to the British as reparations. She went on to a highly successful and popular career as Canadian Pacific's *Empress of Australia*. Ironically, years later, in the spring of 1939, she was indeed selected to serve as a large royal yacht, but for King George V and Queen Elizabeth. The ship carried Their Majesties across the Atlantic on the first leg of the friendship-binding tour of North America in those final months of peace before the Western World was once again plunged into war. *Empress of Australia* proved also to be the longest surviving member of this threesome; she was scrapped in 1952, at the age of 39.

William O'Swald and *Johann Heinrich Burchard* were sold to the Dutch during the war and then, with considerable difficulty caused by the fact that the Allies wanted them as reparations, were finally handed over to their new Amsterdam owners in the first years of peace. They joined Royal Holland Lloyd, but in a short time proved to be too large for that firm's South American passenger services. In 1922, they were sold again, this time to the Americans, to a newly formed company known as United American Lines. It was at this time that they received their best known and best remembered names: the former *O'Swald* became *Resolute* and *Burchard* changed to *Reliance*. Soon transferred to Panamanian registry, to avoid the 'dry ship' status caused by American Prohibition, they soon sailed as transatlantic liners in coordinated services with their original Hamburg America owners. In fact, as Hapag became more and more successful, and once Allied restrictions were eased towards German merchant shipowners, the two liners were sold outright to Hapag and rehoisted the German colours in 1926.

As German liners, they were perhaps best known for their cruising voyages. In this service, they established two of the finest reputations of the late 'twenties and

Top right   Tirpitz *as completed for Hamburg America, but for whom she never sailed commercially* (Willie Tinnemeyer Collection).

Middle right   *In her subsequent career as the British* Empress of Australia, *the former* Tirpitz *was an extremely popular and notable liner, primarily for carrying the British King and Queen to Canada in 1939* (Alex Duncan).

Right   Reliance *and her sister* Resolute *had the classic lines of three-funnel liners* (Hapag-Lloyd).

Above *Dressed in flags during a Northern cities cruise, Reliance is berthed at the Hamburg Overseas Landing Stage for convenient entry into the City itself* (Hapag-Lloyd).

Below *Later repainted in more tropical, heat-resistant white, Reliance is shown at anchor at a small Norwegian port during one of her summertime cruises to the Fjordlands* (Hapag-Lloyd).

early 'thirties. They were especially well known for their long, luxurious voyages, and sample advertising for one of these trips read:

'Change your mind. Give it new beauty, new interests and new experience. Cast off your Occidental worries for a while. Make a cruise around the world. Feel the spell of the Orient . . . the languor of starry, scented nights . . . the mystery of the ancient lands. Watch the monkeys skipping over the walls of Jaipur . . . and a stately Indian squat down in the street to make tea on his portable brazier. Enjoy the musical comedy customs of Korea . . . where a man shows his top-knot thru a stovepipe hat of wire netting. 33 countries to see . . . including Indo-China and Borneo . . . 140 days to absorb them. The luxurious *Resolute*, queen of cruising steamers, to connect them. She is experienced you know . . . for this is her 7th around the world cruise. So sail eastward from New York on January 6th 1930, on "the Voyage of Your Dreams", arriving in every country at the ideal season. Rates from $2,000 and up include an extraordinary programme of shore excursions.'

Another advertisement read:

'To Northern Wonderlands and Russia on the SS *Reliance*. Iceland, North Cape, Norway, Scandinavian and Baltic capitals and a 4-day stay in the Union of the Soviet Socialist Republics. Magnificent scenery—awesome glaciers, the Midnight Sun, snow capped peaks, winding fjords and misty waterfalls. Places and peoples where history and legends date back for centuries. And an opportunity to study the world's greatest social experiment. Sail from New York—June 28th 1930. Duration 36 days to Hamburg—Rates from $800 up including return passage to New York on any steamer of the Line prior to December 31st. Also six cruises from Hamburg—from 11 to 24 days—by the SS *Resolute* and SS *Oceana*.'

Rather oddly within the histories of passenger ships, *Resolute* was sold out of the Hapag fleet in 1935, in what seemed to be the prime of her career. She went on to a far less luxurious task, serving as a troop-ship in the Italian East African campaigns, later becoming a war loss. Hapag might well have regretted the sale of their well-known ship for, three years later, *Reliance* burnt out completely at Hamburg. Her remains eventually went to Nazi munitions factories.

Tirpitz
(Hamburg America Line)

Service Intended for Hamburg-East Coast of South America service, but did not enter German commercial service owing to First World War.
Specifications 21,498 gross tons, 615 × 75 ft (189 × 23 m).
Builder Vulcan Works, Stettin, Germany, 1913–20.
Machinery Steam turbines, twin screw. Service speed 16½ knots.
Capacity 370 first class, 190 second class, 415 third class, 1,000 steerage.

1913 20 Dec: Launched as *Admiral von Tirpitz*.
1914 Feb: Name shortened to *Tirpitz*. Aug: Construction halted owing to war; never completed as intended although rumoured to become Kaiser's wartime review ship in event of British defeat.
1919 Ordered to be completed by Allied command.
1920 Nov: Completed and surrendered to British Government; managed by P&O Lines for troop-ship services.
1921 July: Sold outright to Canadian Pacific Steamships and renamed *Empress of China*, but quickly renamed *Empress of Australia*. Extended refit at Vulcan yards, Hamburg, then completed at John Brown yards, Clydebank, Scotland. Tonnage relisted as 21,860. Used in trans-Pacific service from Vancouver to Far East.
1923 1 Sept: Caught at Yokohama during Great Tokyo Earthquake; undertook heroic rescue work.
1926 Aug–**1927** June: Extensive refit at Glasgow; machinery altered and service speed increased to 19 knots. Accommodation revised as 400 first class, 150 second class and 630 third class. Used in transatlantic service between Southampton and Quebec City and for cruising.
1933 Accommodation revised for 387 first class, 394 tourist class and 358 third class.
1939 May: Carried King George VI and Queen Elizabeth on westbound crossing to Canada. Sept: Converted to troop transport.
1945–52 Peacetime trooping.
1952 Sold to shipbreakers and broken up at Inverkeithing.

Johann Heinrich Burchard/Reliance

(Hamburg America Line)

Service Intended for Hamburg-South America service; later used on Hamburg-Southampton-Cherbourg-New York service as well as extensive cruising.
Specifications 19,980 gross tons, 615 × 71 ft (189 × 22 m).
Builder Tecklenborg Shipyards, Geestemunde, Germany, 1914–20.
Machinery Steam, triple expansion, triple screw. Service speed 16 knots.
Capacity 315 first class, 301 second class, 850 third class.

1914 10 Feb: Launched; construction halted owing to war.
1915 Nov: Completed but soon sold as part of war reparations pact to Dutch. Following Armistice, sale not recognized by Allies. Ship remained idle.
1920 Feb: Renamed *Limburgia*, escaped in fog despite Allied blocking attempts and delivered to Royal Holland Lloyd at Amsterdam. Later entered Amsterdam-Rio de Janeiro, Santos, Montevideo and Buenos Aires service. Unsuccessful.
1922 Sold to United American Lines, US flag; renamed *Reliance*. Tonnage relisted as 19,582 and accommodation restyled for 290 first class, 320 second class and 400 third class. Entered transatlantic service to New York and sailed in conjunction with Hamburg America Line.
1923 Transferred to Panamanian flag owing to American Prohibition laws.
1926 July: Sold outright to Hamburg America Line and returned to German flag; tonnage relisted as 19,527 then as 19,802.
1934 Refitted as full-time cruise-ship; accommodations for 500 first class passengers only.
1937 Further refit and alterations; tonnage relisted as 19,618 and accommodation rearranged for 633 first class and 186 second class.
1938 7 Aug: Destroyed by fire at Hamburg, considered beyond economic repair. Burnt-out remains laid up.
1940 Jan: Sold to Krupps for demolition.
1941 Broken up at Bremerhaven.

William O'Swald/Resolute

(Hamburg America Line)

Service Intended for South American service, later Hamburg-Southampton-Cherbourg-New York as well as extensive cruising.
Specifications 20,200 gross tons, 616 × 72 ft (190 × 22 m).
Builder AG Weser shipyards, Bremen, Germany, 1914–20.
Machinery Steam, triple expansion, triple screw. Service speed 16 knots.
Capacity 335 first class, 284 second class, 469 third class, 857 steerage.

1914 30 Mar: Launched. Aug: Construction halted owing to outbreak of war.
1916 June: Despite hostilities, she and intended sister ship *Johann Heinrich Burchard* (see above) sold to Royal Holland Lloyd of Amsterdam as form of reparations; after War, Allies refused to recognize sale. Following considerable delays, transfer eventually took place.
1920 July: Renamed *Brabantia* under Dutch flag; Amsterdam-Rio de Janeiro-Santos-Montevideo-Buenos Aires service. Unsuccessful.
1922 Sold to United American Lines, US flag; renamed *Resolute*. Refitted for North Atlantic service; tonnage relisted as 19,653 and accommodation restyled for 290 first class, 320 second class and 400 third class. Passenger service run in conjunction with Hamburg America Line, former owners.
1923 Transferred to Panamanian flag owing to American Prohibition laws.
1926 Aug: Sold outright to Hamburg America Line, German flag; tonnage relisted as 19,692. Considerable cruising.
1934 Accommodation restyled for 497 first class passengers only.
1935 Aug: Sold to Italian Government for use as troop transport in Abyssinian War; managed by Lloyd Triestino and renamed *Lombardia*. Accommodation restyled for 103 first class and 4,420 troops; tonnage relisted as 20,006.
1943 4 Aug: Burnt out and sunk during Allied air raid on Naples.
1946 Wreckage salvaged and remains towed to La Spezia for scrapping.

12

Intermediate liners of the 'twenties and early 'thirties

This is a rather mixed group of passenger ships that served primarily, at various times, to renew the German passenger fleet following the devastation of the First World War. Included also are several ships that saw comparatively brief service under German colours, such as the two Red Star liners in the later 'thirties.

Neither Hamburg America nor North German Lloyd had any adequate tonnage by 1919–20, and, compounded by severe Allied restrictions on new-buildings, the renewal of their respective passenger services, especially on the North Atlantic, was slow and at best often fragmented. The careers of the ships in this section frequently reflect this.

The intended Lloyd *Zeppelin* was handed over to the Allies in 1919, then sailed under the British flag for eight years before being sold to her original German owners to become their *Dresden*. The proposed *Munchen* of 1914 never saw German service at all, but

went to the Allies for the remainder of her career. Hapag's rather small *Westphalia* and *Thuringia* were originally intended as freighters, but—in those stark postwar years—were redesigned and completed as passenger ships. Several of the ships in this section went on to become well-known cruise liners, namely Lloyd's *Steuben*, and Hapag's *Milwaukee*, while *Stuttgart* was among the first passenger ships to be assigned to the Nazi Government's Labour Front for use in so-called 'Strength through Joy' cruises. Hapag's *St Louis*, which also served as a cruise-ship, has established a special place in passenger ship history for her Third Reich-inspired voyage from Hamburg to Havana, in May–June 1939, with some 900 Jewish refugees on board. Deliberately denied entry into Cuba, the trip received the intended international press coverage and all to prove the undesirability of European Jews.

Also, several of these ships met with very tragic endings. *Stuttgart* was bombed and destroyed during an

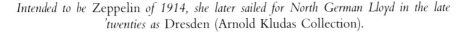

Intended to be Zeppelin *of 1914, she later sailed for North German Lloyd in the late 'twenties as* Dresden *(Arnold Kludas Collection).*

Above *Although evacuated in sufficient time by her passengers and crew, Dresden capsized in June 1934 during a pleasure cruise to Norway (P&O Lines).*

Below *Hamburg-South America Line's* General San Martin *was one of those smaller, now largely forgotten passenger ships that was so often overshadowed by the larger, more opulent liners. What a delightful looking ship she was, however! (Willie Tinnemeyer Collection).*

The cruising liner General von Steuben, *shown with a black hull* (**above**) *while arriving at Venice and in all-white colouring* (**below**) *while at anchor in a Norwegian fjord* (Willie Tinnemeyer Collection).

North German Lloyd's Stuttgart *of 1923 shown in her North Atlantic guise, with a black hull (**above**) then, in the 'thirties, as a 'Strength through Joy' cruising liner (**below**)* (Willie Tinnemeyer Collection).

Amerika *of Hamburg America was the world's largest liner in 1906–07* (Charles Sachs Collection).

Hamburg-Amerika
Linie

Doppelschrauben-Postdampfer „President Grant"

1023 MÜHLMEISTER & JOHLER, HAMBURG. DEP. 2625   Nº 955

Above   President Grant *and her sister were the only six-masted passenger ships to sail the North Atlantic* (Charles Sachs Collection).

Right   Cleveland *and her sister* Cincinnati *were especially popular as long-distance cruising liners* (Charles Sachs Collection).

Below   *A very pleasant rendering of the Hamburg Sud liners* Cap Polonio *and* Cap Norte *at Hamburg* (Charles Sachs Collection).

Hamburg-Amerika
Linie

An Bord
des Dampfers „CLEVELAND"

Der Hamburger Dampfer
IMPERATOR
das größte Schiff der Welt.

Hamburg-Amerika Linie.

With her enormous funnels, Imperator was, in 1913, the largest liner ever built and the first to exceed 50,000 tons (Charles Sachs Collection).

Above   *The Lloyd's* Berlin *of 1925 was sunk twice: first during the war in February 1945, and then, at the age of sixty-one, in August 1986* (Willie Tinnemeyer Collection).

Below   *The fine motor-liner* St Louis, *perhaps best known for her thwarted voyage with Jewish refugees to Havana in June 1939, is shown at New York just afterwards, in that final summer of peace* (Roger Scozzafava).

Above   *Refitted for just 559 first class passengers and advertised as a 'floating spa', Milwaukee is outbound from Hamburg. Robert Ley is in the background on the left (Hapag-Lloyd).*

Below   *During a summer cruise in the 'thirties, Milwaukee is seen in the setting of the magnificent Geirangerfjord (Hapag-Lloyd).*

Allied air attack on occupied Gdynia. Horribly, she was overloaded with wounded soldiers, most of whom perished. *Steuben* was torpedoed in February 1945, just as the Nazis were nearing their defeat, with the loss of 3,000 souls. In peacetime, and although with the loss of far fewer, some 398 in all, the former *Berlin* of 1925, while in her second career as the postwar Soviet *Admiral Nakhimov*, sank following a collision in August 1986. It was listed as the worst passenger ship disaster in peacetime Soviet maritime history.

Several of these ships nonetheless went on to enjoy extremely long careers. The aforementioned *Berlin* was 61 years old when she was lost. Hapag's former *Cordillera*, specially built with her twin sister *Caribia* for the West Indies-Central America run, endured from 1933 until 1979, a career of 44 years. Although sunk during the war, she was eventually salvaged by the Soviets and later revived as the passenger ship *Russ*. *Caribia* reached her 50th year before being retired in 1983. She too went to the Soviets after the war and became their *Ilitch*.

Special note should also be made of the two Red Star passenger liners, *Westernland* and *Pennland*, which sailed under German colours for four years, from 1935 until 1939. The ships had been under the British flag and had sailed between Antwerp, Southampton and New York, but, by 1934, with far less than promising returns. In that financially troubled year, they carried a mere 4,000 passengers in total. The ships, or the Red Star Line itself, could not continue and so there was a scheme to sail them as the 'lowest priced' passenger ships on the Atlantic. The concept included the likes of cafeteria-style dining and was something of a forerunner to the era of the 'no-frills' airlines of the 1970s and 1980s. However, the British Government refused to give its needed approval to the plan, especially as it was anticipating financially troubled times for the far larger and more important Cunard Line. Consequently, both *Westernland* and *Pennland* were sold to Hamburg-based shipper Arnold Bernstein, who continued to run them out of Antwerp under the Red Star banner. Unfortunately, as the Nazi political machine steadily grew, Mr Bernstein, a Jew, was stripped of his holdings and, in that final spring before the outbreak of war, the ships were sold off to Holland America Line. Interestingly, Holland America's last terminal at New York, Pier 40 at the foot of West Houston Street in the Greenwich Village section, and closed to shipping since 1974, still retains a sign marked 'Red Star Line'.

For their time, Hapag's Cordillera *and her sister were quite sizeable passenger-cargo liners*
(Willie Tinnemeyer Collection).

Zeppelin/Dresden
(North German Lloyd)

Service Bremerhaven-Southampton-Cherbourg-New York, also considerable cruising.
Specifications 14,690 gross tons, 570 × 67 ft (175 × 21 m).
Builder Bremer Vulkan Shipyards, Vegesack, Germany, 1915.
Machinery Steam, quadruple expansion, twin screw. Service speed 15½ knots.
Capacity 399 cabin class, 288 tourist class, 284 third class.

1914 9 June: Launched as *Zeppelin*.
1915 Jan: Completed despite outbreak of war, then laid up for duration of hostilities.
1919 Mar: Surrendered to British Government, managed by White Star Line.
1920 Sold outright to Orient Line, British flag. Renamed *Ormuz*; extensively refitted at Belfast then Rotterdam. Tonnage listed as 14,588 and accommodation arranged for 293 first class and 882 third class.
1921 Nov: Entered London-Melbourne-Sydney service via Suez.
1927 Apr: Sold to original North German Lloyd owners; renamed *Dresden*. Refitted and tonnage relisted as 14,690; berthing rearranged for 399 cabin class, 288 tourist class and 284 third class. Transatlantic service and cruising.
1934 20 June: Ran aground during summertime Fjords cruise at Utsire, Norway; 1,000 passengers and crew evacuated. Capsized on following day; 4 killed. Aug: Wreckage sold to local Norwegian firm for scrapping.

Munchen
(North German Lloyd)

Service Did not enter German-flag passenger service owing to First World War.
Specifications 18,940 gross tons, 615 × 71 ft (189 × 22 m).
Builder AG Weser Shipyards, Bremen, Germany, 1914–23.
Machinery Steam, quadruple expansion, twin screw. Service speed 17 knots.
Capacity 229 first class, 523 second class, 690 third class.

1914 Laid down but construction ceased owing to outbreak of war.
1919 Ordered to be completed and then surrendered to the British Government.
1920 23 Mar: Launched, to be owned by Royal Mail Lines, British flag.
1923 Mar: Completed; renamed *Ohio*. Entered Hamburg-Channel ports-New York service.
1925 Began use also as cruise-ship.
1927 Feb: Sold to White Star Line, British flag; renamed *Albertic*. Liverpool-Quebec City-Montreal service, later also assigned to London-Montreal and Liverpool-New York services.
1933 Mar: Laid up.
1934 July: Sold to Japanese shipbreakers. Nov: Delivered for scrapping.

Top left *Like her sister,* Caribia *survived the Second World War and then went on to serve the Soviets for several decades (Hapag-Lloyd).*

Middle left *It had been intended in the mid 'thirties to use* Westernland *and her running-mate* Pennland *as low-fare, cafeteria-style transatlantic passenger ships (Alex Duncan).*

Left Pennland *was sold to Holland America Line in 1939, and then, two years later, was lost in the Aegean while serving as a troop transport (Alex Duncan).*

Westphalia/General Artigas

(Hamburg America Line)

Service Hamburg-New York, later Hamburg-East coast of South America.
Specifications 11,343 gross tons, 495 × 60 ft (152 × 18 m).
Builder Howaldtswerke Shipyards, Kiel, Germany, 1923.
Machinery Steam turbines, single screw. Service speed 13½ knots.
Capacity 150 cabin class, 652 third class.

1917 Planned as Hamburg America freighter *Ammerland* but construction postponed owing to war. Redesigned for passenger service.
1923 19 Jan: Launched as *Westphalia*. May: Transatlantic maiden voyage to New York.
1926 31 Jan: Rescued 27 crew-members from sinking Dutch freighter *Alkaid* in Atlantic.
1929 Refitted for South American service; tonnage relisted as 11,254 and berthing rearranged for 169 cabin class and 392 third class.
1930 Apr: Renamed *General Artigas* and entered service to South America.
1934 Nov: Chartered to Hamburg-South America Line and repainted in their colours.
1936 June: Bought outright by Hamburg-South America.
1940 Converted into accommodation ship for Germany Navy at Hamburg.
1943 25 July: Sunk at Hamburg during British air raid.
1946 Wreckage raised and scrapped.

Thuringia/General San Martin

(Hamburg America Line)

Service Hamburg-New York, later Hamburg-East coast of South America.
Specifications 11,343 gross tons, 495 × 60 ft (152 × 18 m).
Builder Howaldtswerke Shipyards, Kiel, Germany, 1922.
Machinery Steam turbines, single screw. Service speed 13½ knots.
Capacity 159 cabin class, 652 third class.

1917 Ordered as Hamburg America freighter *Havelland*; construction delayed owing to war. Later redesigned for passenger service.
1922 12 Aug: Launched.
1923 Jan: Maiden voyage to New York.
1930 Refitted for South American service and renamed *General San Martin*; tonnage relisted as 11,251. Accommodation rearranged as 169 cabin class and 392 third class.
1934 Mar: Chartered to Hamburg-South America Line.
1936 June: Sold outright to Hamburg-South America Line.
1940 Jan: Began use as accommodation ship for German Navy, then later served as hospital ship. ship.
1945 Evacuated 30,000 people in 11 voyages from German Eastern territories. Oct: Surrendered to British Government at Copenhagen, then refitted as troop-ship at Hamburg. Renamed *Empire Deben* and managed by Shaw Savill Line.
1949 Sold to British shipbreakers and broken up at Newport, Monmouthshire.

Munchen/General von Steuben/Steuben

(North German Lloyd)

Service Bremerhaven-Channel ports-New York, later cruising only.
Specifications 13,325 gross tons, 551 × 65 ft (169 × 20 m).
Builder Vulcan Works, Stettin, Germany, 1923.
Machinery Steam, triple expansion, twin screw. Service speed 15 knots.
Capacity 171 first class, 350 second class, 558 third class.

1922 25 Nov: Launched.
1923 June: Maiden voyage to New York.
1930 11 Feb: Badly damaged at New York berth after cargo caught fire; swamped with water from hoses and sank. Later salvaged and partially repaired at Brooklyn. May: Returned to home waters and extensively refitted; tonnage relisted as 14,690 and accommodation rearranged as 214 cabin class, 358 tourist class and 221 third class.
1931 Jan: Returned to service as *General von Steuben*.
1935 Refitted for full-time use as cruise-ship; 484 first class passengers only.
1938 Name shortened to *Steuben*.
1939 Converted to accommodation ship for German Navy at Kiel, then later served as transport and hospital ship in Baltic.
1945 9 Feb: Left Pillau for Kiel with just under 5,000 on board. Torpedoed on following day by Soviet submarine; sank with loss of 3,000 souls.

Stuttgart

(North German Lloyd)

Service Bremerhaven-Channel ports-New York, later used as 'Strength through Joy' cruise-ship.
Specifications 13,325 gross tons, 551 × 60 ft (169 × 18 m).
Builder Vulcan Works, Stettin, Germany, 1923.
Machinery Steam, triple expansion, twin screw. Service speed 15 knots.
Capacity 171 first class, 338 second class, 594 third class.

1923 31 July: Launched.
1924 Jan: Maiden voyage to New York.
1937 Used solely for cruising.
1938 Sold to the German Labour Front and used for 'Strength through Joy' cruising; managed by North German Lloyd. 990 one-class passengers only.
1939 Converted to hospital ship for German Navy.
1943 9 Oct: While filled with wounded soldiers, bombed then set afire during Allied air raid on Gdynia. Blazing hull later towed to outer harbour and deliberately sunk; considerable loss of life.

Berlin

(North German Lloyd)

Service Bremerhaven-Southampton-Cherbourg-New York, also cruising.
Specifications 15,286 gross tons, 572 × 69 ft (176 × 21 m).
Builder Bremer Vulkan Shipyards, Vegesack, Germany, 1925.
Machinery Steam, triple expansion, twin screw. Service speed 16 knots.
Capacity 220 first class, 284 second class, 618 third class.

1925 24 Mar: Launched. Sept: Maiden crossing to New York.
1928 13 Nov: Rescued survivors from sinking British passenger ship *Vestris*.
1929 Refitted and passenger accommodation revised as 257 cabin class, 261 tourist class and 361 third class.
1938 Oct: Withdrawn from transatlantic service and laid up; later ran two 'Strength through Joy' cruises.
1939 17 July: Boiler explosion off Swinemunde; 17 killed. Repaired, then outfitted as hospital ship for German Navy.
1945 1 Feb: Sank after hitting mine off Swinemunde; abandoned by Germans.
1949 Refloated by Soviets and renamed *Admiral Nakhimov*; extended refit at Warnemunde in East Germany for passenger service.
1957 May: Entered Soviet passenger service for Black Sea Steamship Co; assigned to Black Sea coastal run out of Odessa. Later several transatlantic voyages to Cuba.
1986 31 Aug: Sank eight miles off Novorossisk after collision with Soviet bulk carrier *Petr Vasev*; 398 passengers and crew lost.

St Louis

(Hamburg America Line)

Service Hamburg and Channel ports to New York, considerable cruising.
Specifications 16,732 gross tons, 574 × 72 ft (177 × 22 m).
Builder Bremer Vulkan Shipyards, Vegesack, Germany, 1929.
Machinery MAN diesels, twin screw. Service speed 16 knots.
Capacity 270 cabin class, 287 tourist class, 416 third class.

1928 2 Aug: Launched.
1929 Mar: Maiden voyage to New York.
1939 May–June: Carried 900 Jewish refugees from Germany to Cuba, but denied entry into Havana by Cuban authorities. Well-publicized affair was, in fact, planned Nazi propaganda scheme; later settled when several European countries agreed to accept passengers. Ship returned to European waters, worried passengers disembarked at Antwerp.
1939 Aug: Caught at New York just before the outbreak of war and attempted to return to Hamburg without passengers via Murmansk.
1940 Jan: Reached Hamburg then outfitted as accommodation ship at Kiel.
1944 30 Aug: Badly damaged during Allied air raid on Kiel; later beached.
1946 Remains towed to Hamburg; second funnel gone. Repaired for use as floating hostel in Hamburg harbour.
1950 No longer in use; sold off.
1952 Scrapped at Bremerhaven.

Milwaukee

(Hamburg America Line)

Service Hamburg and Channel ports to New York, considerable cruising.
Specifications 16,669 gross tons, 575 × 72 ft (177 × 22 m).
Builder Blohm & Voss, Hamburg, Germany, 1929.
Machinery MAN diesels, twin screw. Service speed 16½ knots.
Capacity 270 cabin class, 259 tourist class, 428 third class.

1929 20 Feb: Launched.
1929 June: Maiden crossing to New York.
1935 Thoroughly refitted as cruise-ship; accommodation restyled for 559 first class passengers only. Tonnage relisted as 16,754.
1940 Converted for use as German Naval accommodation ship at Kiel.
1945 May: Surrendered to British Government; transferred to Ministry of Transport and managed by Cunard-White Star Line. Renamed *Empire Waveney*.
1946 1 Mar: Completely destroyed by fire while being refitted at Liverpool and sank. May: Salvaged.
1947 Jan: Towed to Glasgow for scrapping. Sept: Final remains towed to Troon for demolition.

Caribia

(Hamburg America Line)

Service Hamburg-West Indies-Central American ports.
Specifications 12,049 gross tons, 524 × 65 ft (161 × 20 m).
Builder Blohm & Voss, Hamburg, Germany, 1933.
Machinery MAN diesels, twin screw. Service speed 17 knots.
Capacity 206 first class, 103 second class, 100 tourist class.

1932 1 Mar: Launched.
1933 Feb: Maiden voyage to West Indies and Central America.
1940 Converted to Naval accommodation ship at Flensburg.
1945 May: Surrendered to British, then awarded to US Government.
1946 Given by US Government to Soviets; renamed *Ilitch* (later restyled as *Ilyich*). Used in Far Eastern waters, mostly between Vladivostock and Kamchatka.
1983 July: No longer listing as sailing.

Cordillera

(Hamburg America Line)

Service Hamburg-West Indies-Central American ports.
Specifications 12,055 gross tons, 524 × 65 ft (161 × 20 m).
Builder Blohm & Voss, Hamburg, Germany, 1933.
Machinery MAN diesels, twin screw. Service speed 17 knots.
Capacity 206 first class, 103 second class, 110 tourist class.

1933 4 Mar: Launched. Sept: Maiden voyage to West Indies.
1939 Sept: Owing to outbreak of war, sailed to Murmansk to avoid capture or attack.
1940 Feb: Finally returned to Hamburg; later outfitted as accommodation ship for German Navy.
1945 12 Mar: Bombed and sank at Swinemunde during Allied air raid.
1949 Salvaged by Soviet Government; towed to Antwerp and later to Warnemunde, East Germany, for repairs and refitting.
1952 Mar: Renamed *Russ*; tonnage relisted as 12,931. Assigned to Far Eastern waters, sailing mostly between Vladivostock and Kamchatka.
1979 Feb: Scrapped at Inchon, South Korea.

Westernland

(Red Star Line)

Service Antwerp–New York via Southampton.
Specifications 16,314 gross tons, 601 × 67 ft (185 × 21 m).
Builder Harland & Wolff Ltd, Belfast, Northern Ireland, 1914–22.
Machinery Steam, triple expansion, triple screw. Service speed 15 knots.
Capacity 550 tourist class passengers.

1913 Ordered, but construction halted after outbreak of war.
1917 19 Apr: Launched as *Regina* for Dominion Line, British flag.
1918 Dec: Completed for use as emergency military transport; fitted with only one funnel and no passenger accommodation.
1920 Returned to builders at Belfast and completed as passenger ship.
1922 Mar: Completed; maiden voyage from Liverpool to Portland, Maine, for Dominion Line. Accommodation listed for 631 cabin class and 1,824 third class passengers.
1925 Dec: Dominion Line taken over by White Star Line, also British flag; *Regina* began sailing for new owners on Liverpool-New York run.
1929 Sold to Red Star Line, also British flag; accommodation rearranged for 350 cabin class, 350 tourist class and 800 third class.
1930 Renamed *Westernland* and used on Antwerp-Southampton-New York service.
1935 Aug: Changed to Red Star Line, German flag; refitted and accommodation reduced to 550 tourist class passengers only.
1939 June: Sold to Holland America Line, Dutch flag; remained on Antwerp service.
1940 May: As Allied troop-ship, *Westernland* temporarily served as seat of exiled Dutch Government at Falmouth.
1942 Nov: Sold outright to British Admiralty; rebuilt at London as fleet repair ship.
1946 Sold to C. Salvesen Ltd, British flag, for conversion to whaling ship, but project never materialized.
1947 July: Delivered to shipbreakers at Blyth, Scotland, and scrapped.

Pennland

(Red Star Line)

Service Antwerp–New York via Southampton.
Specifications 16,332 gross tons, 600 × 67 ft (185 × 21 m).
Builder Harland & Wolff Ltd, Belfast, Northern Ireland, 1913–22.
Machinery Steam, triple expansion, triple screw. Service speed 15 knots.
Capacity 550 tourist class only.

1913 Nov: Laid down as *Pittsburgh* for American Line, but British flag. Construction disrupted by outbreak of war; ship remained incomplete.
1919 Construction resumed.
1920 11 Nov: Launched.
1922 June: Maiden crossing from Liverpool to Boston.
1925 Jan: Sold to Red Star Line, British flag; began Antwerp-New York sailings.
1926 Feb: Renamed *Pennland*.
1935 Transferred to Red Star Line, German flag; accommodation restyled from 600 cabin class and 1,800 third class to 550 tourist class only. Continued in New York service.
1939 June: Sold to Holland America Line, Dutch flag; continued on Antwerp-New York run.
1940 Refitted as troop-ship for use by British Ministry of Transport.
1941 25 Apr: Bombed and sunk by German aircraft in Gulf of Athens.

13
Latin American liners

These seven smaller passenger ships were created primarily for the migrant trade, which gradually resumed in the early 'twenties. The sailed, and often interchangeably for more than one owner, for the three most important German passenger ship firms: Hamburg America, North German Lloyd and Hamburg-South America. They were mostly used in the Latin American trade, to Brazil, Uruguay and Argentina, a fact underlined by their Spanish-sounding names.

Several of these ships had extended careers and went on to sail for other owners after the war. The former *Antonio Delfino* served as Britain's *Empire Halladale*, the ex-*Cap Norte* as *Empire Trooper* and, the longest survivor of all (for 46 years), the one-time *Sierra Morena*, which continued as the Soviet *Asia* until 1970.

Like most of the German passenger ships engaged in Latin American service, Antonio Delfino *of Hamburg Sud had a deliberate Spanish name (Willie Tinnemeyer Collection).*

Above *In the post-war years, from 1945 until 1956, the former* Antonio Delfino *served with the British as the peacetime trooper* Empire Halladale *(J. K. Byass).*
Below *Hamburg-South America's* Cap Norte *later became* Sierra Salvada *for North German Lloyd, but then later reverted to her original name (Willie Tinnemeyer Collection).*

Above *The former* Cap Norte, *now in British Ministry of Transport hands, is shown as* Empire Trooper *at Malta on 18 March 1949* (Michael Cassar).

Below Sierra Cordoba *was restyled in 1935 for 'Strength through Joy' cruising, carrying 1,000 one-class passengers* (Willie Tinnemeyer Collection).

Bahia Castillo/General Belgrano

(Hamburg-South America Line)

Service Hamburg-Rio de Janeiro, Santos, Montevideo and Buenos Aires.
Specifications 9,948 gross tons (later increased to 10,056), 510 × 61 ft (157 × 19 m).
Builder Reiherstiegwerft, Hamburg, Germany, 1913.
Machinery Steam, triple expansion, twin screw. Service speed 12 knots.
Capacity 202 second class, 2,500 steerage.

1913 4 Jan: Launched. Apr: Maiden voyage to South American ports as *Bahai Castillo*.
1914 Aug: Laid up at Hamburg throughout war.
1919 May: Surrendered to British Government and managed by G. Thompson & Co, London.
1922 Sept: Sold to AG Hugo Stinnes, Hamburg (Stinnes Line), German flag; refitted and intended new name *General San Martin* soon changed to *General Belgrano*. Accommodation restyled for 142 second class and 542 steerage. Hamburg-South America service.
1926 Nov: Ship transferred to Hamburg America Line, but remained in South American service; tonnage relisted as 10,121.
1932 Dec: Sold to shipbreakers at Hamburg.

Antonio Delfino/Sierra Nevada

(Hamburg-South America Line)

Service Hamburg-Rio de Janeiro, Santos, Montevideo and Buenos Aires.
Specifications 13,589 gross tons, 526 × 64 ft (162 × 20 m).
Builder Vulcan Works, Hamburg, Germany, 1922.
Machinery Steam, triple expansion, twin screw. Service speed 13½ knots.
Capacity 184 first class, 334 second class and 1,368 steerage.

1921 10 Nov: Launched as *Antonio Delfino*.
1922 Mar: Maiden voyage, Hamburg to South America.
1927 Steam turbines fitted and service speed increased to 15 knots.
1932 Chartered to North German Lloyd and temporarily renamed *Sierra Nevada*.
1934 Resumed sailings for Hamburg-South America Line and reverted to *Antonio Delfino*.
1939 Sept: Managed to return to German waters following outbreak of war.
1940 Outfitted as accommodation ship for German Navy at Kiel.
1943 Moved to Gdynia in Poland.
1945 Jan: Used in evacuation of German Eastern Territories, transporting over 20,000 people.
1945 May: Surrendered to British Government and refitted as troop transport *Empire Halladale*. Tonnage relisted as 14,056 and berthing rearranged for 200 cabin passengers and 843 troops.
1946 Oct: Resumed sailing; managed by Anchor Line for Ministry of Transport.
1955 Oct: Withdrawn from service.
1956 Feb: Sold to shipbreakers at Dalmuir, Scotland.

Top left Lloyd's Sierra Ventana, *shown in the River Elbe, alternated her services mostly between the North Atlantic run to New York and then the Southern run to the East Coast of South America* (Willie Tinnemeyer Collection).

Middle left Der Deutsche *departing from Hamburg during a summer 'Strength through Joy' cruise* (Hapag-Lloyd).

Left Hapag's General Osorio, *completed in 1929, was typical of motor-ship design in the late 'twenties, particularly with her squat funnels* (Willie Tinnemeyer Collection).

Cap Norte/Sierra Salvada
(North German Lloyd)

Service Hamburg-Rio de Janeiro, Santos, Montevideo and Buenos Aires.
Specifications 13,615 gross tons, 526 × 64 ft (162 × 20 m).
Builder Vulcan Works, Hamburg, Germany, 1922.
Machinery Steam, triple expansion, twin screw. Service speed 13½ knots.
Capacity 184 first class, 334 third class, 1,368 steerage.

1922 8 May: Launched. Sept: Maiden voyage to South America.
1927 Steam turbines fitted and service speed increased to 15 knots.
1932 Chartered to North German Lloyd and temporarily renamed *Sierra Salvada*.
1934 Returned to Hamburg-South America Line and reverted to *Cap Norte*.
1939 Oct: While attempting to sail from Pernambuco, Brazil, to Hamburg, intercepted by British cruiser *Belfast* and became prize of war.
1940 Refitted as British troop-ship and managed by British India Line; renamed *Empire Trooper*.
1940 25 Dec: Badly damaged following encounter with German cruiser *Admiral Hipper*; reached Ponta Delgada, Azores, and later repaired and resumed trooping duties.
1949 Converted at Falmouth into peacetime trooper; accommodation restyled for 336 cabin passengers and 924 troops.
1955 May: Sold to shipbreakers and caught fire in yard at Inverkeithing, Scotland; wreck later salvaged and scrapped.

Sierra Cordoba
(North German Lloyd)

Service Bremerhaven-Channel ports-New York, alternating with South American service, Bremerhaven–Rio de Janeiro, Santos, Montevideo and Buenos Aires. Also some cruising.
Specifications 11,469 gross tons, 511 × 61 ft (157 × 19 m).
Builder Bremer Vulkan Shipyards, Vegesack, Germany, 1923.
Machinery Steam, triple expansion, twin screw. Service speed 14 knots.
Capacity 160 first class, 1,143 third class, 762 steerage.

1923 26 Sept: Launched.
1924 Jan: Maiden voyage to South America.
1935 Sold to German Labour Front, managed by North German Lloyd; used solely for 'Strength through Joy' cruises. Tonnage relisted as 11,492 and accommodation restyled for 1,000 single-class passengers.
1940 Outfitted as accommodation ship for German Navy at Kiel.
1945 May: Surrendered to British Government at Hamburg.
1946 13 Jan: Caught fire at Hamburg and damaged beyond repair; 3 killed.
1948 18 Jan: Sank in North Sea while being towed from Hamburg to River Clyde for scrapping.

Sierra Ventana
(North German Lloyd)

Service Bremerhaven-Channel ports-New York, alternating with Bremerhaven-Rio de Janeiro, Santos, Montevideo and Buenos Aires.
Specifications 11,392 gross tons, 511 × 61 ft (157 × 19m).
Builder Bremer Vulkan Shipyards, Vegesack, Germany, 1923.
Machinery Steam, triple expansion, twin screw. Service speed 14 knots.
Capacity 222 first class, 179 second class, 712 third class.

1923 16 May: Launched.
1923 Sept: Maiden voyage to New York.
1935 Sold to Italian Line, Italian flag; renamed *Sardegna*. Troop-ship services for Abyssinian war as well as South American migrant voyages.
1937 Transferred to Lloyd Triestino, also Italian flag.
1940 29 Dec: Torpedoed by Greek submarine while on troop-ship service out of Brindisi.

Sierra Morena/Der Deutsche

(North German Lloyd)

Service Bremerhaven-Rio de Janeiro, Santos, Montevideo and Buenos Aires.
Specifications 11,430 gross tons, 511 × 61 ft (157 × 19 m).
Builder Bremer Vulkan Shipyards, Vegesack, Germany, 1924.
Machinery Steam, triple expansion, twin screw. Service speed 14 knots.
Capacity 157 first class, 1,145 third class, 763 steerage.

1924 3 June: Launched.
1924 Oct: Maiden voyage to South America. Later used also for cruises.
1934 Converted to full-time cruise liner: tonnage relisted as 11,453 and accommodation restyled for 1,000 single-class passengers only. Renamed *Der Deutsche*.
1935 Sold to German Labour Front, but retained North German Lloyd management. Used for 'Strength through Joy' cruises.
1940 Used as troop transport for German Navy, then later stationed at Konigsberg and Gdynia as accommodation ship. Also hospital ship duties.
1945 Jan: Used in evacuation of German Eastern Territories, transporting a total of 34,500 refugees. 3 May: Hit by Allied aerial bombs but managed to reach Kiel; laid up.
1946 Mar: Awarded to Soviet Union as part of reparations agreement, then sent to Warnemunde, East Germany, for full repairs and refitting; renamed *Asia*.
1950 June: Began sailing for Soviets, mostly in Far Eastern waters between Vladivostock and Kamchatka. Tonnage relisted as 12,019 and rebuilt with one funnel.
1970 Broken up.

General Osorio

(Hamburg America Line/Hamburg-South America Line)

Service Hamburg–Rio de Janeiro, Santos, Montevideo and Buenos Aires.
Specifications 11,590 gross tons, 528 × 66 ft (162 × 20 m).
Builder Bremer Vulkan Shipyards, Vegesack, Germany, 1929.
Machinery MAN diesels, twin screw. Service speed 15 knots.
Capacity 228 second class, 752 third class.

1929 20 Mar: Launched. Jun: Maiden voyage to South America.
1934 Nov: Chartered to Hamburg-South America Line.
1936 June: Sold outright to Hamburg-South America and refitted; funnels raised in height.
1940 Began service as accommodation ship for German Navy at Kiel, then later served as target ship.
1944 24 July: Bombed during Allied air raid on Kiel; partially sunk, then later salvaged and repaired.
1945 9 Apr: Again sunk by bombings at Kiel.
1947 Wreckage raised, then sold to British ship-breakers.

14

Hapag quartet

L ike its rival North German Lloyd, Hamburg America Line was all but totally depleted and stripped following the First World War. Rebuilding was slow, cautiously kept under Allied restriction and all the while Hapag's future policy was to avoid very large and overly luxurious liners, and instead concentrate on more moderately sized and more conservatively decorated Atlantic passenger ships. The first two notable newbuildings, placed at just over 20,000 tons and the first of a projected quartet, were specially designed also to restore the travelling public's faith in a German shipping company. Consequently, these first ships used a dated four-mast design, one that was especially intended to remind sea travellers of earlier turn-of-the-century liners. Also, with that booming, enormously profitable era of transatlantic immigration now past (caused mostly by the new American immigration quotas), Hapag sensibly ordered their new liners, twin sister ships that were named *Albert Ballin* and *Deutschland*, with a balanced capacity of some 1,558 passengers and six large cargo holds. These ships, trading between Hamburg and New York in 10 days in each direction, and with stopovers at Southampton and Cherbourg *en route*, consequently earned their revenues from both the passenger and the freight business. Quickly, they proved to be excellent investments.

In Prager's excellent history of Blohm & Voss, considerable mention is made of these new Hapag passenger ships.

'This quartet of the *Albert Ballin* class [the second set of sisters, built in 1926–27, were named *Hamburg* and *New York*], were among the most sought-after and most heavily booked type of ship in North Atlantic service up to the Second World War. With these ships, Hapag had consciously said farewell to expensive prestige fast steamers. Reliability was to take preference over speed. For this reason, these large turbine ships, with Frahm anti-roll tanks in lateral bulges, were intrinsically designed for a speed of only 14.3 knots. Just as much attention was paid to the

transportation of general cargo as was special attention also paid to too crass a demonstration of the passenger facilities for the first, second and third classes. Hapag had very wisely renounced extreme first class luxury. Instead of floating palaces, these ships were well-appointed floating hotels with unobtrusive, genuine comfort. They were also popular with Anglo-Saxon passengers, who regarded them as homely, comfortable "anti seasickness" ships.

'Profitability was the first and last word of the *Albert Ballin* Class ships, which could transport 1,500 or some 1,150 passengers according to vessel size. Four double-ended and four single-ended boilers for each ship were used from the outset and equipped for oil firing. They provided steam to two sets each of four turbines. The twin propeller ships were able to make do with an engine output totalling 13,000 hp. They were a consistent development of the once so successful *Pennsylvania* Class and of the *Cleveland* type. On January 1st 1925, the Liverpool *Journal of Commerce* wrote with regard to the *Albert Ballin* and the *Deutschland*: "During Christmas week, we met one of the German passenger ships of the roll-stabilized design moving smoothly along, while our steamer tossed and rolled so much that we could hardly keep on our feet. These German ships are really the most up-to-date in shipbuilding".

'The four ships of the *Albert Ballin* Class were the first with the cruiser stern. Their double bottom extended the entire length of the ship. Thanks to externally attached anti-roll tanks, the ships were constructed on the double-skin principle, ie they had, so to speak, a double shell plating. It has meanwhile been proved that these extremely safe ships were really built for several decades. At the time this book was going to print [in 1976], two of them were still sailing the seven seas: the 52-year-old *Albert Ballin*, as the passenger vessel *Sovetsky Sojus*, and the 50-year-old *Hamburg*, as the whale factory ship *Yuri Dolgoruki*. In 1945, both ships had fallen victims to seabed mines off Warnemunde and Sassnitz, and capsized. But even the four or five years spent under water do not appear to have harmed them unduly.

'Incidentally, the four ships of the *Albert Ballin* Class were the first passenger vessels to have a real tourist class for the 900 or so passengers in the third class category and in the place of steerage travel as formerly. From now on, nobody had to make their way to the canteen with mug and bowl for

Above *With her passengers on board, the thunderous steam whistle of* Albert Ballin *signals that she is soon to sail from the Cuxhaven terminal* (Hapag-Lloyd).

Below *Rebuilt after the war, the former* Albert Ballin *was given a single, domed funnel as* Sovetsky Sojus, *the largest passenger ship ever to sail for the Soviets* (Frank O. Braynard Collection).

Above *Hapag's* Deutschland *as originally built, before re-engining and lengthening, and with her twin funnels in the original Company mustard colour* (Willie Tinnemeyer).

Below *The same ship, although altered with taller and repainted funnels and an extended bow section,* Deutschland *arrives at New York and is assisted by four Moran tugs. Note that smoke is being released from her second forward mast* (Frank O. Braynard Collection).

Above *Although generally similar to the earlier* Albert Ballin *and her sister,* New York *and her twin sister ship,* Hamburg, *differ most noticeably in having two instead of four masts* (James M. Sesta Collection).

Below *With her extended bow section, fitted in 1933,* Hamburg *is shown loading cargo at Hamburg. The stern section of* Milwaukee *can be seen on the right* (Frank O. Braynard Collection).

the self-service system. Service in the third class (steerage) had been modified on German ships by introducing third class cabins and fourth class dormitories.'

Albert Ballin and her sisters offered notably fine first class quarters in particular. This section occupied six decks and included a large sports deck as well as an open-air bowling alley. The restaurant amenities included a special grill room, with an à la carte menu and an extra entrance fee. The public rooms included a glass-enclosed promenade, a smoking room, writing room, library, ladies' parlour, social hall and terrace café. There was also a children's dining room, indoor tiled pool, gymnasium, lift, gift shop and florist.

The second set of sisters, *Hamburg* and *New York*, while no less popular, differed slightly from the earlier pair. They were approximately 500 tons larger, had two masts instead of four and had somewhat smaller passenger capacities.

Known as the 'Famous Four', and providing a weekly service with a well-known midnight sailing every Wednesday from New York, these ships returned to their builder's yard on two special occasions later in their careers for considerable modification. These events were also detailed in the Blohm & Voss history.

'The four North Atlantic turbine ships *Albert Ballin*, *Deutschland*, *Hamburg* and *New York* had their engine output increased from 15,000 to 28,000 hp in 1929–30 by the installation of new turbines and water-tube boilers. Then they were lengthened in 1933–34 [the first such undertaking with major passenger ships and later used for, among others, several Norwegian cruise-ships in the early 1980s] in order to provide additional outer cabins and reduce fuel consumption. Model experiments at the Hamburg Ship Model Basin had shown that thanks to these measures the propulsion power could be expected to be reduced from 28,000 to 20,000 hp without loss of speed, and that the fuel thus saved would make up for the conversion costs within

two and a half years.

'All four ships were "foreshoed". This lengthening was affected by cutting off the forward quarter 15 metres behind the bows and replacing it with a 25 metre long and much more pointed forward quarter. All four forward quarters were successively built in Dock VI [at the Blohm & Voss yards in Hamburg]. As soon as the old forward quarter had been separated from the ship to be lengthened in Dock V— the old section was scrapped on the spot—Dock VI was towed over to Dock V. Following the line-up of the two docks, the new forward quarter was brought to the ship on cradles. Connecting the two sections was a quick procedure. In detailed operations, only plates had to be attached and riveted. None of these ships was longer than 6 weeks in dock. And, in fact, it turned out that following the lengthening, the ships of the *Albert Ballin* Class reached speeds of over 20 knots.

'Lengthening of the four North Atlantic ships was filmed by newsreel cameras and became familiar throughout the whole of Germany, especially since the *Albert Ballin* Class quartet was a household word even among people living in the interior, far away from Germany's coastline.'

The 'Famous Four' were kept in German or in nearby waters during the Second World War, but—like all other German-flag passenger ships of their era—they would never again sail for their original owners. *Deutschland* and *New York* were destroyed beyond repair and were later broken up, but *Albert Ballin*, which had been renamed *Hansa* in 1935 (at the Third Reich's insistence and because Mr Ballin was Jewish), and *Hamburg* survived. Although both had been sunk, they were selected for extensive salvage and then long refits and restorations by the Soviets. The ex-*Ballin*, as *Sovetsky Sojus*, remains the largest Soviet passenger liner to date. She was scrapped, however, in 1981, just two short years of her sixtieth anniversary. While originally intended to become a passenger ship as well, the former *Hamburg* spent her Soviet-flag years, until withdrawn in 1976, her fiftieth year, as a whaling mother ship. She was renamed *Yuri Dolgoruki*.

Albert Ballin/Hansa
(Hamburg America Line)

Service Hamburg-Southampton-Cherbourg-New York.
Specifications 20,815 gross tons, 627 × 72 ft (193 × 22 m).
Builder Blohm & Voss, Hamburg, Germany, 1923.
Machinery Steam turbines, twin screw. Service speed 15½ knots.
Capacity 251 first class, 340 second class, 960 third class.

1922 16 Dec: Launched.
1923 July: Maiden voyage to New York.
1930 Fitted with new turbines and service speed increased to 19½ knots; tonnage relisted as 20,931.
1934 12 May: Sank North German Lloyd tugboat at Bremerhaven; 7 killed. Jun: Completed extensive refit; modernized and lengthened. Tonnage relisted as 21,131 and length as 677 ft (208 m). Service speed increased to 21½ knots. Accommodation restyled as 204 first class, 361 tourist class, 400 third class.
1935 Oct: Renamed *Hansa*.
1939 Sept: At Hamburg as Second World War started; later used as accommodation ship and then training centre for German Navy.
1945 Jan: Used in evacuation of German Eastern Territories. 6 Mar: Struck mine off Warnemunde while on evacuation voyage out of Gdynia; despite salvage attempts, later sank in shallow water.
1949 Wreckage seized by Soviets and salvaged; underwent extended repairs and refit, first at Antwerp and then Warnemunde. Renamed *Sovetsky Sojus*.
1954 Refit delayed by fire at shipyard while undergoing final stages.
1955 Sept: Entered Soviet passenger service; largest passenger vessel under their colours. Tonnage relisted as 23,009. Used in Far Eastern waters, mostly between Vladivostock and Kamchatka.
1971 Given extended refit at Hong Kong as ship approached fiftieth year.
1980 Renamed *Soyuz*.
1981 Broken up, just short of sixtieth year.

Deutschland
(Hamburg America Line)

Service Hamburg-Southampton-Cherbourg-New York.
Specifications 20,607 gross tons, 627 × 72 ft (193 × 22 m).
Builder Blohm & Voss, Hamburg, Germany, 1923.
Machinery Steam turbines, twin screw. Service speed 15½ knots.
Capacity 221 first class, 402 second class, 935 third class.

1923 28 Apr: Launched.
1924 Mar: Maiden crossing to New York.
1930 May: Fitted with new, more powerful turbines and service speed increased to 19½ knots; tonnage relisted as 20,742.
1934 Modernized and lengthened; service speed increased to 21½ knots and length relisted as 677 ft (208 m). Tonnage changed to 21,046. Accommodation restyled as 200 first class, 360 tourist class, 400 third class.
1940 Used as accommodation ship for German Navy at Gdynia.
1945 Jan: Used in evacuation service of German Eastern Territories; transported 70,000 refugees in seven voyages.
1945 3 May: Bombed and sank during Allied air raid off Neustadt in Bay of Lubeck.
1948 Wreckage raised and scrapped.

Hamburg
(Hamburg America Line)

Service Hamburg-Southampton-Cherbourg-New York.
Specifications 21,132 gross tons, 635 × 72 ft (195 × 22 m).
Builder Blohm & Voss, Hamburg, Germany, 1926.
Machinery Steam turbines, twin screw. Service speed 15½ knots.
Capacity 222 first class, 471 second class, 456 third class.

1925 14 Nov: Launched.
1926 Apr: Maiden crossing to New York.
1929 Aug–**1930** Feb: Extended refit; new turbines, service speed increased to 19½ knots and tonnage re-listed as 21,691.
1933 Further refit and modernization; service speed increased to 21½ knots. Lengthened to 677 ft (208 m) and tonnage relisted as 22,117. Accommodation rearranged for 200 first class, 350 tourist class, 400 third class.
1940 Outfitted as accommodation ship for German Navy at Gdynia.
1945 Jan: Began transport service in evacuation of German Eastern territories; transported 23,000 refugees in three voyages.
1945 7 Mar: While sailing without passengers, struck two mines near Sassnitz and sank.
1950 Claimed by Soviet Government; salvaged and sent to Antwerp and then to Warnemunde for repairs and refitting. Intention to rebuild her as passenger vessel, similar to former *Albert Ballin* (see above), but when reconstruction nearly complete, plans changed and instead rebuilt as whaling 'mother ship'. Renamed *Yuri Dolgoruki*. Completion staggered and delayed.
1960 July: Finally entered Soviet service; tonnage listed as 25,377.
1976 Withdrawn from service; her fiftieth year.
1977 Scrapped.

New York
(Hamburg America Line)

Service Hamburg-Southampton-Cherbourg-New York.
Specifications 21,455 gross tons, 635 × 72 ft (195 × 22 m).
Builder Blohm & Voss, Hamburg, Germany, 1927.
Machinery Steam turbines, twin screw. Service speed 15½ knots.
Capacity 247 first class, 321 second class, 464 third class.

1926 20 Oct: Launched.
1927 Apr: Maiden voyage to New York.
1930 Extensive refit; new turbines and service speed increased to 19½ knots. Tonnage relisted as 21,867.
1934 Further extensive refit; lengthened to 677 ft (208 m) and tonnage relisted as 22,337. Service speed increased to 21½ knots. Accommodation rearranged as 210 first class, 350 tourist class, 400 third class.
1936 7 May: Sank Rotterdam-South America Line freighter *Alphard* in English Channel; all hands rescued.
1939 Aug: Hurriedly left New York to avoid internment, sailed empty via Murmansk.
1939 Dec: Finally reached Hamburg; outfitted as accommodation ship for German Navy at Kiel.
1945 Jan: Used in evacuation service of German Eastern Territories.
1945 3 Apr: Bombed and capsized during Allied air raid on Kiel.
1949 Mar: Wreckage salvaged and towed to Britain for scrapping.

15
The 'Monte' Class and *Cap Arcona*

Regrettably, they proved to be the last of the Hamburg-South America Line's glorious passenger fleet—five handsome two-funnel passenger ships, designed especially for the South American migrant trade, later establishing high reputations for low-fare cruising, and then capped by the Company's largest, fastest and finest liner, the three-stack *Cap Arcona*. The latter ship was one of the most notable liners in all ocean liner history and one that is still well remembered.

The five sister ships known as the 'Monte' Class were built over a period covering seven years. *Monte Sarmiento* and *Monte Olivia* were constructed in 1924–25, *Monte Cervantes* in 1928, then the last pair, *Monte Pascoal* and *Monte Rosa* in 1930–31. All were created by Blohm & Voss, surely the masters of German ocean liner design and construction, and were not surprisingly given significant mention in that firm's history.

'In view of the fact that the difficulties connected with the new [American] laws have made it impossible to a large extent for emigration to North America to be continued, and consequently have resulted in increased emigration to Argentina and Brazil, Hamburg-South America placed orders with Blohm & Voss in 1922 and 1923 for two passenger ships. These vessels, at 13,600 tons, were conceived specifically for emigration traffic and also the seasonal transport of Spanish farmworkers from the Iberian Peninsular to South America. The new buildings were to be able to take on a certain amount of cargo on the home run and were therefore actually combined cargo and passenger ships. They were christened with the names of mountains in Tierra Del Fuego—*Monte Sarmiento* and *Monte Olivia*. These twins were also the first large-scale diesel passenger ships in the German merchant fleet.'

However, there were some problems at the outset for Hamburg Sud and the two new vessels. *Monte Sarmiento* was plagued on her first trip by mechanical troubles, so much so that every day there seemed to be some crisis or another and special repairs had to be made at Buenos Aires, at Rio de Janeiro and then at Lisbon. At one point, while outbound on her homeward voyage, she barely made it to the mouth of a local river. However, with full repairs made upon her return to her builder's yard, and with modification to the subsequent 'Monte' ships, they functioned perfectly thereafter.

Added to this, however, and according to the Blohm & Voss history,

'Scarcely had the technical problems been overcome with the *Monte Sarmiento*, which had gone into service in November 1924, when the Hamburg Sud was compelled to note resignedly in its business report, in March 1925, that the two new 'Monte' ships were hardly capable of fulfilling their intended task: transporting emigrants. Accordingly, "lack of planning by the emigration organizations, in conjunction with foreign currency difficulties and deterrent reports about conditions in the recipient countries, have caused emigration to decline considerably in recent times. The government of the German Reich also takes the view that despite overpopulation of the country, the emigration of German people overseas is not desirable. For this reason—as opposed to governments of other countries—it does not provide any more funds for this purpose."

'In fact, the number of emigrants aboard Hamburg Sud ships dropped from 30,000 in 1924 to 14,000 in 1925. The shipping company therefore hit upon the idea of using the two 'Monte' ships exclusively for recreation and study trips [cruises]. They sailed to South America—with three weeks stay ashore—and to Norway and Spitzbergen, to the Mediterranean, to Morocco, Madeira and the Canary Islands. Hamburg Sud very quickly realized that they had done the right thing with the 'Monte' cruises. These one-class ships with their uniform capacity of some 2,400 passengers were able to offer cruises at minimum prices of 180 to 260 Marks, although they had excellent service and comfortable facilities. With success of this kind, popular tourism at sea caught on to such an extent that already, by 1927, the shipping company ordered the third ship of this class, the *Monte Cervantes*. When the latter was totally

Above   Monte Sarmiento *shown while sailing on a special 'Strength through Joy' cruise in the late 'thirties* (Hamburg-South America Line).

Below   Monte Olivia, *outbound from Hamburg, was a classically handsome ship and identical to the other 'Monte' liners* (Hamburg-South America Line).

Below right   Monte Pascoal *being manoeuvred by one of Hamburg-South America Line's tugs, Sud-Amerika VIII* (Hamburg-South America Line).

wrecked after running on to underwater rocks on Tierra Del Fuego in 1930, the company ordered two more of the same type. Their names were *Monte Pascoal* and *Monte Rosa*, and were both commissioned at the beginning of 1931. As far as the ships of the 'Monte' Class were concerned, there was no world economic crisis. They continued to hold their own with the best. And since at least one of these highly attractive ships was always berthed at the Hamburg Overseas Bridge for exchanging passengers, the 'Monte' Class became a kind of landmark in the Port of Hamburg.'

With the exception of *Monte Rosa*, the last of the group, the other 'Monte' ships were lost in the Second War. *Rosa* went on to British-flag service as the peacetime trooper *Empire Windrush*, and later burnt out and sank in the Mediterranean in 1954. She was, by then, the last survivor of this class.

In the midst of creating the 'Monte' ships, Hamburg Sud also decided to reinforce its luxury service to Latin America. Ordered also from Blohm & Voss, the design of this new flagship was based, to a large extent, on the earlier *Cap Polonio* (see page 72). This new ship became the very finest of all Hamburg Sud liners. Her creation was also specially detailed in the Blohm & Voss history.

'It took 19 months after the order had been placed to complete the legendary *Cap Arcona*. Again fitted with three funnels, the vessel was intended to awaken association with her famous predecessor, the *Cap Polonio*. In fact, however, it was a further devleopment of this former top ship on the South Atlantic run, and was just as modern and successful. The twin-propeller fast steamer *Cap Arcona*, equipped with water-tube boilers and geared turbines, became the flagship of the Hamburg-based merchant fleet in the 'twenties and 'thirties. With 24,000 hp turbine units, she ran at 20 knots, punctually covering the distance between Hamburg and Buenos Aires in 15 days. The shallow navigable waters of the La Plata River also compelled the *Cap Arcona* to have a relatively small draft, but this was made up by the large length and breadth dimensions. The ship provided cabin space for a maximum of 1,434 passengers and this was offered in a first rate manner. All the first class cabins had daylight and private bath. The shipyard thus actually succeeded in constructing a ship which was hardly longer than the 20,500-ton *Cap Polonio*, with three first class passenger decks on top of each other and a cabin area on the boat deck. With the greatest possible lengthening of the superstructure and widening of the beams, it also created cabins for a far larger number of passengers. Because Hamburg Sud took the view that aboard a good tropical vessel, the passengers ought to take their meals in high, airy rooms, which should not be below deck, the *Cap Arcona* had its dining hall built above on the promenade deck, thus providing a wide view of the sea through 20 panorama windows each 5 metres high. Naturally, the ceilings and pillars concealed all the girders of heavy steel construction which provided the necessary strength to the longitudinal structure and inevitably influenced the design of the rooms. The smoke room, festive hall, lounge area and dining halls merged into each other with perfect harmony. Due to all the demands referred to, it was unavoidable that a vessel resulted which had an inordinate number of superlative elements.

Above *Outbound on a summertime cruise, passengers line the outer decks of the* Monte Rosa (Hamburg-South America Line).

Below *A trio of Hamburg Sud liners in the early 'thirties: the three-funnel* Cap Polonio *in the far distance to the left:* Monte Pascoal *in the centre; and* Monte Rosa *to the right* (Hamburg-South America Line).

Above *At anchor,* Monte Rosa *in the Geirangerfjord in 1938. The cruise services of the 'Monte' ships inspired some of the finest and most provocative steamship poster art of the 'twenties and 'thirties* (Hamburg-South America Line).

Below *A dramatic view from the starboard bridge wing of* Monte Pascoal (Hamburg-South America Line).

Above *Several German liners, such as* Monte Olivia *and the giant* Bremen *and* Europa, *carried seaplanes resting in revolving catapults for early versions of air-sea transport* (Hamburg-South America Line).

Below *Now in British hands as* Empire Windrush, *the former* Monte Rosa *is shown at anchor off Spithead in June 1953 during the Coronation Review for Her Majesty Queen Elizabeth II* (Roger Sherlock).

Above   *Under the care of the Hamburg harbour tug* Jan, Cap Arcona *is being readied for her next passage to South America — 15 days to Buenos Aires!* (Hamburg-South America Line).

Below   *Outbound, the superb-looking* Cap Arcona *passes the Landing Stage at Hamburg. She was the largest, fastest and perhaps finest of all Hamburg Sud liners* (Hamburg-South America Line).

Nevertheless, the *Cap Arcona* was internally and externally of striking beauty. Incidentally, all halls on A Deck were also conspicuous for their unusual heights, which was possible by building the units through the normally high boat deck.

'The *Cap Arcona* was extremely cleverly designed, from the heatable salt-water swimming pool with air bubbling plant, to the gymnasium and the sports deck, mainly used as a tennis court, from the large main hospital with operating theatre to the service spaces. She was frequently described as the most wonderful ship of the entire German merchant navy.'

Cap Arcona was left in home waters during the Second World War, but only to suffer one of the most hideously tragic fates of any ship. Bombed out in May 1945, just days before the war ended officially, she capsized and in doing so claimed over 5,000 lives. This disaster (taking more than four times the fatalities of *Titanic*) was surpassed by only one other wartime maritime disaster: an estimated 5,200 souls were killed three months earlier when another German liner, *Wilhelm Gustloff*, was torpedoed in the Baltic. Together, they are the worst maritime tragedies of all time—and yet, surprisingly, two that have been largely forgotten outside Germany itself. To most, it is the *Titanic* sinking that ranks as the most devastating, perhaps because it was not, like the others, a man-made disaster.

Below *With the stern of the cruise-ship* Robert Ley *to the left and a large floating crane and tug to the right,* Cap Arcona *is pleasantly framed in this scene at Hamburg in 1939* (Hamburg-South America Line).

Bottom *Six Hamburg Sud funnels!* Cap Arcona *on the left and the older* Cap Polonio *are berthed together at Hamburg's Overseas Landing Stage* (Hamburg-South America Lane).

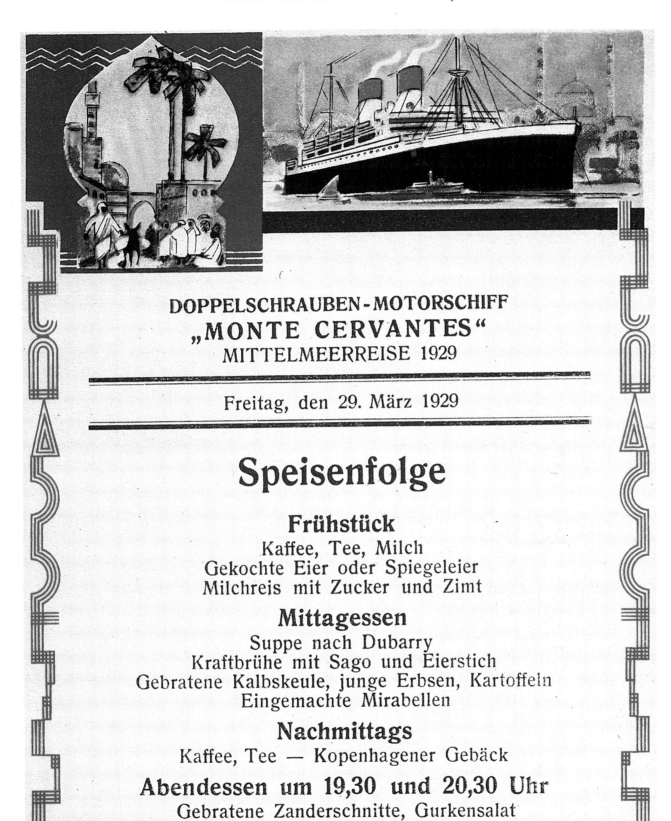

DOPPELSCHRAUBEN - MOTORSCHIFF
„MONTE CERVANTES"
MITTELMEERREISE 1929

Freitag, den 29. März 1929

Speisenfolge

Frühstück
Kaffee, Tee, Milch
Gekochte Eier oder Spiegeleier
Milchreis mit Zucker und Zimt

Mittagessen
Suppe nach Dubarry
Kraftbrühe mit Sago und Eierstich
Gebratene Kalbskeule, junge Erbsen, Kartoffeln
Eingemachte Mirabellen

Nachmittags
Kaffee, Tee — Kopenhagener Gebäck

Abendessen um 19,30 und 20,30 Uhr
Gebratene Zanderschnitte, Gurkensalat
Verschiedene Sorten Wurst
Edamer Käse
Tee

HAMBURG-SÜDAMERIKANISCHE DAMPFSCHIFFFAHRTS-GESELLSCHAFT

A menu dated 29 March 1929, from Monte Cervantes *(Charles Sachs Collection).*

Above *In another Hamburg setting, Hamburg-South America Line's* Monte Sarmiento *and the three-funnel* Cap Polonio (Charles Sachs Collection).

Below *An exceptional rendering of the great* Bremen *of 1929, the last of the German speed queens* (Charles Sachs Collection).

Above Bremen *at sea, with her Lufthansa seaplane just having been launched from her top-deck catapult* (Charles Sachs Collection).

Below *The glamour of midnight sailings, a trademark of North German Lloyd in the 'thirties* (Charles Sachs Collection).

Monte Sarmiento
(Hamburg-South America Line)

Service Hamburg-Rio de Janeiro, Santos, Montevideo and Buenos Aires. Considerable cruising, in European and South American waters.
Specifications 13,625 gross tons, 524 × 66 ft (161 × 20 m).
Builder Blohm & Voss, Hamburg, Germany, 1924.
Machinery MAN diesels, twin screw. Service speed 14 knots.
Capacity 1,328 third class, 1,142 steerage.

1924 31 July: Launched.
1924 Nov: Maiden voyage to South America.
1939 Dec: Outfitted for use as accommodation ship for German Navy at Kiel.
1942 26 Feb: Bombed and sunk during Allied air raid on Kiel.
1943 Wreckage salvaged then towed to Hamburg for scrapping.

Monte Olivia
(Hamburg-South America Line)

Service Hamburg-Rio de Janeiro, Santos, Montevideo and Buenos Aires. Considerable cruising in European and South American waters.
Specifications 13,750 gross tons, 524 × 66 ft (161 × 20 m).
Builders Blohm & Voss, Hamburg, Germany, 1925.
Machinery MAN type diesels, twin screw. Service speed 14 knots.
Capacity 1,372 third class, 1,156 steerage.

1924 28 Oct: Launched.
1925 Apr: Maiden voyage to South America.
1939 Oct: Reached Hamburg after passing through Allied blockade. Used as accommodation ship for German Navy.
1945 Jan: Used to evacuate wounded from German Eastern territories.
1945 3 Apr: Bombed and set afire during Allied bombing of Kiel; burnt out and sunk.
1946–48 Salvaged, then scrapped.

Left *Superb poster art from the 1930s: Lloyd's Ocean Express on the North Atlantic (Charles Sachs Collection).*

Monte Cervantes
(Hamburg-South America Line)

Service Hamburg-Rio de Janeiro, Santos, Montevideo and Buenos Aires. Considerable cruising in European and South American waters.
Specifications 13,913 gross tons, 524 × 66 ft (161 × 20 m).
Builder Blohm & Voss, Hamburg, Germany, 1928.
Machinery MAN diesels, twin screw. Service speed 14 knots.
Capacity 1,354 tourist class, 1,138 steerage.

1927 25 Aug: Launched.
1928 Jan: Maiden voyage to South America.
1928 25 July: Seriously damaged by ice while on summer cruise to Arctic waters; later reached Spitzbergen and given temporary repairs.
1930 22 Jan: Holed by submerged rocks during cruise to Tierra Del Fuego from Buenos Aires. Began to sink; passengers, and later crew, evacuated. All but master saved when she capsized on 24 Jan.
1951 Scrappers began to remove wreckage.
1954 July: Wreckage completely salvaged.
1954 Oct: Finally sank in deep water during attempt to tow wreck to Ushuaia, Argentina.

Monte Pascoal
(Hamburg-South America Line)

Service Hamburg-Rio de Janeiro, Santos, Montevideo and Buenos Aires. Considerable cruising in European and South American waters.
Specifications 13,870 gross tons, 524 × 66 ft (161 × 20 m).
Builder Blohm & Voss, Hamburg, Germany, 1930.
Machinery MAN diesels, twin screw. Service speed 14 knots.
Capacity 1,372 tourist class, 1,036 steerage.

1930 17 Sept: Launched.
1931 Jan: Maiden voyage to South America.
1939 Oct: Returned safely to Hamburg after breaking through Allied shipping blockade.
1940 Jan: Started duties as accommodation ship for German Navy at Wilhelmshaven.
1944 3 Feb: Bombed and sunk during Allied bombing of Wilhelmshaven. May: Salvaged and repaired.
1945 May: Surrendered to British Government but beyond further use; declared surplus.
1946 31 Dec: Loaded with munitions and deliberately sunk by British in Skagerrak.

Monte Rosa

(Hamburg-South America Line)

Service Hamburg-Rio de Janeiro, Santos, Montevideo and Buenos Aires. Considerable cruising in European and South American waters.
Specifications 13,882 gross tons, 524 × 66 ft (161 × 20 m).
Builder Blohm & Voss, Hamburg, Germany, 1931.
Machinery MAN diesels, twin screw. Service speed 14 knots.
Capacity 1,372 tourist class, 1,036 steerage.

1930 4 Dec: Launched.
1931 Mar: Maiden voyage to South America.
1940 Jan: Began service as accommodation ship for German Navy at Stettin.
1942 Used as troop-ship in Norwegian waters.
1943 Oct–**1944** Mar: Served as floating workshop for repairs to battleship *Tirpitz*. Later resumed trooping; later struck mine but repaired and outfitted as hospital ship.
1945 16 Feb: With 5,000 refugees and wounded onboard, struck mine and aft sections badly damaged. Towed to Gdynia with flooded engine room; given temporary repairs, then towed to Copenhagen. Later continued to Kiel. May: Surrendered to British Government at Kiel and sent to South Shields, England, for extensive repairs and refitting. Recommissioned as peacetime troop-ship; tonnage relisted as 14,414. Renamed *Empire Windrush*. Operated by Ministry of Transport and managed by New Zealand Shipping Co.
1954 28 Mar: While homebound from Japan to England, caught fire after engine room explosion in Mediterranean waters; 4 killed. Ship abandoned. Attempts made to take her in tow for Gibraltar, but blistered hulk sank on 29 Mar.

Cap Arcona

(Hamburg-South America Line)

Service Hamburg-Rio de Janeiro, Santos, Montevideo and Buenos Aires.
Specifications 27,650 gross tons, 676 × 84 ft (208 × 26 m).
Builder Blohm & Voss, Hamburg, Germany, 1927.
Machinery Steam turbines, twin screw. Service speed 20 knots.
Capacity 575 first class, 275 second class, 465 third class.

1927 14 May: Launched. Nov: Maiden voyage to South America.
1940 Nov: Began service as accommodation ship for German Navy at Gdynia.
1945 Jan: Began service to evacuate German Eastern Territories; carried 26,000 refugees in three voyages. Apr: sailed with over 5,000 prisoners from concentration camp and almost another 1,000 including guards and crew. 3 May: While still carrying over 6,000 people, attacked by British bombers and set afire. Ship capsized, claiming over 5,000 lives. Wreckage broken up after war.

16
North Atlantic superships

Germany's maritime resurgence following the devastating losses of the First World War was nothing if not completely remarkable. Within a decade of their military defeat and the stripping of almost their entire merchant fleet, two national shipbuilders—AG Weser of Bremen and Blohm & Voss of Hamburg—were busily at work on a pair of near sisters that would not only be among the world's largest ocean liners, but the very fastest afloat and, to some appraisers, among the best decorated. It was an extraordinary rebirth, a brilliant resurgence!

For the most part, newly built superliners were not a part of the 'twenties. Instead, the reigning queens of the North Atlantic were all restored pre-war ships, three- and four-stackers that were, for the most part, lacking in speed and not part of the new age of sleek, more modern decorative stylings. Britain still dominated the Atlantic Ferry, as the transatlantic service was often called, primarily with six large liners: Cunard's *Aquitania, Berengaria* (the former *Imperator*) and *Mauretania* (the Blue Riband champion since 1907), and White Star's *Majestic* (ex-*Bismarck*), *Olympic* and *Homeric* (the intended *Columbus*). The United States had one superliner, *Leviathan* (ex-*Vaterland*), and the French, although still a virtual newcomer to the major leagues of Atlantic shipping, were represented by the four-funnel *France* and two postwar ships, *Paris* and the brand new *Ile de France*. The highly innovative decorative stylings of this last-named ship would, to some extent, influence the two new German speed queens.

John Malcolm Brinnin, in his *The Sway of the Grand Saloon*, aptly wrote:

'In resuming service [after the First World War], the small German ships seemed merely to dog-paddle in the water while fabulous German-built ships under new names, with new oil burners, raced past them *en route* to New York or Southampton. Nevertheless, these little vessels persisted until the moment when Germany would again rock the maritime world with ships as sensational in their time as were the *Kaiser Wilhelm der Grosse* and the *Deutschland* in the first years of the century.

'In conceiving the new *Bremen* and *Europa* [as the new liners were named], the directors of North German Lloyd were concerned first with speed—or, as they put it, "emphatic pronunciation of the principle of rapid speed"—than with size. Also, they wanted a kind of interior decor that would end the Wagnerian emblazonry of the Teutonic phase of La Belle Epoque and, at the same time, suggest a future already adumbrated on the drawing boards of Bauhaus. Thus the new German ships were conceived in the climate of an emergent international aesthetic and its recognition of the beauty of functional objects. Thus, to get a new "German look" in marine interiors, the company's directors had gone to a rising generation of designers whose simple, flat, geometrical surfaces and absence of ornamentation had already begun to influence architecture around the world. The result was a decor of a kind that made the superseded old liners seem as far in the past as a Junker hunting lodge would be from the Potsdam tower.

'Confident they would be winners, determined that the entrance of their new challengers would be dramatic, North German Lloyd staged a sort of two-city launching festival. On consecutive days in August 1928, before an audience of scores of thousands, including a press corps that numbered hundreds, the *Bremen* and then the *Europa* slid down their respective ways. Their joint tonnage made a big splash, and the sister act might have gained even greater coverage if the original plan for simultaneous, record-breaking maiden voyages [set for April 1929] could have been carried out. But the *Europa* suffered serious damage by fire while she was being fitted out and had to hang back for a whole year before she was able to join her mate.'

While *Bremen* triumphantly entered service in the summer of 1929, and immediately snatched the prized Blue Riband from the British, specifically the venerable old Cunarder *Mauretania*, *Europa*'s delay meant that she became the sister with slightly less sparkle, perhaps even less popularity. On the subject of *Bremen's* impressive maiden season, North German Lloyd commented, 'No liner in modern times has so caught the imagination of the public. Already, she has become a legend and a classic. Her name gleams like a new planet'.

August 1928, and the official launching is just days away in this dramatic, highly impressive view of the new speed queen of the North Atlantic, North German Lloyd's 938-ft long Bremen (Hapag-Lloyd).

What a glorious accomplishment and exceptional resurgence: Bremen (**above**) *and then*
Europa, *both superliners, are launched a day apart in August 1928 — the former at Bremen,*
the latter at Hamburg (Hapag-Lloyd).

Above   *Tugs carefully guide the brand new* Bremen *to the outer reaches of the River Weser for her first official trials in the late spring of 1929* (Hapag-Lloyd).

Below   *In the spring of 1930, the two German superliners* Bremen *(on the left) and* Europa *were berthed together for first time at the Columbus Quay at Bremerhaven* (Hapag-Lloyd).

Europa's tragic schedule-disrupting fire was recounted in considerable detail in the Blohm & Voss company history:

'In March 1929, the *Europa* was at least three-quarters finished. A large amount of deck covering of teak and corkolite was already on board and cabin construction had got as far as A Deck. The portholes were ready, and the pipes and cables had been installed. On the night of 25th–26th March, the only personnel aboard were the fire-spotting crew, who regularly made their rounds of the ship and had to clock in at definite times. Shortly after three o'clock in the morning, the look-out man at the middle gangway, near the post on D Deck, noticed a smell of burning and soon afterwards also saw smoke. For reasons which were never entirely clarified, the fire had broken out between frames 122 and 148. The fire spread quickly and engulfed the entire ship. Later, 350 firemen were simultaneously pouring in water from 65 hoses. Due to this enormous burden, which could not flow quickly enough into the lower decks, the *Europa* inevitably became top heavy. She developed a 14.5 degree list to the side away from the quay. Around ten o'clock in the following morning, Hamburg's senior fire official reluctantly gave the order to abandon ship.

'Eventually, the draft was so considerable that water was also able to enter the ship through the open starboard oil bunkering port. Scarcely was the flooded vessel solidly on the river bed and the danger of capsizing past when the shipyard crews and official fire brigades went on board with fresh hosing units. It was not until seven o'clock in the evening that they succeeded in breaking the power of this mammoth fire.

'This most spectacular shipping fire in the port of Hamburg made newspaper headlines. Nobody looking at the largely burnt-out *Europa* in press photographs of the catastrophe would have ever given a penny for the vessel. The necessary flooding of the ship's lower sections had among other things badly damaged the sensitive turbine, boiler and electricity plants. In places where the flames had not actually attacked the ship, the timberwork and many other water-absorbing materials had become useless due to swelling. Even the cork insulation of the turbine and boiler casing was carbonised, the glass plates of the portholes cracked and the alabaster plates of the cabin washbasins had melted. The room temperature must therefore have been about $700°$C. There was no denying the fact that the *Europa* was nothing but a load of scrap resting on the river bed.'

However, neither Blohm & Voss nor North German Lloyd were completely discouraged. They agreed on salvage and so arranged first for divers to seal all the side windows and openings, and then moored a drydock alongside the sunken liner to provide lateral support. On 14 April 1929, the 41,000-ton wreck, including a residue of 3,800 tons of water, was lifted

Europa burning at Hamburg in March 1929 (Ernst Joseph Weber).

Top left *Both* Bremen *and* Europa *had their names spelled out in large letters on the top deck. These were illuminated at night while in port (John Havers Collection).*
Middle left *With her long, lean look and capped by her flat funnels,* Europa — *seen during her eastbound maiden voyage in March 1930 — resembled the bold new age of the superliner. It differed so completely from the earlier designs of the four-stackers* (Roger Scozzafava).
Bottom left *The scene from the Boat Deck of the eastbound* Europa *as* Bremen *makes the run in the opposite direction to New York (Hapag-Lloyd).*
Above Europa *in a rare visit to Hamburg for some special repairs to be made by her Blohm & Voss builders (Hapag-Lloyd).*
Below *As seen from the outbound Hapag liner* New York, Bremen *(left) and* Europa *are again berthed together at the Columbus Quay, Bremerhaven (Hapag-Lloyd).*

Above left *Repainted in wartime camouflage in 1940, both* Bremen *(seen here) and* Europa *made round voyages from Bremerhaven to Hamburg for the purpose of being outfitted for the intended sea invasion of Britain* (Hapag-Lloyd).

Left *Under way for the first time in over five years,* Europa, *now under American command as a troop transport, departs from Bremerhaven for the last time in September 1945. The only survivor of the two German giants of the 'thirties, she will never again return to home waters* (Frank O. Braynard Collection).

Above *Refitted, restyled and refaced:* Liberté, *ex-*Europa, *arrives at New York for her 'second' maiden voyage in August 1950. Cunard's* Caronia *is on the left* (Moran Towing Co).

Right *Waiting for the scrappers: the former* Europa, *stripped and lonely, at anchor at La Spezia in the spring of 1962* (Frank O. Braynard Collection).

from the river. A month later, 6,700 tons of badly damaged steel material had been removed and scrapped. The repair work was close to monumental: much of the fittings had to be replaced, the keel had to be realigned and it was found that the ship had 'sagged' by as much as 19 cm in the fore and aft sections. Her restoration, however, became a matter of pride for every Blohm & Voss worker and, despite their priority attention with day and night shifts on the superliner, they also managed to complete the new Hamburg America liner *Milwaukee* on schedule as well.

On 22 February 1930, the completed *Europa* went

into the North Sea for trials and then two days later docked at her German terminal, the Columbus Quay at Bremerhaven, for the first time. Although ten months late, she had been completely refinished following that near-fatal fire and sinking and then, once in service to New York, performed so well that she took the Blue Riband from her running mate *Bremen*, and during her maiden trip, no less. The pennant eventually went back to *Bremen* in June 1933, but two months later was lost by the Germans forever. The Italian *Rex* became the champion that August.

Fast, luxurious, mighty and impressive, these final German superliners suffered, so it would seem, from only one major infirmity: they carried fewer passengers than expected. Not only was this complicated by the effects of the international Depression, but also by anti-German feelings held mostly by Continental and even American passengers. Initially, and soon after their triumphant maiden sailings, there was some lingering bitterness from the First World War. Later, however, their popularity was reduced further by antagonism and resentment towards the increasingly powerful Nazi regime.

Furthermore, once even larger and faster superliners came into service, such as the French *Normandie* and Britain's *Queen Mary*, in 1935–36, there had been some serious rumours that *Bremen* and *Europa* would be re-engined for higher speed and that they would re-capture the prized Riband and then, even more ambitiously, that the Germans would build two larger and faster superships. Neither scheme ever came to pass.

Teamed in the peak summer season with the smaller and slower *Columbus*, and thereby creating a three-ship weekly service in each direction, *Bremen* and *Europa* were in Germany during the Second World War. Actually, *Bremen* was at New York on 30 August, just two days before the Germans invaded Poland; she was finally permitted to sail, but without passengers. Cautiously, and having been repainted in grey while at sea and maintaining blackout and radio silence, she travelled homeward to Bremerhaven on a specially extended, quite mysterious route via Murmansk and then along the Norwegian coast. She rejoined *Europa* at the Bremerhaven docks in December.

There had been plans to make both liners into large attack transports and troop carriers, especially for the projected sea invasion of Britain, and for this the two exiled German luxury queens made a round trip to Hamburg. The scheme was never realized, however, and the ships returned to Bremerhaven—sadly, never to sail again under German colours. *Bremen* was completely gutted by fire, a blaze started by an unhappy crew-member on an otherwise quiet Sunday afternoon in March 1941. Badly damaged and overloaded with fire-fighting water, she was beyond any sensible repair and consequently her remains were cut up at the dockside. Her last pieces were taken, in fact, to the lower reaches of the River Weser and deliberately sunk.

The neglected, rusting, all-but-forgotten *Europa* was seized by the US invasion forces at Bremerhaven in May 1945. Quickly repaired and refitted, she became the American trooper AP–177, USS *Europa*. In due course, however, she was found to be a troublesome and, perhaps even more significantly, an unsafe ship (at one point, there were no less than eight fires on board in a single day!) and so she was eventually awarded by the United Nations Reparations Commission to the French as compensation for the loss of their glorious pre-war *Normandie*. *Europa* hoisted the Tricolour and was renamed, in a thoughtful gesture following the occupation of France, as *Liberté*. However, just as in her first career, she again sank in port. At Le Havre, in November 1946, she was ripped from her moorings during a ferocious gale and then slammed into the wreckage of another once celebrated pre-war liner, the capsized *Paris*. *Liberté* was badly holed and began to sink, but fortunately in an upright position. Again, just as in March 1929, she had to endure salvage and a delayed delivery.

The former *Europa* first reappeared on the North Atlantic luxury run in August 1950. During the next eleven years, she established an impeccable record and therefore enjoyed a highly successful second career. Succeeded by the brand new *France* in 1962, *Liberté* met her end in that same year at a shipbreaker's yard not far from Genoa in Italy. Some distance from her German birthplace, it was a particularly lonely ending for the very last of Germany's breed of superliners—from those first turn-of-the-century four-stackers to the *Imperator* Class and to her fleet-mate *Bremen*, the most famous of all.

Bremen
(North German Lloyd)

Service Bremerhaven-Southampton-Cherbourg-New York. Some off-season winter cruising.
Specifications 51,656 gross tons, 938 × 102 ft (289 × 31 m).
Builder AG Weser, Bremen, Germany, 1929.
Machinery Steam turbines, quadruple screw. Service speed 27 knots (maximum 28½ knots).
Capacity 800 first class, 500 second class, 300 tourist class, 600 third class.

1928 16 Aug: Launched.
1929 July: Maiden voyage to New York; captured Blue Riband with an average of 27.83 knots westbound and 27.92 knots eastbound
1930 Funnels heightened.
1933 June: After engine refit, surpassed record established by sister ship *Europa* and regained Blue Riband with average of 28.51 knots. Aug: Blue Riband lost to Italian *Rex*.
1937 Tonnage relisted as 51,731.
1939 Aug–Dec: Left New York without passengers, then repainted in wartime grey for extended voyage to home waters via Murmansk and Norwegian coast. Briefly hoisted Soviet colours as disguise.
1940 Jan: Began use as accommodation ship at Bremerhaven. One sailing to Hamburg to be refitted for planned invasion of Britain, but never materialized. Returned to Bremerhaven.
1941 16 Mar: Set afire by crew-member and completely burnt out; partially capsized. Wreckage later scrapped; last remains sunk in River Weser.

Europa
(North German Lloyd)

Service Bremerhaven-Southampton-Cherbourg-New York.
Specifications 49,746 gross tons, 936 × 102 ft (288 × 136 m).
Builder Blohm & Voss, Hamburg, Germany, 1930.
Machinery Steam turbines, quadruple screw. Service speed 27 knots (maximum 28½ knots).
Capacity 687 first class, 524 second class, 306 tourist class, 507 third class.

1928 15 Aug: Launched; intention was for April 1929 completion and simultaneous crossing with *Bremen* on dual maiden voyage to New York.
1929 26 Mar: While fitting out, badly damaged by fire; sank at dock. Completion delayed by nearly a year.
1930 Mar: Maiden crossing to New York. Captured Blue Riband from sister ship *Bremen* with average westbound speed of 27.91 knots.
1933 June: Blue Riband passed back to *Bremen*.
1939 Sept: Laid up at Bremerhaven; later outfitted as accommodation ship for German Navy.
1940 Jan: Sent to Hamburg to be refitted for proposed invasion of Britain, but scheme never materialized. Later returned to Bremerhaven.
1942 Plans to convert ship to aircraft carrier never materialized.
1945 May: Seized by invading US forces at Bremerhaven and later repaired and outfitted for transatlantic trooping. Subsequent problems with onboard fires.
1946 June: Allocated to French Government as reparations; sent to Le Havre. Transferred to Compagnie Générale Transatlantique (French Line) and renamed *Liberté*. 8 Dec: While berthed at Le Havre, ripped away from moorings during gale and rammed sunken wreckage of French Liner *Paris*. Badly holed but sank upright. Later raised and brought to St Nazaire for repairs and extensive refitting.
1949 Oct: Fire onboard while undergoing refit at St Nazaire.
1950 Aug: Resumed commercial service, Le Havre–New York via Southampton or Plymouth. Tonnage relisted as 51,839 and accommodation rearranged for 569 first class, 562 cabin class, 382 tourist class.
1954 Funnels heightened further by addition of domed tops.
1961 Nov: Final sailing from New York; rumoured to become floating hotel at Seattle for 1962 World's Fair; never materialized.
1962 Jan: Delivered to shipbreakers at La Spezia, Italy.

17
Express liners of
the 'thirties

German passenger shippers, namely North German Lloyd, Hamburg America Line and the German-East Africa Line (a firm that has not been mentioned in these pages thus far as it was content with smaller passenger ships under 10,000 gross tons) seemed to develop a fresh enthusiasm for renewing several of their services in the 'thirties. Lloyd looked to the Far East, Hapag to both Latin America and the prestige express run to New York, and German-East Africa to something of a colonial service to the lower half of the African continent.

German-flag passenger and mail service to the Far East had, for the most part, existed merely in name since the start of the First World War. By the early 'thirties, however, and as most other trade routes were appropriately maintained and supported, the Germans again looked to the 'mysterious Orient'. Three years after Hamburg America Line and North German Lloyd merged their passenger services in 1930 under the re-styled title of Hapag-Lloyd, the two firms decided to build three so-called 'East Asia express steamers'. These ships were intended to be not only profitable passenger-cargo vessels, but also special floating representatives of the German nation, as well as being capable of attracting continental as well as British passengers away from the more traditional firms such as P&O, Messageries Maritimes and Lloyd Triestino. Consequently, from the start they were planned as large, quite fast and particularly well-appointed ships.

Scharnhorst and *Gneisenau* were ordered and built directly for Lloyd. The third ship, *Potsdam*, was ordered at first by a specially-created Government affiliate known as the Hanseatic Shipping & Operating Company. Soon after her construction began, however, she was reassigned to Hamburg America ownership, but then this was further complicated when the Hapag-Lloyd operating arrangement was dissolved in February 1934. Furthermore, only Lloyd remained interested in the Far East passenger service and so,

accordingly, *Potsdam* was later sold outright to Lloyd. Once completed, *Potsdam* was affectionately dubbed 'the little *Europa*', mainly because of her trim lines, bulbous bow and cruiser stern. Although used in comparatively brief commercial service, this threesome did, in fact, become well known for the quality of their onboard service as well as their tasteful appointments.

Scharnhorst later became one of the very few German liners to be sunk in wartime action in the Pacific, while *Gneisenau* finished her days the victim of a mine off the Danish coast. Unfortunately, both ships were less than ten years old at the time. *Potsdam* survived and was surrendered to the British at the end of the war in the spring of 1945. She went on to serve them, as with the likes of *Monte Rosa* and *Pretoria*, as a peacetime trooper for the Ministry of Transport. Well known as *Empire Fowey*, she was sold in 1960 to start a third career as the Pakistani pilgrim ship *Safina-e-Hujjaj*, used mostly to ferry Moslem religious pilgrims to and from Jeddah in Saudi Arabia. She was finally broken up in 1976, at the age of 41.

In the African trades, Germany felt—in the 1930s era and long before the age of grand-scale, post-Second War independence—that she would again have colonies in Africa. Colonial possessions were, as well as being important economic outposts, also prestige pieces. Accordingly, Berlin prompted the German-East Africa Line to order two 'prestige steamers'. Although not quite as large or as powerful as Britain's dominant Union-Castle liners, these new Germans— to be named *Pretoria* and *Windhuk*—were among the finest passenger ships ever built for African service. Completed in 1936–37 they were assigned to a rather extensive run between Hamburg and Lourenco Marques (in Portuguese East Africa) and called *en route* at Southampton, Lisbon, Casablanca, Las Palmas, Walvis Bay, Cape Town, Port Elizabeth and Durban.

Built also by the illustrious Blohm & Voss at Hamburg, they were given mention in the history of that ever-productive firm.

Above *The Maierform bow and the* Europa-*style funnel of the Far Eastern combination liner* Gneisenau *are evident in this dockside photograph* (Willie Tinnemeyer Collection).
Below Scharnhorst *and her two sisters were among the finest liners ever to sail in the long-distance Far East service* (Roger Sherlock).

Above *In the post-war colouring of Britain's Ministry of Transport, the former* Potsdam *sailed as* Empire Fowey *and later as the Moslem pilgrim ship* Safina-e-Hujjaj (Alex Duncan).

Below *At the Blohm & Voss shipyards in 1936,* Pretoria *on the left, the incomplete* Windhuk *in the centre and Hapag's three-funnel* Reliance *on the right (Hapag-Lloyd).*

Above *The* Windhuk *(left) and the* Pretoria *in a rare occasion together at Hamburg* (German-East Africa Line).

Below *Imposing ships that appeared larger than the reality,* Pretoria *and her sister were billed by the Berlin Government as 'prestige boats' for the African services* (German-East Africa Line).

Above *The former* Pretoria *shown at Southampton in the 1950s as the Ministry of Transport's* Empire Orwell *(Roger Sherlock).*
Below *Two exiled German liners in far-off waters, and under different flags: the Indonesian* Gunung Djati *on the left is the former* Pretoria; *the* Safina-e-Hujjaj *is the ex-*Potsdam. *The ships are berthed at Jeddah during the Moselm pilgrim season and the year is 1966 (Frank O. Braynard Collection).*

'The arrangement of public rooms on these ships, on the Promenade Deck and A Deck, was especially cleverly conceived. Furthermore, for the first time, the entrance or reception halls, which the passengers entered when going aboard the ships, was built up into a comfortably equipped circulating area. This is a facility which since then was incorporated in all subsequent passenger ships and is now taken for granted as the "lobby". On the *Pretoria* and *Windhuk*, all the offices, doctor's consulting room, shops and hairdressing establishments led to this reception hall.'

However, as with *Scharnhorst* and her sisters, these African liners unfortunately saw a relatively short-lived service. Within three years, they were 'ships at war'. After serving as an accommodation centre and then as an active, white-hulled hospital ship, *Pretoria* was taken as a prize by the invading British in May 1945. She became a peacetime troop-ship, first as *Empire Doon* and then as *Empire Orwell*, until the late 'fifties. Her next career, much like that of the ex-*Potsdam* in the hands of the Pakistanis, was as a Moslem pilgrim ship but under Indonesian colours, and renamed *Gunung Djati*. While thoroughly refitted and converted to diesel propulsion as late as 1973 (at the age of 37!), she remained in Indonesian Government service until 1987, as the troop transport and accom-

modation ship *Kri Tanjung Pandan*. She aroused considerable curiosity, especially as she was the oldest of the surviving large pre-war German liners. In July 1984, while inbound for Djakarta aboard the cruise-ship *Princess Mahsuri*, herself a German-flag ship and better known as *Berlin* of the Peter Dielmann Co, her captain reported to the author that he had indeed seen an otherwise unknown two-funnel ship in port on his last visit, just two weeks earlier. Thoughtfully, he radioed ahead and requested a visit for us. She was then 47 years old and surely a tour on board would have been an extraordinary experience. However, quite unfortunately we received a response some hours later and still some distance from Djakarta that the former *Pretoria* had departed—and for the first time in nearly a year, no less!—on a 'work project' to the island of Timor. The opportunity was lost.

Her sister, *Windhuk*, fled to the safety of neutral Brazil deliberately disguised as the Japanese liner *Santos Maru* in the first months of the Second World War. Later seized outright by the Brazilians, she was soon sold to the US Government, who had her rebuilt (with only one funnel) as the trooper USS *Lejeune*. Laid up after the war, she sat for nearly twenty years in the anonymity and obscurity of a Government reserve

Patira, sailing on her maiden voyage, was intended to reinforce the German shipping presence along the West Coast of South America (Alex Duncan).

fleet. Finally declared surplus, she was broken up, almost without notice, in 1966.

Hapag's *Patria* was, like the *Scharnhorst* trio, built as a 'prestige boat' to reinforce the German presence in Latin America, but along the somewhat more remote West Coast of South America (via the Panama Canal). She too was a rather large combination passenger-cargo liner and, with particularly handsome accommodation, was expected to attract additional Continental passengers as well. She saw little more than a year's commercial service before being plunged into war and later, rather historically, briefly served as the seat of the defeated German Government in May 1945. Afterwards, she was surrendered to the British and intended for use as a peacetime trooper (and as such would have joined the former *Potsdam* and *Pretoria*), but in some re-thinking she was handed over to the Soviets instead. She became their *Rossia* and sailed until 1985, when she was scrapped at the age of 47!

The most ambitious project came, however, at the very end of that rather tumultuous decade of the 'thirties. Despite what some saw as very apparent war clouds on the horizon, there was also simultaneously an air of optimism about, even in as late as 1938. The Munich Pact had been signed, the possibilities of conflict seem more and more remote, and the era of 'peace and prosperity' would continue. The directors at Hamburg America were among those swept up in this misguided enthusiasm. Quite lavishly, they decided to reinforce their North Atlantic express service to New York (and to substantially upgrade their presence in the lucrative off-season American cruise trades) with no less than a trio of 41,000-ton liners, the biggest German liners in almost a decade and second in size only to *Bremen* and *Europa*, which would be their chief rivals. Otherwise, they were modelled to a large extent after another superliner, one of the most outstanding luxury ships of all time, the French *Normandie*. Most noticeably the bow section on the new Germans was almost a direct copy.

Provisionally named (according to Blohm & Voss records) *Vaterland II*, *Imperator II* and *Bismarck II*, the latter two were never even realized. Only *Vaterland* was placed under construction at the Blohm & Voss yards at Hamburg, but only to the point of launching. Notably, the three ships were intended for a 6-day Atlantic service, which was one day more than either *Bremen* or *Europa*, but which, according to Hapag accountants and engineers, was a substantial economic consideration. Surely, if finished, they would have been glorious ships and would have been yet another generation of German superliners.

Again, with further regret and misfortune, the war destroyed these plans. *Vaterland* was launched, although under far less festive circumstances, in that first summer of battle, August 1940. There was no further decision made as to her fate and consequently she was laid up, incomplete and largely ignored thereafter. Her long hull was caught in an Allied air raid in July 1943, and burnt out beyond any form of repair. Her remains were taken in hand by local scrappers after the war in 1948.

Below left   *After the war, Patria was awarded to the Soviets as reparations and there-after spent most of her time in the Black Sea as* Rossia *(Black Sea State Steamship Co).*
Above   *A model of the projected* Vaterland, *one of a planned Hapag trio for the North Atlantic express to New York (Arnold Kludas Collection).*
Below   *With less gaiety and excitement than might have been,* Vaterland *is launched in August 1940 in wartime Hamburg. She would never be completed, but instead bombed out within three years (Arnold Kludas Collection).*

Scharnhorst

(North German Lloyd)

Service Bremerhaven-Southampton-Far East (Hong Kong, Japan, etc) via Mediterranean, Suez and Middle East.
Specifications 18,184 gross tons, 652 × 74 ft (200 × 23 m).
Builder AG Weser, Bremen, Germany, 1935.
Machinery Steam turbo-electric, twin screw. Service speed 21 knots.
Capacity 149 first class and 144 second class.

1934 14 Dec: Launched.
1935 May: Maiden voyage to Far East.
1939 Sept: Kept in Japan owing to outbreak of war in Europe.
1942 Feb: Sold outright to Japanese Navy to become troop-ship. Sept: Instead began conversion at Kure to aircraft carrier.
1943 Dec: Commissioned as carrier; renamed *Shinyo*.
1944 17 Nov: torpedoed by US submarine *Spadefish* some 150 miles north-east of Shanghai.

Potsdam

(North German Lloyd)

Service Bremerhaven-Southampton-Far East (Hong Kong, Japan, etc) via Mediterranean, Suez and Middle East.
Specifications 17,528 gross tons, 634 × 74 ft (195 × 23 m).
Builder Blohm & Voss, Hamburg, Germany, 1935.
Machinery Steam turbo-electric, twin screw. Service speed 21 knots.
Capacity 126 first class, 160 second class.

1935 16 Jan: Launched for Hamburg America Line, but sold to North German Lloyd.
1935 July: Maiden voyage to Far East.
1940 Began service as accommodation ship for German Navy at Hamburg.
1942 Intended for conversion to aircraft carrier but never materialized; instead, sent to Gdynia for further service as accommodation ship.
1945 Jan: Used in evacuation of refugees, prisoners, etc from German Eastern Territories. Jun: Surrendered to British Government and temporarily renamed *Empire Jewel*; extensive repairs and refitting for use as peacetime troop-ship.
1946 Began troop service, renamed *Empire Fowey*; operated by British Ministry of Transport and managed by Orient Line.
1946 Nov: Laid up with engine troubles.
1947–50 Further refit and rebuilding at Glasgow. Service speed changed to 19 knots. Tonnage relisted as 19,121 and accommodation rearranged for 153 first class, 94 second class, 92 third class, 1,297 troops.
1950 Apr: Resumed service.
1960 Mar: Withdrawn from British-flag service; sold to Pan Islamic Steamship Co, Pakistani flag. Renamed *Safina-e-Hujjaj*. Used mostly in pilgrim service between Karachi and Jeddah, later also to East African ports and Hong Kong.
1976 Feb: Withdrawn from service. Oct: Broken up at Gadani Beach, Pakistan.

Gneisenau

(North German Lloyd)

Service Bremerhaven-Southampton-Far East (Hong Kong, Japan, etc) via Mediterranean, Suez and Middle East.
Specifications 18,160 gross tons, 651 × 74 ft (200 × 23 m).
Builder AG Weser, Bremen, Germany, 1935.
Machinery Steam turbines, twin screw. Service speed 21 knots.
Capacity 149 first class, 144 second class.

1935 17 May: Launched.
1936 Jan: Maiden voyage to Far East.
1939 Sept: Laid up at Bremerhaven.
1940 Jan: Began use as accommodation ship for German Navy; later intended for conversion to aircraft carrier, but plan never realized.
1943 2 May: Struck mine off Denmark and sank.

Pretoria

(German-East Africa Line)

Service Hamburg-West and South African ports (Walvis Bay, Cape Town, etc).
Specifications 16,662 gross tons, 577 × 72 ft (177 × 22 m).
Builder Blohm & Voss, Hamburg, Germany, 1936.
Machinery Steam turbines, twin screw. Service speed 18 knots.
Capacity 152 first class, 338 tourist class.

1936 16 July: Launched. Dec: Maiden voyage to African ports.
1939 Sept: Kept in German waters owing to outbreak of war; first used as accommodation ship for German Navy and later as hospital ship.
1945 Jan: Began service to evacuate German Eastern territories. May: Seized by invading British forces; later outfitted as troop-ship *Empire Doon*. Operated by Ministry of Transport and managed by Orient Line.
1948–49 Extensively refitted; service speed changed to 16 knots. Tonnage relisted as 18,036 and accommodation rearranged for 359 passengers, 1,108 troops. Renamed *Empire Orwell*.
1958 Chartered to Pan Islamic Steamship Co of Karachi for pilgrim services, then later in same year sold to Blue Funnel Line Ltd, British flag; converted to pilgrim ship at Glasgow. Tonnage relisted as 17,891 and accommodation restyled for 106 first class, 2,000 pilgrims. Renamed *Gunung Djati*.
1959 Mar: Entered pilgrim service for Blue Funnel Line between Indonesia, Middle East and Jeddah.
1962 Sold outright to Indonesian Government; owners later listed as Pelni Line, Indonesian flag, then Arafat Line, also Indonesian flag.
1973 Major refit; converted to motor-ship at Hong Kong and repaired following shipyard fire.
1977 Reclassified as troop transport and accommodation ship by the Indonesian Government. Renamed *Kri Tanjung Pandan*.
1986 Reached fiftieth year of service.
1987 Sold for scrapping at Kaohsiung, Taiwan.

Windhuk
(German-East Africa Line)

Service Hamburg-West and South African ports (Walvis Bay, Cape Town, etc).
Specifications 16,662 gross tons, 577 × 72 ft (177 × 22 m).
Builder Blohm & Voss, Hamburg, Germany, 1937.
Machinery Steam turbines, twin screw. Service speed 18 knots.
Capacity 152 first class, 338 tourist class.

1936 27 Aug: Launched.
1937 Apr: Maiden voyage.
1939 Sept: Caught at Lobito at beginning of Second World War. Nov: Sailed for Santos disguised as Japanese liner *Santos Maru*. Laid up.
1942 Jan: Officially seized by Brazilian Government. May: Sold to US Government; commissioned as troop transport USS *Lejeune*. Refitted with accommodation for 4,660 troops; second funnel removed.
1948 Feb: Laid up at Tacoma, Washington.
1966 Aug: Declared surplus and sold to shipbreakers at Portland, Oregon.

Patria
(Hamburg-America Line)

Service Hamburg-West Indies, Panama Canal and West Coast of South America.
Specifications 16,595 gross tons, 584 × 74 ft (180 × 23 m).
Builder Deutsche Werft, Hamburg, Germany, 1938.
Machinery MAN diesels, twin screw. Service speed 16 knots.
Capacity 185 first class, 164 tourist class.

1938 15 June: Launched. July: Nearly capsized in drydock; recovered with only slight damage. 12 Jul: Departed from Hamburg on maiden voyage, Baltic cruise. Aug: Maiden voyage to South America.
1939 Oct: Became accommodation ship and floating power station at Stettin.
1942 Moved to Flensburg.
1945 May: Surrendered to British invasion forces and temporarily served as seat of German Government.
1945 July: Refitted at Belfast as British troop-ship *Empire Welland*. Operated by Ministry of Transport, managed by Furness Withy & Co. Tonnage relisted as 17,870.
1946 Feb: Transferred at Liverpool to Soviet Union as reparations; renamed *Rossia*. Briefly served on North Atlantic run between Leningrad, then Odessa, and New York, but mostly in Black Sea service out of Odessa. Later also made several crossings to Havana.
1985 Sold to Pakistani breakers and temporarily renamed *Aniva* for delivery voyage to Gadani Beach. Scrapped just short of fiftieth year in service.

Vaterland
(Hamburg America Line)

Service Intended for North Atlantic service, Hamburg-Southampton-Cherbourg-New York. Also cruising.
Specifications 41,000 gross tons, 824 × 98 ft (253 × 30 m).
Builder Blohm & Voss, Hamburg, Germany, 1940.
Machinery Turbo-electric engines, twin screw. Service speed 23½ knots (maximum of 25½ knots).
Capacity 354 first class, 435 tourist class, 533 third class.

1940 24 Aug: Launched despite outbreak of Second World War; shortly afterwards laid up, incomplete.
1943 25 July: Heavily bombed and completely burnt out during Allied air raids on Hamburg harbour.
1948 Wreckage scrapped.

18
Two special cruise-ships

The so-called 'Kraft durch freude' ('Strength through Joy') had, in that politically-dominated period in German history during the 1930s, a sea-going cruise organization that offered inexpensive holiday voyages to German, and in particular Nazi party, workers and their families. This programme had begun in 1934, first using passenger ships that had been hard hit by the Depression and might be otherwise out of work such as Lloyd's *Stuttgart*, *Berlin* and *Der Deutsche*. The concept of single-class cruising, open to all passengers without any form of class distinction or shipboard separation, was—to a large extent—based on the earlier cruise services of the Hamburg Sud 'Monte' ships. The basic concept, according to Prager's history of Blohm & Voss, was that,

'Admittedly, the trips could only be booked by way of the Deutsche Arbeitsfront [the German Labour Front] and to this extent compelled the individual—if he was really interested in such a trip—to be kindly disposed towards the place of work, the Arbeitsfront itself and to the [Nazi] party. For an enormously large number of "national comrades", a sea journey with one of these big, white ships was the first encounter with the sea and sea travel altogether; for the great majority of them, it was also an event which a few years earlier could not even have been thought about. Men and women, who during their life had scarcely travelled beyond the provincial capital, were now seeing the Norwegian fjords, the Bay of Naples, the Canary Islands and Spitzbergen.

'There had never been plans for such an institution, but as in so many cases, clever propaganda experts of the Nazi regime discovered a demand here which could be admirably exploited for their purposes. One could simultaneously get laid-up ships moving again and then provide workplaces for unemployed seamen, the joy of taking holidays could be roused by new destinations, and by the necessity to provide reliefs for the holiday-makers, employers would be forced to engage more workers. During the sea journey, the "national comrade" not only remained within reach, but he was unable to spend any valuable foreign currency. The money he spent on board flowed back to Germany, of course.'

The success and popularity of these 'Strength through Joy' cruises was such that, by 1937, orders were placed for two specially-built and quite large passenger liners. *Wilhelm Gustloff* came from Blohm & Voss and was commissioned in the spring of 1938. While owned by the German Workers' Front, her cruise management and staffing were handled by a more experienced firm, Hamburg–South America Line. The slightly larger, although similar-looking, *Robert Ley* followed a year later in the spring of 1939. She was managed by Hamburg America. Both ships were run purely for passengers and had no cargo-carrying provisions whatsoever, and because of their leisurely, all-cruise nature, they were comparatively slow ships, making only 15½ knots maximum. They were both fitted with extremely sophisticated fire-safety systems as well as large searchlights, which were fitted to the foremasts and mostly used to floodlight night-time coastal settings for the enjoyment of the passengers.

Wilhelm Gustloff was described in Prager's history:

'She was, in fact, a remarkable vessel in many respects. She became the pacesetter for construction of special cruising ships, even down to the present day. All 1,465 passengers were allowed to have only outside cabins. This was achieved by a cunning new type of cabin arrangement. A larger, four-bedded inner cabin surrounded a smaller two-bed outer cabin and was connected by a light passage with the outer wall and the porthole. Incidentally, the *Wilhelm Gustloff* was the world's first sea-going ship on which, according to instructions, the crew had to be accommodated in exactly the same manner as the passengers. A further demand on her owner's part was for large free decks without disturbing ventilator heads, winches and deck equipment so that there was ample space for all passengers for deck chairs and enough space for sports and games. The "German Office for Travelling, Wandering and Holiday Organization" also called for large, bright halls with seating accommodation for every holidaymaker and without having to use the dining halls for this purpose.

'No objective observer could deny the fact that the dining and public rooms were of sound, unobtrusive beauty.

The first of the so-called 'Strength through Joy' cruise-ships, Wilhelm Gustloff, *is sent down the ways on 5 May 1937 (Frank O. Braynard Collection).*

Similar looking, but with noticeably different details and differences within their dimensions,
Wilhelm Gustloff (**above**) *and* Robert Ley (**below**) *were surely among the least fortunate*
passenger liners.

This applied to the music room with dance floor and library, the staircases, the circulating areas, the gymnasium and the tiled swimming pool.'

Again victims of the war, these two ships were destroyed within two months of one another in the final days of the conflict, the early spring of 1945. *Wilhelm Gustloff* was hideously torpedoed and then capsized while evacuating the Eastern Territories, which were then in retreat. Her loss ranks as the worst tragedy in maritime history: some 5,200 refugees, prisoners, wounded soldiers and crew-members were lost. Some say the actual figure—still vague because of the lack of actual passenger lists and record-keeping—stands as high as 5,400. This horrific disaster has been the subject of several German books and films, but—quite surprisingly—has been given comparatively scant attention abroad.

Robert Ley was bombed out during an Allied air raid on Hamburg in March 1945. There had been reports that she would be salvaged and repaired, and then surrendered to the Soviets for use as the passenger ship *Josif Stalin*. This never came to pass, and instead her twisted remains were towed to Britain in 1947 and then scrapped. Neither ship even reached a decade of service.

Wilhelm Gustloff
(German Workers' Front/Hamburg-South America Line)

Service 'Strength through Joy' workers' cruises.
Specifications 25,484 gross tons, 684 × 77 ft (210 × 24 m).
Builder Blohm & Voss, Hamburg, Germany, 1938.
Machinery MAN diesels, twin screw. Service speed 15½ knots.
Capacity 1,465 tourist class passengers only.

1937 5 May: Launched.
1938 Apr: Maiden cruise. Also sailed to Tilbury (London) for use as floating 'polling station' outside three-mile limit for Germans living in Britain.
1939 Sept: Transferred to German Navy and refitted as hospital ship.
1940 Nov: Became accommodation ship at Gdynia.
1945 30 Jan: Used for evacuation of German Eastern territories; loaded with 6,100 refugees and wounded soldiers, ordered to German port. However, on same day was hit by three torpedoes from Soviet submarine. Later capsized and all but 904 lost; worst maritime tragedy of all time.

Robert Ley
(German Workers' Front/Hamburg America Line)

Service 'Strength through Joy' workers' cruises.
Specifications 27,288 gross tons, 669 × 78 ft (206 × 24 m).
Builder Howaldtswerke Shipyards, Hamburg, Germany, 1939.
Machinery MAN diesels, twin screw. Service speed 15½ knots.
Capacity 1,774 tourist class passengers only.

1938 29 Mar: Launched.
1939 Apr: Maiden cruise. Sept: Transferred to German Navy and outfitted as hospital ship; stationed at Gdynia.
1940 Further service as accommodaiton ship.
1945 Jan: Began service in evacuation of German Eastern territories. 24 Mar: Bombed and burnt out during Allied air raids on Hamburg.
1947 June: Towed to Britain and scrapped.

19
Post-war revival

In 1945, just as in 1918–19, the German liner companies were devastated: their ships were either sunk, beyond repair or seized as prizes of war, mostly by the British and the Soviets. Once again, the likes of North German Lloyd and the Hamburg America Line, which had owned some of the mightiest and most luxurious liners (as well as two of the world's largest cargo ship fleets) were left with little more than a few harbour tugs and coastal freighters. Plans for renewal and rebuilding were halted at first and then sluggish, especially when considering the Allied shipping restrictions for German shipowners, the unavailability of home shipyards and the lingering war debts and other financial constraints. At best, by the late 'forties only a handful of small freighters with 2–12 passenger berths had been created. The passenger liner trade would have to wait.

The directors at the Hamburg America Line evidently saw limited potential in the renewal of liner services (although never again would they own a large ocean liner), but instead they managed two North Atlantic liners of the early 'fifties, Home Lines' 21,500-ton *Italia* and 10,200-ton *Homeland*. Both ships flew the Panamanian flag and, since Home Lines' operational base was at Genoa, they were otherwise generally regarded as Mediterranean-owned ships. They sailed between Hamburg (Cuxhaven), Southampton, Cherbourg, Halifax and New York, specifically carrying large numbers of westbound German migrants and returning with some of the first post-war waves of German-American tourists. This service was subsequently extended to Canada, to the St Lawrence River ports of Quebec City and Montreal, using not only *Italia* but also the 24,900-ton *Homeric*.

In 1957, Hapag decided also to experiment, albeit quite briefly, in renewed luxury cruising. It purchased Swedish Lloyd's 7,700-ton *Patricia* and refitted her with 249 all-first-class berths as the West German flag *Ariadne*. She sailed in Northern waters, to the Mediterranean and West Africa, and across the

Atlantic to the West Indies and South America, but with rather limited success. She was sold in 1960 to Eastern Steamship Lines of Miami and was placed under Liberian colours. She retained her German name, but thereafter remained in Caribbean waters.

Hapag did, however, eventually join North German Lloyd in building a series of six combination passenger-cargo liners, each with de luxe quarters for 86 first class passengers, in 1953–54. Each company built three of them and they are generally regarded as the first post-war passenger ships in the West German fleet and so, while they are approximately 9,000 tons and therefore below the 10,000-ton limit that has been used in this book, an exception has been made to include them.

The ships were designed especially for the long-haul Far Eastern service and were almost identical. Not only adequate cargo carriers, trading to a most important manufacturing area, they were also purposely intended to revive the prestige passenger service (especially for businessmen and their families) of the late 'thirties that had been run by *Potsdam* and her two running-mates. *Hamburg*, *Hannover* and *Frankfurt* were owned by the Hamburg America Line, and *Bayernstein*, *Hessenstein* and *Schwabenstein* by North German Lloyd. While *Hannover* made two introductory sailings to New York, the ships were otherwise used exclusively in 95-day round-trip voyages, supplemented by six 12-passenger freighters as well. The routing took them from Hamburg, Bremerhaven, Antwerp, Rotterdam and Southampton to Genoa, Port Said, Djibouti, Penang, Singapore, Hong Kong, Yokohama, Shimizu, Nagoya and Kobe. In addition to their passenger roles, cargo was an important revenue: general goods outwards, then returning with products such as rubber, coconut oil, latex, textiles and mass-produced, inexpensive manufactured goods, especially from Japan and Hong Kong.

For nearly a decade, they served successfully. By 1966–67, however, they were outmoded and were replaced by large-capacity, high-speed cargo ships.

Above *At the very beginning of her career, Hapag's Hannover made two special trans-atlantic crossings to New York. The ship docked, however, at the Company's freight terminal at 17th Street in Brooklyn (Frank O. Braynard Collection).*

Below Frankfurt *and her five sisters of the joint North German Lloyd-Hamburg America Far Eastern service were among the finest post-war combination ships* (Schiffsfotos).

Above Bayernstein *and her two Lloyd sisters were noticeably different from the three Hapag ships in that they did not have tapered funnel tops.* (Hapag-Lloyd).

Below *The former* Schwabenstein *prepares to depart from Bremerhaven for the last time, having been sold and repainted in the colours of Orient Overseas Line* (Wolfgang Fuchs).

Above Gripsholm *as she appeared in 1954, with her North German Lloyd funnel colours but sailing for the so-called Bremen-Amerika Line* (North German Lloyd).

Below *Rebuilt from the French* Pasteur *of 1939, the 697-ft long* Bremen *was post-war flagship of the North German Lloyd passenger fleet* (Howard Whitford).

Above Berlin, *the former* Gripsholm *of 1925, was the first post-Second World War liner to sail for the Germans* (Ernest Arroyo).

Below Europa *of 1953, the ex-*Kungsholm *of Swedish American Line, was one of the finest transatlantic liners of her time* (Author's Collection).

Idle ex-Germans: the former George Washington, Amerika, Kronprinzessin Cecilie *and* Kaiser Wilhelm II *in Chesapeake Bay, 1939* (Ted Hindmarsh Collection).

Above *Another midnight sailing: German Atlantic's* Hanseatic *is about to sail from New York on a seven-week cruise around continental South America in October 1969* (Bill Miller).

Below *A poetic view of* Europa, *then in use as a full-time cruise-ship, as she arrives at Lisbon* (Luis Miguel Correia).

Above   *The last remaining bulkhead terminals, built by Hamburg America and North German Lloyd in 1905–06, desolate and awaiting demolition at Hoboken in the autumn of 1982* (Bill Miller).

Below   *Just across from the great towers of Lower Manhattan, the enormous funnels of the likes of* Imperator *and* Kronprinzessin Cecilie *once stood above these terminal roof-tops at Hoboken* (Bill Miller).

Above *In the final years of her long 41-year career,* Berlin *is outbound on a cruise. Note the Christmas tree perched above her wheelhouse* (Luis Miguel Correia).

Below *After 1971,* Bremen *was sold to the Greek-flag Chandris Group and sailed as a cruise-ship, both in European and Caribbean waters* (Michael D. J. Lennon).

The six original combination liners were then sold to the ever-expanding C.Y. Tung Group, placed under the Liberian flag and used in the Orient Overseas Lines' service between the United States and the Far East via Panama. Another decade or so of service followed until the last of these ships was broken up in 1979.

Rather brief mention should be made also at this point of the Hamburg-South America Line. This company decided not to revive its Latin American liner services, but did, however, build six specially fitted freighters, with 28 passenger berths each, between 1951 and 1953. They were *Santa Ines*, *Santa Teresa*, *Santa Catarina*, *Santa Elena*, *Santa Isabel* and *Santa Ursula*, and they sailed on the same pre-war run to Rio, Santos, Montevideo and Buenos Aires. They too were replaced by larger, faster freighters (and still later by even larger container-ships) in the 1960s. Later sold to foreign-flag owners, all have since been scrapped.

As for North German Lloyd, soon after it completed its three ships for the Far Eastern 'combo service', it entered into an agreement in 1954 with Swedish American Line, to operate their 19,100-ton *Gripsholm*

(built in 1925) on a revived transatlantic service between Bremerhaven and New York. For that first year, this service was provided by the so-called Bremen-America Line and, while *Gripsholm* retained her Swedish registry and white hull colouring, she was repainted with North German Lloyd funnel colours. A year or so later, in January 1955, she was sold outright to Lloyd, repainted completely in their colours and, being transferred officially to the West German national colours, became the first post-war German ocean liner. It was ten years since the war had ended and sixteen years since a German liner made a commercial crossing to New York. Her name was changed to *Berlin* and this revival of German-flag passenger service on the North Atlantic meant that a successful future was assured. Expansion was soon necessary.

Lloyd was still unable to undertake the building of a brand new passenger liner, however. Instead, it was quite fortunate to obtain the laid-up French liner *Pasteur*, which, at over 30,000 tons, was one of the largest liners ever planned for the Europe-South America run. She was last used as a peacetime trooper sailing to politically troubled Indochina, and although

An unusual occasion: both Berlin *and* Bremen *arriving in New York harbour and passing under the Verazzano Narrows Bridge at the same time. The time is a Saturday afternoon in April 1965* (North German Lloyd).

Above *Initially,* Europa, *the former* Kungsholm *of 1953, was painted in the traditional North German Lloyd black hull for transatlantic service* (Michael Cassar).

Below *When restyled as a year-round cruise-ship,* Europa *adopted an all-white hull and later the new Hapag-Lloyd funnel markings* (Schiffsfotos).

there had been some thought to rebuilding her for transatlantic service with French Line (who were then also sailing the former *Europa* of 1930 as *Liberté*), she was put on the sales lists and went quite quickly to the Germans. After a lavish and thorough rebuilding, she re-emerged in July 1959 as the national flagship, the 'new' *Bremen*. On her maiden passage to New York, she met the outbound *Berlin* in Manhattan's Upper Bay; it was a proud and symbolic moment. Although it had been fourteen years since the war had finished, and while their earlier liner fleet had been far larger, Lloyd once again had a two-ship transatlantic service and, in *Bremen*, one of the finest ships in that trade.

The enthusiastic mood at Lloyd's Bremen head-quarters did not, however, lead to larger liners or to any dramatic renaissance in the form of a German superliner, such as the rival French did with their *France* in 1962. Clearly, the Germans, like several other far-sighted companies in Atlantic service, saw the new age of jet aircraft as an unbeatable threat (the first commercial jet airliner crossed the Atlantic in the autumn of 1958, just over six months before *Bremen* made her debut, and within a short time the airlines had secured nearly two-thirds of all transatlantic clientele). Therefore, while the older, slower *Berlin* still relied largely on tourist class and migrant traffic, the far more luxurious *Bremen* had to be more competitive and earn her way by emphasizing the alternative of a 'sea-going hotel to Europe', and a tropical off-season cruise-ship. However, she would in fact prove to be the last of the German transatlantic liners when she ran the final sailing from New York to Bremerhaven in December 1971. Unfortunately, as she slipped past those same Hoboken docks where so many of her grand predecessors had once berthed, she was less than half-filled, in the darkness of night and barely noticed by the general public at all. The curtain had fallen.

Lloyd added *Europa* in 1965–66, but primarily as a replacement for the then 41-year-old *Berlin*. While the newer ship ran for several seasons on the Atlantic with class-divided passengers, she was used increasingly and then permanently, with all-first-class berthing, as a cruise-ship. She remained with the Germans until handed over to a Panamanian-flag subsidiary of the Costa Line of Italy in 1981. Earmarked for further periodic German cruising, she was renamed *Columbus C*, adopting the name of the famed North German Lloyd liner of the 'twenties and 'thirties as a marketing technique aimed at the older, wealthier German cruise market. Sadly, she was lost in July 1984 when she sank at the Spanish port of Cadiz during a Mediterranean cruise.

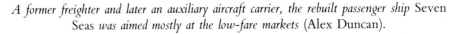

A former freighter and later an auxiliary aircraft carrier, the rebuilt passenger ship Seven Seas *was aimed mostly at the low-fare markets* (Alex Duncan).

Above   *One of the last three-funnel liners, Canadian Pacific's* Empress of Scotland *was a pre-war speed champion but on the trans-Pacific run. She was gutted completely in 1958, and became the two-funnel* Hanseatic *(J. K. Byass).*

Below   *Modernized, streamlined and lengthened,* Hanseatic *is seen during a wintertime cruise at anchor off Port-au-Prince, Haiti (Everett Viez Collection).*

Above *Just before sailing for Europe in September 1966, Hanseatic caught fire at her New York pier. United States and Queen Mary are in the background (Willie Tinnemeyer Collection).*

Below *Damaged beyond economic repair, the 36-year-old Hanseatic was towed to Hamburg and then delivered to local shipbreakers (Schiffsfotos).*

When Hamburg America Line and North German Lloyd decided to merge in 1970, so as to become more competitive internationally as well as to cut mounting operational costs, the management saw de luxe, up-market luxury cruising as their future role in passenger ship operations, but only with a single-ship schedule—first with the aforementioned *Europa* (the ex-*Kungsholm* of 1953) and then with a brand new, specially designed liner, the next *Europa*, built in 1981 (and dealt with in the next chapter).

Two other West German flag companies, created in the 'fifties and aiming at the still buoyant transatlantic trade, also began with second-hand tonnage. The Europe-Canada Line, organized by a Dutch partnership between Holland America Line and Royal Rotterdam Lloyd (but which selected West German registry so as to use then less costly German labour), was interested in the migrant, student and low-fare tourist trades to Eastern Canada and periodically to New York. It used the rebuilt, former auxiliary aircraft carrier *Seven Seas*, which sailed for little more than ten years.

The other entrant represented that earlier partnership between Hamburg America Line and the Italian-based, multi-national-owned Home Lines. In 1957, the so-called Hamburg Atlantic Line was formed and bought one of the world's last three-funnel liners, Canadian Pacific's *Empress of Scotland*, which dated from 1930. She was totally rebuilt at Hamburg and then entered service to New York in the summer of 1958. As *Hanseatic*, she developed a sound popularity, a very definite rival to Lloyd's *Berlin* and its *Bremen* in particular. However, she was so seriously damaged by a fire at her New York pier in September 1966 that she had to be scrapped. Her success and popularity were such, however, that the newly formed German Atlantic Line of 1967 soon thereafter introduced a 'new' *Hanseatic*, the former Israeli liner *Shalom*. More details about this firm are included in the next chapter.

The transatlantic service to New York—for which so many liners included in this book were created, such as *Kaiser Wilhelm der Grosse* and her four-funnel fleetmates, the giant *Imperator* trio and the speedy *Bremen* and *Europa* of the 'thirties—is now virtually desolate (with the exception of Britain's *Queen Elizabeth 2*, which plies this historic trade for about six months of each year). Otherwise, profitable service has long since been defeated by the age of the jetliner. Even the

docks, the Columbus Quay at Bremerhaven and the slips along New York's once aptly named 'Luxury Liner Row', are largely changed and unrecognizable. In August 1985, while returning from a three-week cruise to Greenland aboard the cruise-ship *Astor* (included in the following chapter), we arrived at Cuxhaven and passed through the aged, now rarely used passenger terminal. Momentarily, I thought back to the age of *Imperator*, *Vaterland* and the *Albert Ballin* quartet. Recently, Hamburg's luxurious Atlantic Hotel released a commemorative book on its history, and included were photos of the great German liners taken in the days when many hotel guests had just arrived or were about to entrain at the Cuxhaven terminal (about two hours from Hamburg itself).

At New York, where there is now far less visible shipping, Hapag-Lloyd ships now carry containers (but not passengers) and bear such names as *Nurnburg Express* and *Stuttgart Express*. Even the main Company offices, which had been located for so long in the traditional 'steamship row' of Lower Manhattan, have now relocated to the outer reaches of New York harbour, to a modern complex on Staten Island. The ships have not called at the once busy Hudson River docks for some years, but go instead to the vast container terminals of Elizabethport, New Jersey, located some fifteen miles west of the City. More recently, there have been even further changes. In December 1986, while at Manaus, Brazil, during an Amazon River cruise, we were berthed near *Hapag Lloyd Brasil*. A more traditional breakbulk freighter, she carried German officers, a multinational deck crew and was registered in Panama. Six months afterwards, while on a summertime visit to Hamburg, the containership *Sierra Express* was in one of the big Blohm & Voss drydocks undergoing extensive repairs. After over sixty years, the original Hamburg America striped funnel colours (which were retained even after the Hapag-Lloyd merger) were being removed. In this current age of computerized shipping and home office efficiency, the Company directors have decided on new funnel colours for their two dozen or so cargo-ships. These new markings match those on the cruiseship *Europa*, on the Company's tugs and, diverse in its investments and enterprises, the Hapag-Lloyd passenger aircraft fleet. So little now reflects the earlier days of most of the ships mentioned in this book.

Hamburg
(Hamburg America Line)

Service Hamburg and Bremerhaven-Far East via Suez Canal (ports of call included Antwerp, Rotterdam, Southampton, Genoa, Port Said, Suez, Aden, Penang, Port Swettenham, Singapore, Miri, Manila, Hong Kong, Yokohama, Nagoya and Kobe; homewards also include Colombo and Marseilles).
Specifications 8,959 gross tons, 538 × 64 ft (165 × 20 m).
Builder Bremer Vulkan Shipyards, Vegesack, Germany, 1954.
Machinery MAN diesels, single screw. Service speed 16½ knots.
Capacity 86 first class.

1954–66 Far Eastern passenger-cargo service; afterwards sold to C.Y. Tung Group and placed under Liberian flag as *Oriental Warrior*. Used on North America–Far East service via Panama for Orient Overseas Lines. Continued to carry passengers.
1972 25 May: Caught fire off east coast of Florida; abandoned by passengers and crew. Adrift for two days before being taken in tow; later destroyed.

Hannover
(Hamburg America Line)

Service Hamburg and Bremerhaven-Far East via Suez Canal (for ports see listing under *Hamburg*).
Specifications 9,008 gross tons, 538 × 64 ft (165 × 20 m).
Builder Bremer Vulkan Shipyards, Vegesack, Germany, 1954.
Machinery MAN diesels, single screw. Service speed 16½ knots.
Capacity 86 first class.

1954–66 Far Eastern passenger-cargo service; afterwards sold to C.Y. Tung Group and placed under Liberian flag as *Oriental Inventor*. Continued to carry passengers in North America-Far East service via Panama for Orient Overseas Lines.
1973 Downgraded to freighter service only.
1976 Used in worldwide tramping service.
1978–79 Broken up in Far East.

Frankfurt
(Hamburg America Line)

Service Hamburg and Bremerhaven-Far East via Suez Canal (for ports see listing under *Hamburg*).
Specifications 8,974 gross tons, 538 × 64 ft (165 × 20 m).
Builder Bremer Vulkan Shipyards, Vegesack, Germany, 1954.
Machinery MAN diesels, single screw. Service speed 16½ knots.
Capacity 86 first class.

1954–66 Far Eastern passenger-cargo service; afterwards sold to C.Y. Tung Group and placed under Liberian flag as *Oriental Hero*. Continued to carry passengers in North America-Far East service via Panama for Orient Overseas Lines.
1973 Downgraded to freighter service only.
1976 Used in worldwide tramping service.
1978–79 Broken up in Far East.

Bayernstein
(North German Lloyd)

Service Hamburg and Bremerhaven-Far East via Suez Canal (for ports see listing under *Hamburg*).
Specifications 8,999 gross tons, 538 × 64 ft (165 × 20 m).
Builder Bremer Vulkan Shipyards, Vegesack, Germany, 1954.
Machinery MAN diesels, single screw. Service speed 16½ knots.
Capacity 86 first class.

1954–66 Far Eastern passenger-cargo service; afterwards sold to C.Y. Tung Group and placed under Liberian flag as *Oriental Lady*. Continued to carry passengers in North America-Far East service via Panama for Orient Overseas Lines.
1973 Downgraded to freighter service only.
1976 Used in worldwide tramp service.
1978–79 Broken up in Far East.

Hessenstein
(North German Lloyd)

Service Hamburg and Bremerhaven-Far East via Suez Canal (for ports see listing under *Hamburg*).
Specifications 8,929 gross tons, 538 × 64 ft (165 × 20 m).
Builder Bremer Vulkan Shipyards, Vegesack, Germany, 1954.
Machinery MAN diesels, single screw. Service speed 16½ knots.
Capacity 86 first class.

1954–66 Far Eastern passenger-cargo service; afterwards sold to C.Y. Tung Group and placed under Liberian Flag as *Oriental Musician*. Continued to carry passengers in North America–Far East service via Panama for Orient Overseas Lines.
1973 Downgraded to freighter service only.
1976 Used in worldwide tramp service.
1978–79 Broken up in Far East.

Schwabenstein
(North German Lloyd)

Service Hamburg and Bremerhaven-Far East via Suez Canal (for ports see listing under *Hamburg*).
Specifications 8,955 gross tons, 538 × 64 ft (165 × 20 m).
Builder Bremer Vulkan Shipyards, Vegesack, Germany, 1953.
Machinery MAN diesels, single screw. Service speed 16½ knots.
Capacity 86 first class.

1953–66 Far Eastern passenger-cargo service; afterwards sold to C.Y. Tung Group and placed under Liberian flag as *Oriental Ruler*. Continued to carry passengers in North America-Far East service via Panama for Orient Overseas Lines.
1973 Downgraded to freighter service only.
1976 Used in worldwide tramp service.
1978–79 Broken up in Far East.

Berlin
(North German Lloyd)

Service Bremerhaven–New York, occasionally via Southampton and/or Halifax. In later years, annual sailing to Quebec City and Montreal. Also cruising from New York and Bremerhaven.
Specifications 18,600 gross tons, 590 × 74 ft (181 × 23 m).
Builder Sir W.G. Armstrong-Whitworth & Co, Newcastle, England, 1925.
Machinery B & W diesels, twin screw. Service speed 16½ knots.
Capacity 98 first class, 878 tourist class.

1924 26 Nov: Launched as *Gripsholm* for Swedish American Line.
1925 Nov: Maiden voyage, Gothenburg-New York. Tonnage listed as 17,993 and accommodation arranged for 127 first class, 482 second class, 948 third class. Transatlantic service and extensive cruising.
1932 Repainted with white hull.
1937 Major refit; tonnage relisted as 18,134.
1940–46 Used as International Red Cross 'exchange ship' for diplomats, refugees, prisoners, etc.
1946 Mar: Resumed Swedish American commercial service to New York.
1949–50 Major refit at Kiel. New funnels fitted, accommodation restyled for 210 first class and 910 tourist class, given new bow and lengthened from 573 to 590 ft (176 to 181 m). Tonnage relisted as 19,105.
1953 Dec: Final sailing, Gothenburg-New York.
1954 1 Feb: Began sailing for newly formed Bremen-America Line (Swedish American Line and North German Lloyd partnership); retained original name, but used on Bremerhaven-New York service.
1955 Jan: Bought outright by North German Lloyd, West German colours; renamed *Berlin*. First post-war German passenger liner on North Atlantic run.
1966 Nov: Delivered to shipbreakers at La Spezia, Italy.

Bremen

(North German Lloyd)

Service Bremerhaven-Southampton-Cherbourg-New York. Also winter cruising from New York to Caribbean and occasionally from Bremerhaven.
Specifications 32,336 gross tons, 697 × 88 ft (214 × 27 m).
Builder Chantiers de L'Atlantique, St Nazaire, France, 1939.
Machinery Steam turbines, quadruple screw. Service speed 23 knots.
Capacity 216 first class, 906 tourist class.

1938 15 Feb: Launched as *Pasteur* for Compagnie Sud-Atlantique, French flag; intended for France-Brazil-Argentina service.
1939 Sept: Commercial maiden voyage cancelled owing to outbreak of Second World War; laid up at Brest for safety.
1940–46 Used as troop-ship by British Government; managed by Cunard-White Star.
1946–56 Peacetime trooping for French Government, sailing mostly to Indochina. Capacity listed as 4,000 troops.
1957 Jan: Laid up; offered for sale. Rumoured to be refitted for French Line transatlantic service to New York. Sept: Purchased by North German Lloyd, West German flag; renamed *Bremen*. To Bremerhaven for complete rebuilding.
1957–59 Rebuilt for transatlantic service; tonnage increased from 29,253 to 32,336.
1959 July: Maiden crossing to New York; West Germany's largest post-war liner.
1971 Dec: Ended German transatlantic passenger service. Sold to Chandris Group, Greek flag; renamed *Regina Magna*. Thereafter used for cruising only: Scandinavia, Mediterranean and Caribbean.
1974 Oct: Laid up at Perama, Greece.
1977 Sold to Philippine Singapore Ports Corporation, Philippine flag; left Piraeus under tow for Jeddah, Saudi Arabia, for use as floating hotel. Renamed *Saudi Phil 1*.
1978 Mar: Renamed *Filipinas Saudi 1*. Accommodation listed as 3,600 workers.
1980 Apr: Sold for scrapping at Kaohsiung, Taiwan. Jun: Sank while being towed from Jeddah to Kaohsiung.

Seven Seas

(Europe-Canada Line)

Service Bremerhaven and/or Rotterdam-Le Havre-Southampton-Quebec City-Montreal or New York (occasional calls at Halifax). Wintertime around-the-world cruises as floating university.
Specifications 12,575 gross tons, 492 × 69 ft (151 × 21 m).
Builder Sun Shipbuilding & Drydock Co, Chester, Pennsylvania, 1940.
Machinery Sulzer diesels, single screw. Sevice speed 16½ knots.
Capacity 20 first class, 987 tourist class.

1940 Completed as *Mormacmail*, C3-type freighter, for Moore McCormack Lines, US flag.
1941 Mar: Transferred to US Navy and rebuilt as auxiliary aircraft carrier; renamed USS *Long Island*.
1941–46 Military service.
1946 Apr: Decommissioned from active service and laid up.
1948 Mar: Sold to Caribbean Land & Shipping Co, Panamanian flag; renamed *Nelly*. Rebuilt as immigrant ship.
1949–55 Australian migrant service.
1955 Apr: Purchased by Europe-Canada Line (Caribbean Land & Shipping Co, Geneva, and Holland America Line/Royal Rotterdam Lloyd partnership); renamed *Seven Seas*, Panamanian flag. Entered transatlantic service.
1955 July: Transferred to West German flag; rumour of renaming to *Bremen*, but never materialized.
1965 18 July: Immobilized in North Atlantic by engine-room fire.
1966 Repairs completed. Sept: Became floating hostel at Rotterdam for foreign workers of Verolme Shipyards; permanently moored.
1977 4 May: Left Rotterdam under tow bound for scrapyards at Ghent, Belgium.

Hanseatic

(Hamburg Atlantic Line)

Service Hamburg (Cuxhaven)-Southampton-Cherbourg-New York. Winter cruising from Port Everglades, Florida, to Caribbean, occasionally from New York and Hamburg.
Specifications 30,029 gross tons, 672 × 83 ft (207 × 25 m).
Builder Fairfield Shipbuilding & Engineering Co, Glasgow, Scotland, 1930.
Machinery Steam turbines, twin screw. Service speed 21 knots.
Capacity 85 first class, 1,167 tourist class.

1929 17 Dec: Launched as *Empress of Japan* for Canadian Pacific Steamships, British flag.
1930 June: Special maiden voyage from Liverpool to Quebec City. Aug: Southampton–Vancouver via Suez and Hong Kong, thence regular transpacific service between Vancouver and Far East.
1931 Apr: Record Pacific run from Yokohama to Victoria (British Columbia) in 7 days, 20 hrs, 16 mins. Fastest liner in Pacific service until 1939.
1939 Aug: Requisitioned for troop-ship service by British Government.
1942 Oct: Renamed *Empress of Scotland* after Japan's entry into war.
1948 Released from military service and extensively refitted. Tonnage listed as 26,313. Accommodation restyled for 458 first class, 250 tourist class.
1950 May: Maiden post-war sailing from Liverpool to Quebec City.
1951 Nov: Carried Princess Elizabeth (later Queen) and Duke of Edinburgh from Portugal Cove, Newfoundland, to Liverpool.
1952 May: Masts shortened by 40 ft so as to proceed to Montreal.
1957 Nov: Withdrawn from Canadian Pacific service and laid up at Liverpool, then Belfast.
1958 Jan: Sold for £1 million to newly created Hamburg Atlantic Line, West German flag; provisionally renamed *Scotland*, then formally *Hanseatic*. Thoroughly rebuilt at Howaldtswerke Shipyards, Hamburg, for £1.4 million. Three funnels replaced by two, accommodation increased from 708 to 1,252 berths, new bow fitted, overall length increased from 666 to 672 ft (205 to 207 m), tonnage relisted as 30,029. July: Maiden crossing as German liner to New York.
1966 7 Sept: Badly damaged by fire at New York's Pier 84; laid up at Brooklyn shipyard. 10 Oct: Arrived under tow in Hamburg for further inspection; found to be beyond economic repair. Sold to Eisen & Metall of Hamburg for demolition.

Europa

(North German Lloyd)

Service Bremerhaven-Southampton-Cherbourg-New York, but mostly cruising from New York, Bremerhaven and Genoa. Voyages from 7 to 100 days. days.
Specifications 21,514 gross tons, 600 × 77 ft (185 × 24 m).
Builder De Schelde Shipyards, Flushing, Holland, 1953.
Machinery B & W diesels, twin screw. Service speed 19 knots.
Capacity 122 first class, 721 tourist class; later changed to 769 single-class.

1952 18 Apr: Launched as *Kungsholm* for Swedish American Line, Swedish flag.
1953 Nov: Maiden crossing, Gothenburg-New York via Copenhagen. Tonnage listed as 21,141 and accommodation arranged for 176 first class, 626 tourist class.
1961 Nov: Refitted.
1965 Oct: Sold to North German Lloyd, West German flag; renamed *Europa*.
1966 Jan: Maiden crossing to New York.
1970 North German Lloyd merged with Hamburg America Line to form Hapag-Lloyd; hull and funnels repainted in new colours.
1971 Transatlantic service discontinued; assigned to full-time cruising.
1980 Oct: Sold to Costa Line, Panamanian flag.
1981 Oct: Delivered to Costa Line; renamed *Columbus C*. South American cruising, and later in European waters.
1984 29 Jul: During Mediterranean cruise, struck breakwater at Cadiz and later sank at berth; beyond economic repair and declared a constructive loss.
1984 Nov: Salvaged and offered for sale.
1985 Mar: Delivered to Spanish shipbreakers.

20
Cruising liners

Cruising—mostly to tropical, sun-filled destinations, on the so-called 'warm water' routes—has been the mainstay of passenger shipping for at least the past twenty years. Shipowners interested in remaining (as well as surviving) in liner operations, especially following the collapse of the once traditional, class-divided, prosperous trades such as the transatlantic service, had to make a large transition. That last port-to-port crossing of *Bremen* in late 1971 was more than just a historic termination of over a century of service; it also signified a complete change of thought for the future, for the managers and especially the passenger division of Hapag-Lloyd. The era of shipboard transport was over, replaced by leisure at sea. Thus a new generation of liners had to be purposely built—with top-deck pools and sunning areas, private plumbing in even the lowest-priced cabin, large lounges, discos, night-clubs, casinos and complete shopping centres, saunas, closed circuit television, cinema and conference rooms, gymnasiums and health facilities, dietary menus and buffet luncheons at the pool-side. In short, they had to be white-hulled 'floating resorts that moved'.

The North American cruise trade, particularly to the Caribbean from such ports as Miami, Port Everglades and San Juan, has been immensely successful. It has exceeded the $4 billion-per-year level for the combined cruise companies based in the United States. More and increasingly larger ships, more advanced and more thoughtfully designed and decorated (with the likes of 12-channel television in every cabin and six-deck-high entrance foyers with glass-covered elevators shuttling up and down) have entered service. The world's largest ocean liner is the Norwegian-owned cruise-ship *Sovereign of the Seas* at 74,000 gross tons, 874 ft (269 m) in length and with accommodation for a maximum of 2,600 passengers. In tonnage, she easily surpasses all of the ships mentioned in these pages including the 54,000-ton *Vaterland*, which, in 1914, was the largest ship afloat of any kind. Of course, we have

also reached and now passed the age of the 550,000-ton supertanker as well. Plans are already in hand for 80,000-ton and 90,000-ton cruise liners, the biggest passenger ships ever (surpassing the mightiest of all, the Cunard Line's original *Queen Elizabeth*, built in the late 'thirties and placed at 83,600 tons) and, most ambitious of all, plans have resumed for an eventual 200,000-ton liner that will carry as many as 5,000 passengers and cost over $500 million.

European and Europe-based cruising has not been as wildly successful or as widely expansive, however. Consequently, in this final chapter on German ocean liners, only two of the listed cruise-ships remain (in the summer of 1987) under national colours. The problems for this final group of cruising liners have been largely financial. Generally, it has been too expensive to sail them under the German flag—and with German crews and German tax laws. Secondly, actual service from German ports, namely Bremerhaven and Hamburg, is strictly limited to the peak summer months of June, July and August for trips to the Baltic capitals, the Norwegian fjords, around the British Isles and occasionally on more adventurous jaunts to places like Greenland, Iceland and the Scottish isles. Otherwise, passenger operators must reposition their liners to ports such as Genoa or Piraeus (Greece), and then offer air-sea tours to their clientele. At an average of $275 (about £150) per day, passengers want to spend every ship-board day at least in mild weather, if not warm sunshine.

Furthermore, on all current long cruises, say to South America, East Africa and the Far East, air-sea segments are offered whereby passengers join the ship at places such as Rio or Callao (Lima), Durban or Mombasa, Hong Kong or Singapore, and then remain on board for two, three or even four weeks. (Recently, on a 100-day around-the-world cruise, only 300 out of the 750 passengers made the complete round voyage. All others were continuously changing 'segment passengers'.) Lastly, and perhaps most significant to this final look at German ocean liners, the Germans themselves are not as cruise-oriented as their North American counterparts. There is far more alternative holiday travel in economically prosperous West Germany—ski holidays, motor trips to 'the mountains' as well as to Scandinavia and Italy, and air tours to sunny, beach-filled isles like the Canaries, Majorca and Crete. Furthermore, cruising to many Germans is widely seen as the domain of 'older, richer' travellers and this in itself is limiting.

All of these final liners are one-class cruise-ships. German Atlantic Line, a privately owned successor to the earlier Hamburg Atlantic Line (but without the involvement of its Hamburg America and Home Lines partners) bought its first ship, Israel's Shalom, in 1967 and then recommissioned her as the 'second' Hanseatic (the earlier liner had burned and been scrapped less than two years before). So enthusiastic and optimistic was this new company that it invested not only in the otherwise quickly diminishing North Atlantic trade between Cuxhaven, the Channel ports and New York, but also soon ordered a brand new, highly luxurious liner, a 24,600-tonner and the first to be built in a West German shipyard since 1940. The transatlantic service was soon abandoned, however, and Hanseatic and then the new Hamburg, introduced in the spring of 1969, were used solely for cruising, mostly on long, diverse and expensively-priced trips. Sailing both in European as well as North American service (and for a time coordinated with the illustrious Norwegian America Line), German Atlantic's success coupled with its too rapid expansion was seriously limiting. By the summer of 1973, strained even further by the dramatic increases

in marine fuel oil costs, the company was near bankruptcy. Hanseatic was soon sold off, going to Home Lines to become its Doric, and then, in a bid to capitalize on her supposedly more popular name, the four-year-old Hamburg was quickly renamed Hanseatic. She lasted a mere three months before her owners collapsed completely. Sold to the Soviets and becoming Maxim Gorky, she has been, quite ironically and almost ever since, chartered back to the Germans, to the giant Neckermann travel organization, for worldwide cruising.

The little Boheme, built on a car ferry design but modified as a cruise-ship for the early years of steadily increasing Caribbean cruising out of Florida in the 1970s, was a highy successful ship. She flew the German colours until sold in 1981, and then transferred to the Panamanian flag, the most popular 'flag of convenience' of all. Berlin, completed in 1980, was built for a newcomer to German cruising, the Dielmann Co of Neustadt in Schleswig-Holstein. Her purpose was to serve as a yacht-like cruise-ship, offering smaller, more intimate quarters and atmosphere. She has had moderate success after an unsuccessful charter to the Singapore-based Blue Funnel Cruises, who ran her as Princess Mahsuri, and has been lengthened and given increased accommodaiton for worldwide service.

The creation of the 18,800-ton Astor, built at Hamburg in 1981, was a bold, momentarily encouraging but otherwise completely unsuccessful attempt by an otherwise inexperienced passenger ship firm to enter the luxury cruise business. Her owners, the HADAG Co of Hamburg, had previously owned nothing larger than excursion steamers and harbour ferries, but

The former Shalom *of 1964, German Atlantic's* Hanseatic *had a comparatively short-lived career under the West German flag, from 1967 until 1973 (Schiffsfotos).*

Above Hamburg *of 1969 was the first brand new luxury liner to be built in a West German shipyard since 1940* (German Atlantic Line).

Below *Another view of a luxurious* Hamburg, *with her 'hour glass' funnel, which became a specially recognizable feature of the ship* (Roger Sherlock).

Still sailing in German passenger service, but under charter to the Neckermann organization, the former Hamburg *flies the Soviet colours as* Maxim Gorky *(Luis Miguel Correia).*

wished to rival the continuing success of Hapag-Lloyd, who were simultaneously building their own new de luxe liner, the 33,800-ton *Europa*. While *Astor* was a beautifully decorated liner and popular to some extent (especially as she had been featured in a German version of American television's 'Love Boat' series), her success and therefore her profits were less than encouraging. Within two years, by the autumn of 1983, she was being offered for sale and finally went to South Africa, as an attempt by the South African Marine Corporation (Safmarine Lines) to revive the discontinued, once highly popular Southampton-to-Cape Town 'mailboat' service, which was last offered by Union-Castle Line in 1977. Unsuccessful as this was, and although she was also used for some cruising, she was sold once again in August 1985 to the East German Government who sail her as the *Arkona*. She was replaced by a new, improved and slightly larger *Astor*, completed at Kiel in early 1987, which was owned by the UK-based Morgan Leisure Ltd, but registered in Mauritius. She too has been sold, to the Soviets in 1988.

Since most of the ocean liners mentioned in these pages belonged to either Hamburg America Line or North German Lloyd, it is rather fitting that the last liner is Hapag-Lloyd's *Europa*. She is one of the most beautifully decorated of all current cruise-ships and a ship regarded by many to be in the very top class of cruise-ship categories. At nearly 34,000 tons, she usually carries no more than 600 passengers (although 758 is her maximum capacity) in what are best described as 'exceptionally spacious quarters'. The atmosphere is akin to an exclusive sea-going club, with superb, starched white, almost heel-clicking service and superb cuisine served on impeccable china. She has been, until quite recently, all but exclusively a 'German ship for German passengers' in tone. Now, in the United States, she is being openly marketed to American travellers for the first time. Her itineraries and destinations are continuously diverse, such that some of her passengers, who remain on board for several consecutive cruises, will not repeat a port-of-call. While she makes occasional, mostly summertime sailings from Bremerhaven, she tends more to roam the globe (following a pattern set by earlier liners such as *Reliance* and *Resolute*). While there have been shorter voyages to the nearby Baltic and Norwegian fjords, she also cruises in the Mediterranean and Black seas, to West Africa and the Canaries, and on special longer trips to such areas as the Amazon River, Alaska and the North American Pacific Coast, East African and the Indian Ocean islands, and out to the Far East and Australia. After six years of service, there are few ports which she has not visited.

Above *The Wallenius Lines' Boheme operated out of Miami by the Commodore Cruise Lines was the most popular Caribbean cruise-ship in Florida service for some years (Schiffsfotos).*
Below Berlin, *here arriving at Lisbon, has since been lengthened and given extended passenger accommodation to make her more profitable (Luis Miguel Correia).*

Above   *Hapag's bid to enter luxury cruise service with* Astor *of 1981 was quite unsuccessful, lasting but two years. She is now in East German hands as* Arkona (Antonio Scrimali).

Below   *Hapag-Lloyd's current* Europa, *one of the most luxurious cruise liners of the present-day generation, outbound from Hamburg in her maiden season* (Hapag-Lloyd).

In October 1987, *Europa* made her second call at New York, as part of a two-month-long cruise to North and South America. It was a two-day visit and most of her passengers were 'in transit', camera-toting tourists off on bus trips to a variety of local attractions. The few passengers that were actually 'landed' were almost assuredly air-sea tour participants, returning to Germany or elsewhere in Europe by air. No doubt others were also arriving by air and then joining the ship for a further portion of her cruise. It is, as has been said so often, a completely different passenger ship business today for the last of the big German liners.

Europa—with her stout funnel placed aft, her oval-shaped bow and squared stern, and her unique passenger configuration (cabins forward, public rooms aft)—is an heiress of sorts to the great and grand legacy of the German ocean liner: the gilded opulence of *Kaiser Wilhelm der Grosse*'s first class; the race for the Blue Riband and the challenge with Imperial Britain; the 3,352 steerage berths on the likes of *President Grant* of 1907, on board which passengers paid as little as $10 per person for 'the voyage of a lifetime' to America;

the genius of Albert Ballin; the Kaiser's fascination with the *Imperator* Class and the plan to take the royal family on a post-First World War celebratory victory cruise around the world in no less than the 56,000-ton *Bismarck*; the impressive resurgence of the 'twenties; the plan for the dual, record-breaking maiden voyages of *Bremen* and *Europa* in 1929; 'Strength through Joy' cruising; and those more sinister endings such as the hideous demise of *Wilhelm Gustloff* with as many as 5,200 casualties and still the worst maritime tragedy of all time. And finally, in 1971, *Bremen* running the last German-flag passage on the North Atlantic.

In all, it is a wonderful fleet, assembled in something of a glorious review in these pages, which were prompted by the 75th anniversary of the commissioning of the mighty and majestic *Imperator*. With *Kaiser Wilhelm der Grosse*, the coverage actually begins in 1897, over 90 years ago. However, there is no doubt yet more to be written, in greater detail and highlighted by enlightening personal anecdotes and recollections, about these ships, this fleet of *German Ocean Liners of the 20th Century*.

Hanseatic

(German Atlantic Line)

Service Hamburg (Cuxhaven)-Southampton-New York; mostly cruising, in North American and European waters.
Specifications 25,338 gross tons, 629 × 82 ft (193 × 25 m).
Builder Chantiers de L'Atlantique, St Nazaire, France, 1964.
Machinery Steam turbines, twin screw. Service speed 20 knots.
Capacity 148 first class, 864 tourist class; 650 single-class for cruises.

1962 10 Nov: Launched; original name to be *King Solomon*, then *King David* before choice of *Shalom*. Owned by Zim Lines, Israeli flag; flagship and largest liner in Israeli merchant fleet.
1964 Apr: Entered service from Haifa and other Mediterranean ports to New York; also off-season Caribbean cruising.
1964 Oct: Refitted at Schiedam, Holland; accommodation restyled for 148 first class, 1,018 tourist class.
1964 26 Nov: Rammed Norwegian tanker *Stolt Dagali* off Ambrose Light, New York; 19 killed on board tanker. $575,000 damage later repaired at Brooklyn shipyard.
1967 May: Sold to German Atlantic Line for £5.6 million.
1967 Nov: Delivered to German Atlantic, West German flag; renamed *Hanseatic*.
1967 Dec: Maiden cruise.
1969 Transatlantic sailings discontinued; cruising only.
1973 Aug: Sold to Home Lines, Panamanian flag; renamed *Doric*. Refitted and accommodation restyled for 945 single-class.
1974 Jan: Entered Home Lines service; winters from Port Everglades to Caribbean, remainder of year between New York and Bermuda.
1981 Jan: Sold to Royal Cruise Lines, Greek flag.
1982 Feb: Delivered to Royal Cruise and renamed *Royal Odyssey*. Accommodation restyled for 798 single-class. Entered cruise service in Northern Europe and Mediterranean waters, later North America and South Pacific.
1988 Oct: Sold and transferred to Regency Cruises, Panamanian flag; renamed *Regent Sun*. Caribbean and European cruising.

Hamburg

(German Atlantic Line)

Service Occasional 'positioning voyages' Hamburg (Cuxhaven)-Southampton-New York, but mostly long and luxurious cruising to Pacific Mediterranean, South America, North Cape, etc. Sailings from New York, Port Everglades, San Francisco, Los Angeles as well as Cuxhaven and Genoa.
Specifications 24,692 gross tons, 642 × 90 ft (197 × 28 m).
Builder Deutsche Werft, Hamburg, West Germany, 1969.
Machinery Steam turbines, twin screw. Service speed 21 knots.
Capacity 600 cruise passengers (790 maximum berths).

1966 1 Apr: Ordered as West Germany's first newly built post-war passenger liner.
1968 21 Feb: Launched. Intended for summer season transatlantic service to New York and off-season cruising, but near completion owners revised plans to full-time cruise service.
1969 Jan: Delayed by engine problems. Mar: Maiden cruise, Hamburg-South America. Jun: Maiden crossing to New York.
1972 Feb: Began cruising in Pacific waters from California.
1973 Sept: Despite owners' increasing financial problems, renamed *Hanseatic* for further service. Dec: Withdrawn from service and ended operations for German Atlantic Line. Laid up then reportedly sold to Ryutsu Kaiun K K, Japanese Flag; never materialized. Later sold to Robin International, Liberian flag, as agents for Black Sea Steamship Co, Odessa. Renamed *Maxim Gorky*, Soviet flag.
1974 Feb: Briefly chartered to United Artists as floating 'prop' for film *Juggernaut*; temporarily renamed *Britannic* and used in waters off Scotland.
1974–75 Soviet-flag cruising from New York.
1975 Nov: Damaged by bomb explosion at San Juan during Caribbean cruise. Dec: Reassigned to European-based cruising, often sailing under charter to Neckermann organization of Frankfurt. Still in Soviet service.

Boheme

(Wallenius Lines)

Service 7-day cruises from Miami to Caribbean ports.
Specifications 10,328 gross tons, 441 × 68 ft (136 × 21 m).
Builder Wartsila Shipyards, Turku, Finland, 1986.
Machinery Sulzer diesels, twin screw. Service speed 21 knots.
Capacity 480 cruise passengers only.

1968 12 Feb: Launched.
1968 Nov: Completed; entered North American cruise service, managed and operated by Commodore Cruise Lines, Miami.
1981 Sold to Sally Shipping GmbH, but transferred to subsidiary, Hanseatic Caribbean Shipping Co, Panamanian flag. Remained in Caribbean cruise service.
1986 Sold to International Association of Scientologists for conversion to seagoing religious retreat. Renamed *Freewinds*; owner listed as San Donato Properties Corp, Panamanian flag. Laid up at Curacao.

Berlin

(Reederi Peter Deilmann)

Service Cruising from German ports in Northern waters, also Mediterranean and Caribbean voyages and occasional longer cruises to Indian Ocean and Far Eastern waters.
Specifications 7,813 gross tons; 402 × 56 ft (124 × 17 m).
Builder HDW Shipyards, Kiel, West Germany, 1980.
Machinery Diesels, twin screw. Service speed 17½ knots.
Capacity 330 cruise passengers.

1980 Completed for cruising with German passengers.
1982–84 Chartered to Blue Funnel Cruises, Singapore, but retained West German registry; temporarily renamed *Princess Mahsuri*. South-east Asian and Pacific cruising from Singapore as well as Australian ports; unsuccessful.
1984 Dec: Returned to owners and European waters. Reverted to original name.
1986 Nov: Refitted and lengthened to 458 ft (141 m); tonnage increased to 10,000. Accommodation extended for 470 cruise passengers.
1986 Jan: Began cruising in Caribbean waters during winter season.

Astor

(HADAG)

Service Cruising in Northern European and Mediterranean waters, later to North and South America.
Specifications 18,835 gross tons, 538 × 74 ft (165 × 23 m).
Builder HDW Shipyards, Hamburg, West Germany, 1981.
Machinery MAN diesels, twin screw. Service speed 18 knots.
Capacity 638 cruise passengers only.

1980 16 Dec: Launched for HADAG (Hadag Seetouristik & Fahrdienst AG); intended name *Hammonia*, but changed to *Astor*.
1981 21 May: Fire damage while still at shipyard; completion delayed by four months.
1983 Oct: Unsuccessful as West German passenger ship; sold to South African Marine Corporation (Safmarine Lines), South African flag, but retained original name.
1984 Feb: Handed over to South Africans and later used to resume Cape Town-Southampton mail service; also considerable cruising.
1985 July: Registry changed to Bahamas. Aug: Sold and delivered to East German Government (Deutsche Seereederi); renamed *Arkona*. Began cruising from Rostock, later chartered for use in West German cruise trades.

Europa

(Hapag-Lloyd)

Service Year-round cruising (7 to 100 days); sailings from Bremerhaven and Genoa.
Specifications 33,819 gross tons, 655 × 93 ft (201 × 29 m)
Builder Bremer Vulkan, Vegesack, West Germany, 1981.
Machinery MAN diesels, twin screw. Service speed 21 knots.
Capacity 758 cruise passengers only.

1980 22 Dec: Launched.
1981 Dec: Delivered to Hapag-Lloyd.
1982 Jan: Maiden cruise from Genoa to North African ports.
1985 July: Damaged during special cruise to Greenland; repaired and resumed service.

Epilogue

I last visited Bremerhaven, once the German gateway for transatlantic liners, in the summer of 1982. In earlier years, in the 'thirties, the giant *Bremen* and *Europa*, among others, berthed alongside the famed Columbus Quay. Then, after the war, other notable passenger queens like *United States*, *America* and *France* called. There was also another *Bremen*, and another *Europa* as well. But by the time of my visit, and just as with other ports such as Southampton, Le Havre and Cherbourg, the pace had lessened noticeably, the tone quite different. Today, Bremerhaven is essentially a cargo and a shipyard port (with the latter facilities handling such recent tasks as the transformation of *France* into *Norway*, the lengthening of the three Royal Viking Line cruise-ships, the face-lifting of several Soviet passenger ships and the re-engining of *QE2*). The remains of the Columbus Quay now mostly receive summer cruise-ships bound for Scandinavia and the Baltic and, at that time, the every-other-day schedule of an 8,000-ton ferry out of Harwich, England. But even that has changed. By that December, *Prins Oberon* had made her last run from Bremerhaven since her owners, DFDS-Prins Ferries, decided to place their efforts on the North Sea–German trade out of Hamburg. But if the port of Bremerhaven itself has changed, it has at least two very notable possessions: the presence of the German Maritime Museum and its librarian, the well-known ocean liner historian and author Arnold Kludas. In both, those earlier more colourful days are alive and well.

The Museum, located in the heart of the City and along the riverbank, is one of the finest of its kind in the world. It is housed in a modern complex, centring around a main structure which was completed in 1975, a mere four years after the initial founding of the Museum itself. Other progress has been equally remarkable. As befits what is the National Maritime Museum, the site already had six preserved and restored vessels: several tugs, a lightship and a four-masted schooner, *Saute Deern*, dating from 1919.

However, the interior is a particular treasure chest, especially to the passenger ship enthusiast. A centrepiece is the 12-ft long model of that grand three-stacker, *Cap Arcona*. Six 'sister' models were built when the liner itself was new, in 1927, but five were destroyed in the war. This magnificent remainder, surely in the top class of ocean liner modelling, is presently valued at over $250,000. Sitting nearby is another perfectly detailed miniature, although in a smaller scale, Hamburg America's *Reliance* of 1920.

The model collection, now numbering over 50 items, also includes a rather extraordinary acquisition. A 2-ft long model of the giant *Imperator*, the largest liner in the world in 1913, rests in a glass case in flood-lit perfection. This gem of a piece is done completely in sterling silver, down to every last lifeboat (there were 83 of them on board) and even to every strand of rigging. The model was made for the Vulkan Shipyards of Hamburg in 1912 as a present to the Kaiser, who had consented to launch the liner. However, the Kaiser was so thrilled with the ship's creation and the superlative distinctions she brought to Imperial Germany that he in turn gave the model to Albert Ballin, then the resident genius and guiding force of the Hamburg America Line, the ship's owners. Graciously, Ballin accepted the exquisite piece. Later, even after his death in 1919, it remained with the Ballin family. However, its more recent history is somewhat clouded, at least according to Arnold Kudas. Its whereabouts were unknown for some years. Then, in 1978 and rather mysteriously it was presented to the Museum, not by the Ballin family, but by the original German silversmiths who made it.

Other intriguing ocean liner items include furnishings, woodwork and deck pieces. A complete first class bedroom from *Cap Polonio*, the flagship of the Hamburg-South America Line fleet in 1914, has been added to the Museum. The liner itself was scrapped in 1935 at a dockyard site less than a mile away, and most of the passenger furnishings were sold off to a local hotel. Then, some forty years later, when the Museum opened, several items of furniture were contributed by the present hotel owners. Other furnishings come from *Kaiser Wilhelm der Grosse*, the first of the Atlantic's four-stackers and the first of the so-called 'superliners', dating from 1897. There are also mirrored wood panels and carvings from another of Germany's grand turn-of-the-century four-funnel queens, *Kronprinzessin Cecilie*. Such pieces remained with that exiled liner almost to the very end of her days, even as she lay rusting in the backwaters of Chesapeake Bay in the late 'thirties (the ship had been seized by the US Government during the First World War and, while used as a troop-ship, was never again involved in peacetime service). The mirrors and the wooden pieces came off her just before final demolition at Baltimore in 1940. They were presented to the Museum by Ralph E. Whitney of St Petersburg, Florida.

The 400lb bronze bell from *Imperator* dominates a prized collection of others—from the likes of at least two earlier liners named *Bremen* and from *Cap Polonio*. *Imperator*'s bell, although made in Germany for a German-flag liner, had actually spent most of its seventy-odd years in America. In 1919, when the ship first revisited New York after a long wartime lay-up at Hamburg, the bell was removed and hauled ashore. It was evidently considered inappropriate, particularly as the ship briefly became USS *Imperator* and then went on to Britain as reparations, becoming *Berengaria* for Cunard.

The bell went first to a private collector in, of all rather unlikely places, Booth Bay in Maine. From there, it passed on to the Bath Maritime Museum and then on to another collector at Brooksville, another Maine location. An American named Alli Ryan was instrumental in getting the bell back to its rightful home, in Germany. Together with Arnold Kludas, who crossed the North Atlantic to make the final preparations, the bell was delivered to the Museum in 1979. Rather symbolically, it was shipped in a Hamburg America container-ship, an heiress of sorts to the legacy of such earlier ships as *Imperator*.

Other interesting pieces at the Museum include a tapestry from one of the lounges of the Blue Riband holder *Bremen* of 1929. It seems to be one of the few items rescued from that exceptional vessel before her sudden and fatal demise by fire along the Bremerhaven docks in March 1941. Her last remains, the final pieces of her double bottom, still poke above the waters of the River Weser in a position not too distant from the Museum itself. Glass showcases contain other North German Lloyd and Hamburg America memorabilia: uniforms, brass buttons, silver pieces, china and even printed items such as menu cards, daily programmes and passenger lists. The art collection is a revolving

one. During my visit, there was a notably outstanding collection on view that included some superb works on German transatlantic steamers of the teens and 'twenties. A spectacular boat deck view of *Columbus* at sea is indelibly etched in my memory.

Arnold Kludas supervises the Museum's Library, containing over 25,000 volumes on international shipping, 10,000 photos, 15,000 ship's plans and other archival material; it is the only Museum in Germany to have *Lloyd's Register* from 1878 to the present. Kludas himself has a superb first-hand knowledge of the collection, and together with a small staff, he records and organizes a continual daily flow of new acquisitions and seemingly endless array of magazines, newsletters and reports on topics ranging from Danish fisheries to shipbuilding in South Korea to Nile River boats.

Kludas is, in a word, brilliant. He has a sharp knowledge combined with a strong, deliberate energy that allows for almost total devotion to this, his favourite subject. His personal accomplishments are almost legendary, certainly most impressive. He has written 28 different books to date, including the six-volume *Great Passenger Ships of the World* series, which is regarded by many to be the finest work of its kind, surely the classic reference piece. These were published in the mid-'seventies, first in German and then later published in English. The sixth volume is an update which first appeared in 1983 and was then revised further still in 1987. Other Kludas titles have included a three-volume set on all the ships of Hamburg America Line (including every tug, tender and coaster, and a work used by that noted firm itself), fleet histories of both the Hamburg-South America and German-East Africa lines, another work entitled *German Hospital Ships During World War II* and even one on *German Reefers* (refrigerated cargo ships).

Kludas was born in what is now part of East Germany. His early fascination with ships began with a visit to the port of Hamburg, a fascinating place that still retains a 'ship-moving, barge-filled, working port' atmosphere to this day. He joined the illustrious Blohm & Voss shipyards at Hamburg in 1955, a year after they were permitted by the Allies to resume their shipbuilding division. Kludas was assigned to their 'standardization and rationalization' department, preparing outlines for the production of ships. He had eighteen years at the Yard, including a final three as librarian for the company's staff library. Beginning in 1972, and for four years afterwards, he was an editor with the now-defunct Stalling Publishing Company, best known in Germany for their maritime titles. He joined the Bremerhaven Museum in 1976 as librarian.

The Maritime Museum at Bremerhaven is more

than worth the time and effort of a visit. Its fascinating displays and historic pieces must be seen by any maritime enthusiast. Its future seems assured, the size of the collection ever growing. Kludas himself remains as busy as ever (at the time of writing, he has a multi-volume set on all German passenger ship companies well in hand). There is yet more to come on the subject of German ocean liners.

Bibliography

Bonsor, N.R.P. *North Atlantic Seaway* (Volumes 1–5). Jersey, Channel Islands: Brookside Publications, 1975–80.

Bonsor, N.R.P. *South Atlantic Seaway*. Jersey, Channel Islands: Brookside Publications, 1983.

Braynard, Frank O. *Leviathan: Story of the World's Greatest Ship* (Volumes 1–5). New York: South Street Seaport Museum, 1972–81.

Braynard, Frank O. *Lives of the Liners*. New York: Cornell Maritime Press, 1947.

Braynard, Frank O. and Miller, William H. *Fifty Famous Liners* (Volumes 1–3). Wellingborough: Patrick Stephens Ltd, 1982–86.

Brinnin, John Malcolm. *The Sway of the Grand Saloon*. London: Macmillan London Ltd, 1972.

Cairis, Nicholas T. *North Atlantic Passenger Liners Since 1900*. London: Ian Allan Ltd, 1972.

Crowdy, Michael (editor). *Marine News* (1964–87). Kendal, Cumbria: World Ship Society.

Devol, George (editor). *Ocean & Cruise News* (1980–87). Stamford, Connecticut: World Ocean & Cruise Society.

Dunn, Laurence. *Passenger Liners*. Southampton: Adlard Coles Ltd, 1961.

Eisele, Peter (editor). *Steamboat Bill* (1966–87). New York: Steamship Historical Society of America Inc.

Hodgins, Eric. *Ocean Express: The Story of the Bremen and the Europa*. New York: North German Lloyd, 1932.

Horton White, A.G. *Ships of the North Atlantic*. London: Sampson Low, Marston & Co Ltd, 1937.

Kludas, Arnold. *Great Passenger Ships of the World* (Volumes 1–6). Wellingborough: Patrick Stephens Ltd, 1972–76, 1986.

Kludas, Arnold. *The Ships of the German-Africa Line*. Oldenburg: Verlag Gerhard Stalling AG, 1975.

Kludas, Arnold. *The Ships of the Hamburg Sud 1871–1951*. Oldenburg: Verlag Gerhard Stalling AG, 1976.

Miller, William H. *The Great Luxury Liners 1927–54*. New York: Dover Publications Inc, 1981.

Miller, William H. *Transatlantic Liners 1945–80*. Newton Abbot, Devon: David & Charles Ltd, 1981.

Miller, William H. *The First Great Ocean Liners 1897–1927*. New York: Dover Publications Inc, 1984.

Prager, Hans Georg. *Blohm & Voss: Ships and Machinery for the World*. Herford: Koehlers Verlagsgesellschaft, 1977.

Schmidt, Robert and Kludas, Arnold. *Die Deutschen Lazarettschiffe in Zweiten Weltkrieg*. Stuttgart: Motorbuch Verlag, 1978.

Shaum, John H. and Flayhart, William H. *Majesty at Sea*. Wellingborough: Patrick Stephens Ltd, 1981.

Witthoft, Hans Jurgen. *Hapag-Lloyd*. Herford: Koehlers Verlagsgesellschaft, 1979.

Across the Atlantic. New York: Hamburg America Line, 1912.

Die Hapag-Riesen: Der Imperator Klasse. Hildesheim: Olms Presse, 1978.

Die Lloyd-Schnelldampfer. Hildesheim: Olms Presse, 1975.

Der Ozean-Express. Hildesheim: Olms Presse, 1976.

Appendix I:
The 25 largest German ocean liners

	Name	Date built	Gross tonnage	Owner
1	*Bismarck	1914–22	56,551	Hapag
2	Vaterland	1914	54,282	Hapag
3	Imperator	1913	52,117	Hapag
4	Bremen	1929	51,656	NGL
5	Europa	1930	49,746	NGL
6	*Vaterland	1940	41,000	Hapag
7	Europa	1981	33,819	Hapag-Lloyd
8	Hindenburg/Columbus	1914–23	32,354	NGL
9	Bremen	1939	32,336	NGL
10	*Columbus	1913–22	32,000	NGL
11	Hanseatic	1930	30,029	Hamburg Atlantic
12	Cap Arcona	1927	27,650	Hamburg Sud
13	Robert Ley	1939	27,288	Workers' Front
14	George Washington	1909	25,570	NGL
15	Wilhelm Gustloff	1938	25,484	Workers' Front
16	Hanseatic	1964	25,338	German Atlantic
17	Hamburg	1964	24,692	German Atlantic
18	Kaiserin Auguste Victoria	1906	24,581	Hapag
19	New York	1927	22,337	Hapag
20	Amerika	1905	22,225	Hapag
21	Hamburg	1926	22,117	Hapag
22	Europa	1953	21,514	NGL
23	*Tirpitz	1913–20	21,498	Hapag
24	Albert Ballin	1923	21,131	Hapag
25	Deutschland	1923	21,046	Hapag

* Did not sail commercially for German owners.

Appendix II:
The 25 longest German ocean liners

	Name	Date built	Overall length in ft(m)	Owner
1	*Bismarck	1914–22	956 (294)	Hapag
2	Vaterland	1914	950 (292.25)	Hapag
3	Bremen	1929	938 (288.5)	NGL
4	Europa	1930	936 (288)	NGL
5	Imperator	1913	919 (282.75)	Hapag
6	*Vaterland	1940	824 (253.5)	Hapag
7	Hindenburg/Columbus	1914–23	775 (238.5)	NGL
8	*Columbus	1913–22	774 (238)	NGL
9	George Washington	1909	723 (222.5)	NGL
10	Kronprinzessin Cecilie	1907	707 (217.5)	NGL
11	Kaiser Wilhelm II	1903	707 (217.5)	NGL
12	Kaiserin Auguste Victoria	1906	705 (217.5)	Hapag
13	Amerika	1905	700 (215.25)	Hapag
14	Bremen	1939	697 (214.5)	NGL
15	Deutschland	1900	684 (210.5)	Hapag
16	Wilhelm Gustloff	1938	684 (210.5)	Workers' Front
17	Hamburg	1926	677 (208.25)	Hapag
18	New York	1927	677 (208.25)	Hapag
19	Albert Ballin	1923	677 (208.25)	Hapag
20	Deutschland	1923	677 (208.25)	Hapag
21	Cap Arcona	1927	676 (208)	Hamburg Sud
22	Hanseatic	1930	672 (206.75)	Hamburg Atlantic
23	Robert Ley	1939	669 (206)	Workers' Front
24	Kronprinz Wilhelm	1901	664 (204.25)	NGL
25	Cap Polonio	1914–15	662 (203.75)	Hamburg Sud

* Did not sail commercially for German owners.

Appendix III:
Major German passenger ship losses 1939–45

Date of loss	Name	Circumstances
1939 Dec	*Columbus*	Scuttled off Virginia, USA
1941 16 Mar	*Bremen*	Destroyed by fire at Bremerhaven
1942 26 Feb	*Monte Sarmiento*	Bombed and sunk at Kiel
1943 2 May	*Gneisenau*	Mined and sunk off Denmark
25 July	*General Artigas*	Destroyed in air raid on Hamburg
25 July	*Vaterland*	Destroyed in air raid on Hamburg
9 Oct	*Stuttgart*	Bombed at Gdynia
1944 30 Aug	*St Louis*	Damaged in air raid at Kiel
17 Nov	*Scharnhorst*	Torpedoed and sunk near Shanghai
1945 30 Jan	*Wilhelm Gustloff*	Mined in the Baltic
1 Feb	*Berlin*	Mined off Swinemunde
9 Feb	*Steuben*	Torpedoed in the Baltic
16 Feb	*Monte Rosa*	Mined off Gdynia
6 Mar	*Hansa (ex-Albert Ballin)*	Mined off Warnemunde
7 Mar	*Hamburg*	Mined near Sassnitz
24 Mar	*Robert Ley*	Bombed at Hamburg
3 Apr	*Monte Olivia*	Bombed at Kiel
3 Apr	*New York*	Bombed at Kiel
9 Apr	*General Osorio*	Bombed at Kiel
3 May	*Cap Arcona*	Bombed and sunk in the Baltic
3 May	*Deutschland*	Bombed and sunk in Lubeck Bay

Appendix IV:
General reference table for German ocean liners

Name	Owner	Date built	Gross tonnage	Dimensions in feet	Machinery	Speed	Number of passengers
Albert Ballin	Hapag	1923	20,815	627 × 72	Steam turb	15½	1,551
Amerika	Hapag	1905	22,225	700 × 74	Quad expan	17½	2,662
Antonio Delfino	Hamb Sud	1922	13,589	526 × 64	Trip expan	13½	1,886
Astor	Hadag	1981	18,835	538 × 74	Diesel	18	638
Bahia Castillo	Hamb Sud	1913	9,948	510 × 61	Trip expan	12	2,702
Barbarossa	NGL	1897	10,769	548 × 60	Quad expan	14½	2,392
Bayernstein	NGL	1954	8,999	538 × 64	Diesel	16½	86
Berlin	NGL	1909	17,323	613 × 69	Quad expan	19	3,212
Berlin	NGL	1925	15,286	572 × 69	Trip expan	16	1,122
Berlin	NGL	1925	18,600	590 × 74	Diesel	16½	976
Berlin	Deilmann	1980	7,813	402 × 56	Diesel	17½	330
Bismarck	Hapag	1914–22	56,551	956 × 100	Steam turb	23½	3,500
Blucher	Hapag	1902	12,334	550 × 62	Quad expan	16½	2,102
Boheme	Wallenius	1968	10,328	441 × 68	Diesel	21	480
Bremen	NGL	1897	10,552	550 × 60	Quad expan	14½	2,330
Bremen	NGL	1929	51,656	938 × 102	Steam turb	27	2,200
Bremen	NGL	1939	32,336	697 × 88	Steam turb	23	1,122
Cap Arcona	Hamb Sud	1927	27,650	676 × 84	Steam turb	20	1,315
Cap Finisterre	Hamb Sud	1911	14,503	591 × 65	Quad expan	16½	1,389
Cap Norte	Hamb Sud	1922	13,615	526 × 64	Trip expan	13½	1,886
Cap Polonio	Hamb Sud	1914–15	20,576	662 × 72	Trip expan	17	1,555
Cap Trafalgar	Hamb Sud	1914	18,805	613 × 72	Trip expan	17	1,587
Caribia	Hapag	1933	12,049	524 × 65	Diesel	17	409
Cincinnati	Hapag	1909	16,339	603 × 63	Quad expan	15½	2,827
Cleveland	Hapag	1909	16,960	607 × 63	Quad expan	15½	2,841
*Columbus	NGL	1913–22	32,000	774 × 82	Trip expan	18	2,750
Columbus	NGL	1914–23	32,354	775 × 83	Trip expan	19	1,792
Cordillera	Hapag	1933	12,055	524 × 65	Diesel	17	419
Der Deutsche	NGL	1924	11,453	511 × 61	Trip expan	13	1,000
Deutschland	Hapag	1900	16,502	684 × 67	Quad expan	22½	2,050
Deutschland	Hapag	1923	20,607	627 × 72	Steam turb	15½	1,558
Dresden	NGL	1915	14,690	570 × 67	Quad expan	15½	971
Europa	NGL	1930	49,746	936 × 102	Steam turb	27	2,124
Europa	NGL	1953	21,514	600 × 77	Diesel	19	843
Europa	Hapag	1981	33,819	655 × 93	Diesel	21	758
Frankfurt	Hapag	1954	8,974	538 × 64	Diesel	16½	86

Name	Owner	Date built	Gross tonnage	Dimensions in feet	Machinery	Speed	Number of passengers
Friedrich der Grosse	NGL	1896	10,531	546 × 60	Quad expan	14½	2,423
General Artigas	Hapag	1923	11,254	495 × 60	Steam turb	13½	561
General Belgrano	Hamb Sud	1913	10,056	510 × 61	Trip expan	12	684
General Osorio	Hapag	1929	11,590	528 × 66	Diesel	15	980
General San Martin	Hapag	1922	11,251	495 × 60	Steam turb	13½	561
General von Steuben	NGL	1923	14,690	551 × 65	Trip expan	15	793
Gneisenau	NGL	1935	18,160	651 × 74	Steam turb	21	293
George Washington	NGL	1909	25,570	723 × 72	Quad expan	18½	2,679
Graf Waldersee	Hapag	1899	12,830	586 × 62	Quad expan	13	2,546
Grosser Kurfurst	NGL	1900	13,182	581 × 62	Trip expan	15	2,989
Hamburg	Hapag	1900	10,532	521 × 60	Quad expan	15½	2,170
Hamburg	Hapag	1926	21,132	635 × 72	Steam turb	15½	1,149
Hamburg	Hapag	1954	8,959	538 × 64	Diesel	16½	86
Hamburg	Germ Atl	1969	24,692	642 × 90	Steam turb	21	790
Hannover	Hapag	1954	9,008	538 × 64	Diesel	16½	86
Hansa	Hapag	1900	16,333	684 × 67	Steam turb	17½	1,386
Hansa	Hapag	1923	21,131	677 × 72	Steam turb	19½	965
Hanseatic	Hamb Atl	1930	30,029	672 × 83	Steam turb	21	1,252
Hanseatic	Germ Atl	1964	25,338	629 × 82	Steam turb	20	1,012
Hessenstein	NGL	1954	8,929	538 × 64	Diesel	16½	86
Imperator	Hapag	1913	52,117	909 × 98	Steam turb	23	4,601
Kaiser Friedrich	NGL	1898	12,481	600 × 63	Quad expan	19	1,350
Kaiser Wilhelm II	NGL	1903	19,361	707 × 72	Quad expan	23	1,888
Kaiser Wilhelm der Grosse	NGL	1897	14,349	655 × 66	Trip expan	22	1,970
Kaiserin Auguste Victoria	Hapag	1906	24,581	705 × 77	Quad expan	17½	2,780
Kiautschou	Hapag	1900	10,911	540 × 60	Quad expan	15½	2,210
Konig Albert	NGL	1899	10,643	521 × 60	Quad expan	15½	2,175
Konigin Luise	NGL	1897	10,566	552 × 60	Quad expan	14½	2,400
Kronprinz Wilhelm	NGL	1901	14,908	664 × 66	Quad expan	22½	2,761
Kronprinzessin Cecilie	NGL	1907	19,360	707 × 72	Quad expan	23	1,808
Main	NGL	1900	10,067	520 × 58	Quad expan	14½	3,451
Milwaukee	Hapag	1929	16,669	575 × 79	Diesel	16½	957
Moltke	Hapag	1902	12,335	550 × 60	Quad expan	16	2,102
Monte Cervantes	Hamb Sud	1928	13,913	524 × 66	Diesel	14	2,492
Monte Olivia	Hamb Sud	1925	13,750	524 × 66	Diesel	14	2,528
Monte Pascoal	Hamb Sud	1930	13,870	524 × 66	Diesel	14	2,408
Monte Rosa	Hamb Sud	1931	13,882	524 × 66	Diesel	14	2,408
Monte Sarmiento	Hamb Sud	1924	13,625	524 × 66	Diesel	14	2,470
*Munchen	NGL	1914–23	18,940	615 × 71	Quad expan	17	1,442
Munchen	NGL	1923	13,325	551 × 65	Trip expan	15	1,079
New York	Hapag	1927	21,455	635 × 72	Steam turb	15½	1,032
Patria	Hapag	1938	16,595	584 × 74	Diesel	16	349
Patricia	Hapag	1899	13,023	585 × 62	Quad expan	13	2,489
Pennland	Red Star	1913–22	16,332	600 × 67	Trip expan	15	550
Pennsylvania	Hapag	1897	12,891	579 × 62	Quad expan	13	2,724
Potsdam	NGL	1935	17,528	634 × 74	Steam turb	21	286
President Grant	Hapag	1903–07	18,072	616 × 68	Quad expan	14½	3,830
President Lincoln	Hapag	1903–07	18,168	616 × 68	Quad expan	14½	3,828
Pretoria	Hapag	1898	12,800	586 × 62	Quad expan	13	2,579

Name	Owner	Date built	Gross tonnage	Dimensions in feet	Machinery	Speed	Number of passengers
Pretoria	Germ-E Afr	1936	16,662	577 × 72	Steam turb	18	490
Prinz Friedrich Wilhelm	NGL	1908	17,082	613 × 68	Quad expan	17	2,519
Prinzess Irene	NGL	1900	10,881	540 × 60	Quad expan	15½	2,354
Reliance	Hapag	1914–20	19,582	615 × 71	Trip expan	16	1,010
Resolute	Hapag	1914–20	19,653	616 × 72	Trip expan	16	1,010
Rhein	NGL	1899	10,058	520 × 58	Quad expan	14½	3,451
Robert Ley	Wkrs' Front	1939	27,288	669 × 78	Diesel	15½	1,774
St Louis	Hapag	1929	16,732	574 × 72	Diesel	16	973
Scharnhorst	NGL	1935	18,184	652 × 74	Turbo-elec	21	293
Schwabenstein	NGL	1953	8,955	538 × 64	Diesel	16½	86
Seven Seas	Eur-Canada	1940	12,575	492 × 69	Diesel	16½	1,007
Sierra Cordoba	NGL	1923	11,469	511 × 61	Trip expan	14	2,065
Sierra Morena	NGL	1923	11,430	511 × 61	Trip expan	14	2,065
Sierra Nevada	NGL	1922	13,589	526 × 64	Steam turb	15	1,886
Sierra Salvada	NGL	1922	13,615	526 × 64	Steam turb	15	1,886
Sierra Ventana	NGL	1923	11,392	511 × 61	Trip expan	14	1,113
Steuben	NGL	1923	14,690	551 × 65	Trip expan	15	484
Stuttgart	NGL	1923	13,325	551 × 60	Trip expan	15	1,103
*Tirpitz	Hapag	1913–20	21,498	615 × 75	Steam turb	16½	1,975
Thuringia	Hapag	1922	11,343	495 × 60	Steam turb	13½	811
Vaterland	Hapag	1914	54,282	950 × 100	Steam turb	23	3,909
*Vaterland	Hapag	1940	41,000	824 × 98	Turbo-elec	23½	1,322
Victoria Luise	Hapag	1900	16,703	684 × 67	Steam turb	17½	487
Westernland	Red Star	1914–22	16,314	601 × 67	Trip expan	15	550
Westphalia	Hapag	1923	11,343	495 × 60	Steam turb	13½	802
Wilhelm Gustloff	Wkrs' Front	1938	25,484	684 × 77	Diesel	15½	1,465
Windhuk	Germ-E Afr	1937	16,662	577 × 72	Steam turb	18	490

Quad expan = Quadruple expansion
Trip expan = Triple expansion
Steam turb = Steam turbine
Turbo-elec = Turbo-electric

* Did not sail in commercial service for German owners.

Index

Admiral Hipper, 120
Admiral Nakhimov, 112
Admiral von Tirpitz, 95
Aeolus, 33
Agamemnon, 23
Albert Ballin, 127
Albertic, 109
Alkaid, 110
Alphard, 128
America, 54
Amerika, 54
Ammerland, 110
Aniva, 164
Antonio Delfino, 119
Arabic, 60
Arkona, 196
Astor, 196
Audacious, 60

Bahia Castillo, 119
Barbarossa, 30
Batavia, 41
Bayernstein, 184
Belgia, 41
Belgravia, 41
Berengaria, 86
Berlin (1909), 60
Berlin (1925), 112
Berlin (1925, ex-Gripsholm), 185
Berlin (1980), 196
Bismarck, 87
Blucher, 34
Boheme, 196
Borussia, 34
Brabantia, 96
Brasilia, 40
Bremen (1897), 31
Bremen (1929), 153
Bremen (1939), 186
Britannic, 195
Bulgaria, 40
Burdigala, 47

Caledonia, 87
Canada, 40
Cap Arcona, 142

Cap Finisterre, 71
Cap Norte, 120
Cap Polonio, 72
Cap Trafalgar, 72
Caribia, 113
Carmania, 72
Catlin, 55
Cincinnati, 61
City of Honolulu, 30
City of Los Angeles, 33
Cleveland, 61
Columbus (1913–22), 91
Columbus (1914–23), 91
Columbus C, 187
Constantinople, 31
Cordillera, 113
Covington, 61

Der Deutsche, 121
Deutschland (1900), 22
Deutschland (1923), 127
Doric, 195
Dresden, 109

Edison, 31
Edmund B Alexander, 54
Elbe V, 37
Empire Deben, 110
Empire Doon, 163
Empire Fowey, 162
Empire Halladale, 119
Empire Jewel, 162
Empire Orwell, 163
Empire Trooper, 120
Empire Waveney, 113
Empire Welland, 164
Empire Windrush, 142
Empress of Australia, 95
Empress of China, 60, 95
Empress of India, 60
Empress of Japan, 187
Empress of Scotland (1906), 55
Empress of Scotland (1930), 187
Eolo, 32
Europa (1930), 153
Europa (1953), 187

Europa (1981), 196

Ferdinando Palasciano, 32
Filipinas Saudi I, 186
Frankfurt, 184
Freewinds, 196
Freiderich der Grosse, 30

General Artigas, 110
General Belgrano, 119
General Osorio, 121
General San Martin, 110, 119
General von Steuben, 111
George Washington, 55
Gneisenau, 163
Graf Waldersee, 37
Grenadier, 71
Gripsholm, 185
Grosser Kurfurst, 33
Gunung Djati, 163

Hamburg (1900), 32
Hamburg (1926), 128
Hamburg (1954), 184
Hamburg (1969), 195
Hanover, 184
Hansa (1900), 22
Hansa (1923), 127
Hanseatic (1930), 187
Hanseatic (1964), 195
Hanseatic (1969), 195
Havelland, 110
Hercules, 40
Hessenstein, 185
Highflyer, 19
Hindenburg, 91
Homeric, 91
Hudson, 32
Huron, 30
Hyperion, 91

Ilitch, 113
Imperator, 86
Incemore, 23
Instructor, 54
Irishman, 41

Italia, 32

Johann Heinrich Burchard, 96

Kaiser Friedrich, 47
Kaiser Wilhelm II, 23
Kaiser Wilhelm der Grosse, 21
Kaiserin Auguste Victoria, 55
Karlsruhe, 33
Kiautschou, 34
King Alexander, 31
Konig Albert, 32
Konigin Luise, 31
Kri Tanjung Pandan, 163
Kronprinz Wilhelm, 22
Kronprinzessin Cecilie, 23
Kungsholm, 187

Lejeune, 164
Leopoldina, 34
Leviathan, 87
Liberte, 153
Limburgia, 96
Lombardia, 96
Long Island, 186
Loughborough, 31

Main, 47
Majestic, 87
Maxim Gorky, 195
Mercury, 30
Michigan, 41
Milwaukee, 113
Mobile, 61
Moltke, 34
Monte Cervantes, 141
Monte Olivia, 141
Monte Pascoal, 141
Monte Rosa, 141
Monte Sarmiento, 141
Monteith, 60
Montlaurier, 60
Montnairn, 60
Mormacmail, 186
Mount Vernon, 23
Munchen (1914–23), 109
Munchen (1922), 111

Nansemond, 37
Nelly, 186
New Rochelle, 32
New York (American), 37
New York (1927), 128

Nipponia, 37
Norseman, 38

Ohio, 109
Omar, 31
Oriental Hero, 184
Oriental Inventor, 184
Oriental Lady, 184
Oriental Musician, 185
Oriental Ruler, 185
Oriental Warrior, 184
Ormuz, 109

Pasteur, 186
Patria, 164
Patricia, 37
Pavia, 35
Pennland, 114
Pennsylvania, 37
Pesaro, 34
Petr Vasev, 112
Philippines, 40
Pittsburgh, 114
Pocahontas, 33
Polonia, 41
Potsdam, 162
Powhatan, 32
President Arthur, 34
President Fillmore, 32
President Grant, 48
President Lincoln, 48
Pretoria, (1898),
Pretoria (1936), 163
Princess Mahsuri, 196
Princess Matoika, 34
Prinz Freidrich Wilhelm, 60
Prinzess Alice, 34
Prinzess Irene, 33

Red Cross, 32
Regent Sun, 195
Regina, 114
Reliance, 96
Republic, 48
Rhein, 47
Riga, 41
Robert Ingham, 22
Robert Ley, 168
Rossia, 164
Royal Odyssey, 195
Russ, 113

Safina-E-Hujjaj, 162

St Louis, 112
Sardegna, 120
Saudi Phil I, 186
Scharnhorst, 162
Schwaben, 91
Schwabenstein, 185
Scotia, 48
Scotland, 187
Servian, 48
Seven Seas, 186
Shalom, 195
Shinyo, 162
Sierra Cordoba, 120
Sierra Morena, 121
Sierra Nevada, 119
Sierra Salvada, 120
Sierra Ventana, 120
Slavonia, 33, 41
Sovetsky Sojus, 127
Soyuz, 127
Spadefish, 162
Steuben, 111
Stolt Dagali, 195
Stuttgart, 111
Suffren, 84
Susquehana, 47

Taiyo Maru, 71
Teutonia, 34
Thuringia, 110
Tirpitz, 95
Tirpitz (battleship). 142
Transbalt, 41

Vaterland (1914), 87
Vaterland (1940), 164
Vestris, 112
Victoria Luise, 22
Vineta, 72
Volturno, 33
Von Steuben, 22

Westernland, 114
Westphalia, 110
White Palace, 34
Wilhelm Gustloff, 168
William O'Swald, 96
Windhuk, 164

Yuri Dolgoruki, 128

Zeppelin, 109
Zero, 33